Base Camp Reno

101 Hikes from Sage to Snow

IMBRIFEX

Base Camp Reno

101 Hikes from Sage to Snow

Christopher
and Elizabeth Barile

IMBRIFEX BOOKS

IMBRIFEX BOOKS
8275 S. Eastern Avenue, Suite 200
Las Vegas, NV 89123
imbrifex.com

BOOKS

Editor: Vicki Adang
Cover and Book Designer: Sue Campbell Book Design
Author Photo: Sarah Ann Grant
All cover and interior photos by the authors except as follows: Sarah Ann Grant: pages 17, 37; Flickr/dHReno: page 264; Rick Cooper: page 265

Library of Congress Cataloging-in-Publication Data
Names: Barile, Christopher, author. | Barile, Elizabeth, author.
Title: Base camp Reno: 101 hikes from sage to snow / Christopher and Elizabeth Barile.
Description: First edition. | Las Vegas, NV: Imbrifex Books, 2022. | Includes index. | Summary: "Reno: A Base Camp for All Seasons Ideally positioned between the spectacular peaks and lakes of California's Sierra Nevadas and the vast and varied Great Basin of Nevada, Reno is an unparalleled hub for exploring the natural beauty and grandeur this region offers. The area's four-season climate combined with year-round sun guarantees that every day can be a great day to go exploring."—Provided by publisher.
Identifiers: LCCN 2021051408 (print) | LCCN 2021051409 (ebook) | ISBN 9781945501586 (trade paperback) | ISBN 9781945501593 (epub)
Subjects: LCSH: Hiking—Nevada—Reno—Guidebooks. | Trails—Nevada—Reno—Guidebooks. | Hiking—Sierra Nevada (Calif. and Nev.)—Guidebooks. | Trails—Sierra Nevada (Calif. and Nev.)—Guidebooks. | Reno (Nev.)—Guidebooks. | Sierra Nevada (Calif. and Nev.)—Guidebooks. | LCGFT: Guidebooks.
Classification: LCC GV199.42.N3 B37 2022 (print) | LCC GV199.42.N3 (ebook) | DDC 796.510979355—dc23
LC record available at https://lccn.loc.gov/2021051408
LC ebook record available at https://lccn.loc.gov/2021051409

First Edition: April 2022

Printed in Canada

IMBRIFEX® is registered trademark of Flattop Productions, Inc.
Reno.basecampguides.com | Imbrifex.com | BasecampGuides.com

For Juniper and Sage
Climb every mountain, grow in curiosity, pursue truth,
and most of all, love with your whole heart, mind, and soul.

Contents

Steamboat Ditch, Hike 46

Before You Hit the Trail

Reno is one of the best metropolitan areas in the country for outdoor recreation. While Lake Tahoe ski resorts and casinos generate the most tourism revenue, the hiking opportunities are truly special and do not cost a dime. Reno is positioned at the interface between the Sierra Nevada Mountains and the Great Basin Desert. Vast mountain ranges surround the city in all directions. The mountainous topography and the sunny four-season climate combine to make for outstanding hiking conditions any time of the year.

Located less than 10 miles from the California-Nevada state line, Reno is situated in the middle of a dichotomy of landscapes between the two states. Eastern California is epitomized by the Sierra Nevadas, one of the snowiest and highest places in the country. In contrast, the Great Basin Desert is Nevada's most conspicuous feature. The Great Basin gives Nevada the distinctions of being the most arid state, the state with the most mountain ranges, and the most isolated state in terms of its population distribution among the contiguous United States. What is the end result for a hiker with a base camp in Reno? You get to choose between the best of either world, and oftentimes you will experience both during the same hike!

The California-Nevada dichotomy is an oversimplification, though, and many hikes in this book will lead you through country that shatters this paradigm. Consider, for instance, the enormous swath of lush subalpine terrain of the Carson Range in Nevada or the sage-covered hillsides and red rock canyons in the Petersen Range in California. Regardless, you can hike in snow, sage, or sand, along peaceful meadows and creeks, and upon exhilarating craggy cliffs and summit tops. Whether it is a two-hour reprieve or an all-day adventure, *Base Camp Reno* is your guide to finding the perfect hike that is less than a 90-minute drive from downtown. All trailheads are accessible with a low-clearance two-wheel-drive vehicle, and all but three of the trailheads have no entrance fee. Get outside and happy hiking!

How to Use this Book

The 101 guides to hikes in this book are divided into 10 geographical regions, with each region containing roughly 10 hikes. Each hike contains a trail map, an "At a Glance" box, and a detailed hiking description.

The "At a Glance" box has several metrics to help you choose a hike. The difficulty rating is ranked on a scale from very easy to easy, hard, and epic. The difficulty rating is calculated based on the number of calories burned during the hike (see Appendix D). This means that a short, steep hike may be given a rating of hard, while a long, flat hike may be rated as easy.

The "At a Glance" box also contains

- The distance of the hike
- A very approximate amount of time the hike will take
- The solitude, or popularity, of the hike (e.g., heavy use, medium use, light use, complete solitude)
- The walking surfaces encountered (e.g., road, foot trail, off trail)
- Land ownership (e.g., National Forest, Bureau of Land Management)
- The best seasons for the hike
- The transportation methods of other users (e.g., hikers, bikers, equestrians, off-highway vehicles (OHVs))
- Any interesting features of the hikes (e.g., waterfalls, petroglyphs, colorful rocks)
- Common large animals on the trail (e.g., wild horses, antelope).

The elevation gain for each hike is also listed. This value is the total elevation gain throughout the hike, not just the difference between the highest and lowest elevations. For instance, a loop hike over rolling hills where you climb 100 feet and descend 100 feet and do that five times would have an elevation gain of 500 feet.

Lastly, the book contains numerous appendices that organize the hikes by different categories and will aid you in finding the ideal hike quickly.

Throughout the book, we chose to use the colloquial terms "Sierras" and "Sierra Nevadas" to refer to the Sierra Nevada mountain range, though we are aware that this might be controversial.

The 10 Geographical Regions

MOST OF THE 101 HIKES IN THIS BOOK ARE WITHIN A 35-MILE RADIUS OF DOWNTOWN RENO. For most hikes, this translates to less than an hour drive from downtown. Although reaching some of the trailheads requires traveling on dirt roads, every trailhead is navigable by low-clearance two-wheel-drive vehicles.

The most defining landscapes in the Greater Reno area are mountains, so the hikes are organized into 10 geographical regions based on distinct mountain ranges. These 10 regions form sections 2 through 11 of the book and are organized starting from the northwest and ending with the southeast. The regions progress from west to east and then north to south in the same way that you read a page from left to right and top to bottom. The hikes within each region are listed in the same order.

The Northeastern Sierras

The first mountain range group described contains the Verdi, Bald, and Diamond Mountain Ranges of the northeastern Sierra Nevadas. Near the California-Nevada border, the Verdi and Bald Mountain Ranges each stretch for 12 miles in a north-south orientation between Sierra Valley and the Truckee River. The Diamond Mountains stretch for 50 miles from the southeast at Beckwourth Pass to their northwestern terminus near Susanville, where the Sierra Nevadas as a whole end and give way to the Cascades. Elevations in the region range from 5,500 feet at the valley floors to Babbitt Peak at 8,760 feet. Prominent peaks in this region, such as Verdi and Ladybug Peaks, are visible while driving on I-80 heading west from Reno. Regional geology is a mix of granite uplifted by the Sierra Nevadas and younger igneous rocks from recent

Adams Peak, Hike 2

volcanism in the nearby southern Cascades.

The area contains four large reservoirs, numerous isolated meadows, verdant springs, and perennial creeks. Expect spectacular summer wildflower displays in the lower meadows. The vibrancy and diversity of larger vegetation in the region is also impressive and includes sagebrush, mountain mahogany, aspen, white fir, red fir, western white pine, and Jeffrey pine. The eastern side of Babbitt Peak contains the rare Washoe pine and is one of only two places in the world where pure stands of this enigmatic tree exist.

With an average of 30 inches of annual precipitation, the region is about four times wetter than Reno. Snowfall can be heavy in the winter, but the generally gentle slopes of the area and large valleys make the region excellent for snowshoeing. Fantastic hiking opportunities exist all year round in these mountains, and in summer, the dense forests afford miles of shade you can use to escape the downtown heat.

The Petersen Mountains

From the Highway 395 corridor in Long Valley lying around 4,500 feet, the Petersen Mountains to the east rise sharply, topping out at an elevation of 7,857 feet. Passersby cannot help but notice the stark contrast between these rocky and seemingly barren desert peaks and the greener Sierra Nevada ranges to the west. For the few people fortunate enough to get out of their cars and climb these mountains, they will be treated to a world of surprises.

Precipitation spillover from the Sierra Nevada results in about 15 inches of annual precipitation, twice the amount Reno receives, and supports a wide variety of life in these desert ranges. While sage-juniper forests dominate dry areas, piñon trees, ponderosa pines, and incense cedars are found in wetter high-elevation ravines. Springs on the eastern slopes support stands of aspen and willow. Numerous riparian habitats support water-loving plants such as wild roses, wild onions, and cattails.

Common animals in the region include golden eagles, Swainson's hawks, antelope, rabbits, and, most impressively, deer. Each fall, a herd of approximately 3,000 deer migrate to the Petersen Mountains from the Sierra Nevadas. As a result, you are almost guaranteed to see deer in this region on even a short hike from November to April.

Regional geology is dominated by granodiorite, an igneous rock that contains more darker-colored minerals than granite, and sandy soils deposited by ancient waterways. Additionally, pockets of beautiful iron-rich red and yellow rock formations dot the landscape.

This region also contains the Little Petersen Range several miles east of the main Petersen Range, which offers several pleasant and less strenuous hiking adventures. Hiking is enjoyable year-round with the exception of hot days in July and August.

Red Rock Cliffs, Hike 13

The North Valleys

The North Valleys area consists of a series of isolated pockets of mountains that rise precipitously from valley floors north of Reno. The region's climate is classically high desert with sage-juniper woodland blanketing the landscape.

The top of Dogskin Mountain is the highest point in the region at 7,486 feet and contrasts sharply with flat valleys with elevations as low as 4,200 feet. Although the southern valleys are either dotted with ranch homes or contain the Spanish Springs suburbs, the northern portion of the area marks the beginning of an enormous swath of open public land that extends well past the Oregon border. After a 20-minute drive from downtown, you will reach remote landscapes and quickly forget that you were just in an urban area with nearly half a million people.

Warm Springs Mountain, Hike 22

Despite the arid terrain, the region contains two large lakes, Swan Lake and Silver Lake. The blue waters of these oases contrast beautifully with the surrounding desert scenery and serve as important resting grounds for hundreds of species of migratory birds.

Sedimentary rocks characterize valley geology, whereas diorite and monzonite, volcanic rocks with nearly equal mixtures of light and dark minerals, are exposed in the mountains. Eroded spherical granite boulders are scattered throughout the region, the most striking of which are found in the aptly named Moon Rocks outcroppings.

Winter, spring, and fall are all good times to hike in this region. The heat and heightened rattlesnake activity make for less pleasant hiking in the summer. Winter is perhaps the best season for hiking, particularly when there is a light dusting of snow in the area. The lack of trees in the area gives you outstanding views of snowier peaks in all directions while your foreground glistens in shades of white and sage green.

The Pah Rah Range

The Pah Rah mountain range is the largest in the Reno-Sparks area and is a prominent landscape across the region, which is characterized by high desert climate and mostly arid vegetation. However, because the ridgeline is high and tops out at 8,366 feet at Virginia Peak, large swaths of the area host denser vegetation than is typical of lower desert landscapes.

Several creeks feed riparian canyons that contain cottonwoods, aspen, and willows. Wildflowers in these areas are surprisingly diverse and include desert paintbrush, lupine, larkspur, and desert peach.

The Pah Rahs consist predominantly of light-colored rhyolite and soft tuff, rock derived from volcanic ash. The mountains stretch for about 20 miles in a north-south trending arc from the Truckee River in Sparks to Pyramid Lake.

Whereas tens of millions of people visit Lake Tahoe each year, few visitors know of Pyramid Lake, which is equally large and sits at the region's low point at 3,800 feet. Pyramid Lake is the only home to the endangered cui-ui sucker fish and one of the few habitats of the large Lahontan cutthroat trout, which can reach over 40 pounds. In addition to supporting fish, Pyramid Lake provides crucially important bird habitat for migratory birds. The lake's Anaho Island is one of the world's largest breeding grounds for the American white pelican. Each year, nearly 10,000 pelicans lay their eggs on the island's rocky shores. Other notable water birds that breed here include terns, gulls, egrets, herons, and cormorants.

This region also covers portions of the adjacent Virginia Mountains, not to be confused with the Virginia Range described in its own section. These mountains contain large swaths of colorful rock formations, and the views to the north offer

spectacular views of Pyramid Lake. Like the Pah Rahs, the Virginia Mountains host a wide variety of habitats due to a significant range in elevations. Tule Peak, the highest desert peak in the Greater Reno area at 8,723 feet, rises nearly 5,000 feet above nearby Pyramid Lake.

Because of the region's topographical variety, the desert landscapes described in this section can be enjoyably hiked any time of the year. Spring and fall make for excellent times to visit the region's high points, shaded creeks give you respite from summer heat, and Pyramid Lake is a wonderland in the winter.

Spanish Springs Peak, Hike 36

Truckee Meadows

Even though the Reno-Sparks metropolis lies in Truckee Meadows, there are still a plethora of excellent hiking opportunities here that take you to local creeks, peaks, and waterfalls. Given the nearby population density, it is understandable that many of these hikes are among the most popular in the book.

The most prominent landform in the area is Peavine Peak, which gradually rises north of the Truckee River to an elevation of 8,266 feet. All of the hikes in this region give you excellent views of the surrounding mountains, including snow-capped Mount Rose Wilderness and the Verdi and Virginia Ranges.

Hunter Creek Falls, Hike 47

Most of the described hikes can be completed in half a day and are enjoyable year-round. Adventures include first-class wildflower displays in Dog Valley, navigating through conifer forests on West Peavine, and peaceful strolls along the mighty Truckee River.

Donner Pass

When you hike the Donner Pass region, you are in the heart of the northern Sierra Nevadas. Backcountry lakes, countless pristine streams, endlessly deep forests, and rugged mountain peaks are just some of the features that await you.

More than anything, though, the region is characterized by snow. The town of Truckee, which lies nine miles east of the pass proper, ranks as one of the snowiest

Castle Peak, Hike 56

cities in the United States. Mountain peaks, the highest of which is Mount Lola at 9,148 feet, routinely receive over 30 feet of snow! Snow fields can linger at higher elevations until September. As a result, summer and early fall are the easiest times to hike in the Donner Pass region. Snowshoeing in the spring and winter can also be immensely enjoyable.

Several kinds of rocks make up the Donner Pass area, but like most of the Sierra Nevadas, none is more striking or prevalent as granite. Trails will frequently take you over smooth granite slabs and past enormous fields of granite boulders.

Forests consist of numerous tree species, the most common of which are red fir, lodgepole pine, Jeffrey pine, and western juniper. Common mammals include squirrels, chipmunks, mule deer, and black bears. The region hosts a variety of transient bird species, and among the year-round bird residents are mountain chickadees, dark-eyed juncos, and owls.

The Donner Pass region is one of the best places in the West to view mountain wildflowers. You can chase colorful flowers as they bloom progressively later at higher elevations. In the absence of other information, a rule of thumb is to look for wildflowers at 6,000 feet in May, 7,000 feet in June, 8,000 feet in July, and 9,000 feet in August.

North Lake Tahoe

Nothing compares to Tahoe. Hike after hike, season after season, vista after vista, the lake never ceases to disappoint.

Lake Tahoe, with a shoreline elevation of 6,224 feet, is the largest alpine lake in North America and the third largest freshwater alpine lake in the world. Recreational activities in the area abound, and although people take plenty of advantage of them, there always seem to be enough trails for everybody, especially outside of the popular Memorial Day to Labor Day window.

Each season has its own visitation perks. In winter, snowshoe the flat shoreline and rim trails. In spring, enjoy the snow-free shore surrounded by snow-capped peaks. In summer, stay away from the popular shores and take in breathtaking high-elevation views of the lake. In fall, revel in majestic fall foliage alongside any of the numerous tributaries that feed the lake.

Lake Tahoe consists of a deep granite water bowl, and the lack of sediment renders the water the clearest in the nation. This hiking region also features adventures to beautiful Spooner and Marlette Lakes with adjoining vistas of Lake Tahoe.

Forests in Northwest Lake Tahoe consist of white firs, red firs, Jeffrey pines, ponderosa pines, lodgepole pines, aspen, and the magnificent sugar pine, which bears the world's longest pine cones. Hundreds of species of wildflowers bloom in lakeside meadows in the summer. Large fauna include black bears, coyotes, deer, and beavers.

Sand Harbor, Hike 68

The Carson Range

The Carson Range is an eastern spur of the northern Sierra Nevadas that mostly lies in Nevada. Here in these rugged, wild, and snowy mountains is where the misperception of Nevada as barren desert is most obviously obliterated. Enjoy clear lakes, rushing streams, picturesque waterfalls, and breathtaking panoramas.

At the heart of this range lies 32,000 acres of gorgeous roadless terrain in Mount Rose Wilderness. The region ranges in elevation from 5,000 feet at the foothills near Washoe Lake to 10,776 feet at the summit of Mount Rose.

Naturally, this extremely large range of elevations gives rise to an impressive variety of flora and fauna. For example, the treeless alpine zones above 10,000 feet are one of the few homes of the pika, an adorably squeaky rabbit. Black bears, deer, rabbits, frogs, and mountain chickadees also frequent the region.

Wildflower viewing at upper elevations in the summer is fantastic, and representative families are buttercups, marigolds, shooting stars, larkspurs, and paintbrushes. All of the conifer species described in this book can be found in this region, including the rare Washoe pine.

Uplifted zones along the eastern portion of the Carson Range formed the mountains millions of years ago, and fault lines continue to uplift the mountains and periodically cause regional earthquakes. As a result of this tectonic activity, the eastern slopes of the Carson Range are exceedingly steep, with some locations gaining more than 2,500 feet of elevation in only 0.75 miles of lateral distance.

As a result of its position to the east of the rest of the northern Sierra Nevadas, the Carson Range receives about half as much snow as the Donner Pass area, which significantly extends the dry hiking season. Snow-free hiking at middle elevations is usually possible from April to December. Tahoe Meadows, a large subalpine meadow at 8,400 feet, is a popular snowshoeing destination in the winter and spring.

Chickadee Ridge, Hike 81

The Virginia Range

The desert mountains of the Virginia Range form the eastern boundary of Reno south of the Truckee River and receive far fewer visitors than the Carson Range to the west. Only the edge of this vast region is visible from a downtown vantage point.

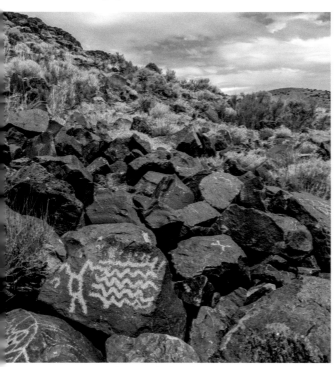

Lagomarsino Petroglyphs, Hike 87

The Virginia Range stretches for about 10 miles east of Reno and runs about 17 miles north to south, giving you endless hiking opportunities in little-touched desert country. Hidden gems include colorful canyons and Native American petroglyphs.

The elevation ranges from 4,300 feet near the Truckee River to 7,864 feet at the top of Mount Davidson. Treeless sage land prevails at lower elevations, but the sage is widely interspersed with Utah juniper trees above 5,000 feet. Piñon trees, filled with their delicious pine nuts, become increasingly common above 6,000 feet. Stands of ponderosa pines and mountain mahogany live in wetter, high-elevation ravines.

The geology of the Virginia Range is characterized by a mixture of igneous rocks, such as basalt, andesite, and rhyolite, formed from volcanism in the area tens of millions of years ago. In some areas, crisscrossing faults have created steep and folded topography that exposed the veins of silver and gold of Virginia City fame.

Cliffside rocky outcroppings make excellent homes for approximately 100 bighorn sheep. Wild horses are so prevalent that you are almost certain to see them on each hike. Deer, rattlesnakes, rabbits, hawks, spotted towhees, and mountain bluebirds are common.

Because summer days are typically too hot, winter, fall, and spring are excellent times to hike in the Virginia Range.

Carson City and Beyond

Just 30 miles south of Reno, Carson City is an easily accessible hiking destination. This section covers hiking in the immediate vicinity of Carson City and the desert areas farther to the east.

The lower portions of the Carson River flow near Carson City, providing wetland habitat for birds, including pelicans, egrets, herons, and bald eagles. The Carson Range rises precipitously from the floors of the valleys, resulting in an impressive westward backdrop while hiking.

This section also covers the Flowery Range, a narrow 15-mile mountain belt oriented on a southwest-northeast axis. Extensive gold and silver mining has occurred in the Flowery Range since the 1850s, and despite ongoing mining activity in select spots, the range offers several outstanding and isolated desert hiking experiences. The mountain range is named for a few weeks in late spring when wildflowers carpet the hillsides in brilliant yellows and reds.

The Lahontan Valley is east of the Flowery Range and is home to some of the starkest desert landscapes in northern Nevada. The lowlands here are only at 4,000 feet, and the hot summer temperatures combined with high salinity in the soil preclude sagebrush from growing. Instead, the vegetation is dominated by

Bently Heritage Trail, Hike 101

salt-tolerant plants such as greasewood and shadscale. In some areas called *playas*, there is no vegetation at all.

Despite the barren landscapes, these deserts feature hidden treasures. Geothermal hot springs are common. There is also a high concentration of Native American petroglyphs. Several thousand years ago, this region was not arid. Instead it was a fertile marshland and a favorite hunting and foraging spot.

Climate and Weather

THE GREATER RENO AREA CLIMATE CONSISTS OF FOUR TRUE SEASONS WITH WARM, DRY summers and cool, snowy winters. The city of Reno itself lies in the Great Basin Desert in the rain shadow of the Sierra Nevadas. It receives no more than an average of 1 inch of precipitation every month. Some years, no rain falls at all in July and August. The majority of annual precipitation falls as snow during the winter months. Mostly, though, it is dry, and six out of seven days, there is no precipitation. On most of the days it does rain or snow, it only does so for a few hours. The lack of precipitation means low rates of cloud cover. In fact, Reno is the northernmost place in the world that is sunny at least 75 percent of the time during the day. Couple clear, sunny, and dry air with mountainous terrain, and you get phenomenal hiking conditions with vistas featuring excellent visibility.

The area's dry climate also gives rise to very large (30–50°F) daily temperature swings, so dressing in layers is important at all times of the year. Rapid night-

Rocky Peak, Hike 96

time cooling frequently results in gusty late afternoons and evenings. These windy conditions are particularly pronounced on treeless desert landscapes and exposed summit tops. To predict if it will be windy, look for lens-shaped, or lenticular, clouds. This class of clouds only forms ahead of high wind events in mountainous regions.

Unlike Reno and the desert mountains to the east, the Sierra Nevadas receive much larger quantities of precipitation. Snowfall is highly dependent upon elevation with high-elevation summits above 10,000 feet routinely receiving over 30 feet of snow annually. In addition to elevation, snow levels are enhanced by moisture accumulation over large bodies of water. As such, so-called lake-effect snow is prevalent in areas near

Lake Tahoe and Pyramid Lake. Thunderstorms producing rain and hail are most common in August and September, but even high in the Sierras, they occur relatively rarely. Those who have hiked in the Rocky Mountains or lived in the Midwest might be surprised by the lack of daily afternoon summer thunderstorms.

Because the greater area contains both the Sierras and the Great Basin Desert, the weather an hour drive from downtown in any direction is highly variable. When choosing where to hike, use this variability to your advantage. In general, the farther east you travel, the less likely it will rain or snow. At the same time, higher elevations will be cooler than lower elevations. Under dry conditions, air temperature decreases 5.4°F every 1,000 feet you climb.

	ELEVATION	TEMPERATURE
DOWNTOWN RENO	4,506 feet	90°F
LAKE TAHOE	6,224 feet	81°F
MOUNT ROSE TRAILHEAD	8,912 feet	66°F
MOUNT ROSE SUMMIT	10,776 feet	56°F

You can use this fact to estimate what the temperature will be at different elevations, even if there are no weather stations available. For example, suppose the forecasted high is an uncomfortable 90°F in downtown Reno (elevation 4,506 feet). Under normal conditions, the temperature on Mount Rose Summit (elevation 10,776 feet) would then be a pleasant 56°F.

Lastly, because most storm systems originate from the Pacific Ocean and must pass over rugged Sierra Nevada terrain to reach Reno, weather forecasts here are notoriously unreliable, especially several days in advance. Always check the weather forecast the morning before your hike.

Flora and Fauna

BECAUSE THE HIKES IN THIS BOOK SPAN FROM THE GREAT BASIN DESERT TO THE SIERRA Nevadas, you will walk through numerous flora and fauna habitats. The climate, elevation, soil, precipitation, and topography all factor into the plants and animals that live in these different zones. For simplification, the book covers four broad vegetative zones. At lower elevations east of the Sierras, you will hike through sagebrush steppe and then transition to piñon-juniper woodland at higher elevations. In the Sierras, you will pass through montane forests (6,000–9,000 feet) until reaching subalpine forest and the tree line at higher elevations. The following plants and animals are common in these zones, but this list is by no means comprehensive. Remember to respect wildlife, and give them their space. We are the ones intruding on their homes.

Big sagebrush

Sagebrush Steppe

If there is one plant that dominates the hikes and smells in the Greater Reno area, it is sagebrush, the state flower of Nevada. Sagebrush refers to a broad family of blue-gray plants, but the most common and important one here is big sagebrush. Big sagebrush has incredible ecological tolerance, meaning you will find it on nearly every hike regardless of the environmental conditions. Its scientific name is *Artemisia tridentata*, which can help you remember how to identify it. The thin, somewhat fuzzy leaves have three lobes or are three-toothed like a trident. Several other large, rounded shrubs are regularly spaced and can easily be confused for sagebrush. These sagebrush look-alikes include rabbitbrush, bitterbrush, and stiff sagebrush.

Rubber rabbitbrush (*Ericameria nauseosa*) has thin, pointed blue-gray leaves and bursts into bright, showy yellow blooms in autumn. As its name implies, rubber can be derived from it. Rabbits, however, do not have a particular culinary affinity for rabbitbrush. Instead, jackrabbits use it as shelter. Bitterbrush (*Purshia tridentata*), also called antelope brush, is an excellent food source for deer and antelope, though as the name suggests, it tastes bitter and has a pronged leaf. Bitterbrush can be distinguished from the other medium-sized shrubs by its extensive branching and greener leaves. Bitterbrush is often associated with balsamroots. In the late spring, bitterbrush produces lovely yellow flowers.

Curl-leaf mountain mahogany in blossom

Mormon tea (*Ephedra nevadensis*) looks like a woody thicket of bright green nodular twigs. Tribal people used these plants for medicinal purposes. Boiling a handful of the twigs for 15 minutes produces a flavorful tea, but be warned that it is highly caffeinated and was the inspiration for the medicine ephedrine.

Curl-leaf mountain mahogany (*Cercocarpus ledifolius*) is a shrubby, slow-growing, gnarled tree of the rose family. The misleading association with mahogany is due to its dense wood, which sinks in water. The tree is covered with green curled leaves and fuzzy hair. The hairs reflect light, cooling the plant. In the spring, it produces small pale yellow flowers. Some groves are so thick they are impenetrable.

Arrowleaf balsamroots (*Balsamorhiza sagittata*) are the most common drought-tolerant wildflower in sage country. Their fuzzy, large silvery leaves grow up from a large taproot. Each stalk forms a single bright yellow flower head. Their resinous root was used by indigenous people for food.

Mule deer (*Odocoileus hemionus*) are the most common large mammal in the Greater Reno area. With large ears like a mule, tan body, and black-tipped tail, they are recognizable as they move through different vegetative zones with the seasons. The buck grows antlers that are shed yearly. When startled, a mule deer will bound over the terrain with stiff-legged jumps with all four hooves hitting the ground simultaneously.

Arrowleaf balsamroot flowers

Although less common, the black-faced, cinnamon-colored pronghorn (also called the American antelope, *Antelocapra americana*) also lives in sage country. Pronghorns have horns, which, unlike antlers, grow throughout the animal's lifetime. Despite the name and horns, they are not related to antelopes or goats. Pronghorns are the fastest animal in the Western Hemisphere, making 20-foot bounds, and have been recorded at 70 miles per hour for three to four minutes at a time. The animal's typical cruising speed is 30 miles per hour, which it can maintain for 15 minutes. Herds of pronghorn are typically larger than mule deer, and you can distinguish startled pronghorns by their characteristic white rumps.

A mule deer bounding on the slopes of Peavine Mountain

Nuttall's cottontails (*Sylvilagus nuttallii*) and black-tailed jackrabbits (*Lepus californicus*) are the most common rabbits and hares in the Reno area sage steppe. Nuttall's cottontails are about 14 inches long, grayish-brown, and prefer grasses but will eat sagebrush and juniper "berries." Black-tailed jackrabbits are about twice the size, gray with black tails, and have large hind legs and ears. They hop 5–10 feet at a time. When panicked, they can hop upwards of 20 feet and up to 35 miles per hour.

The sage scrub provides home to numerous birds. The western meadowlark (*Sturnella neglecta*) is a medium-sized bird with a bright yellow belly and a cheerful, watery, flute-like call. It nests on the ground and eats insects. The California quail (*Callipepla californica*) is a medium-sized ground bird with a distinct "chi-ca-go" call. Both the male and female have striking plumes on their heads. When startled, they will fly away with labored flapping.

Garter snakes are common, nonvenomous snakes in the area.

We have seen many different snakes on our hikes in Nevada and California, most of which slither away as soon as they sense us. The Great Basin rattlesnake (*Crotalus lutosus*) is the only venomous snake in the Greater Reno area. Rattlesnakes are most active from April through October and usually hibernate in dens in the winter. If you hear the rattle, you are too close to the snake. This is their warning for you to stop, listen, and move quietly away from the snake. Give them a 15-foot radius and trek off trail around them. A forest ranger once told us that the most common phrase said before a snake bite is "Hold my beer! Watch this!" Snakes tend to like rocks for sunbathing, protection, and finding prey, but you can also find them in ravines, canyons, meadows, forests, and woodpiles. If you are bitten, call 911 immediately so the hospital can get ready for you. It is not recommended to run after you have been bitten because it may cause the venom to spread faster. Also, do not suck out the venom because it will prolong treatment and cause more damage.

Wild horses

Watching a group of wild horses (*Equus ferus*) gallop across sage country is an unforgettable experience. To many, the wild horse is the ultimate symbol of freedom and the West. The truth is that these beautiful animals are nonnative because they were expelled from North America at least 10,000 years ago only to be reintroduced much later by Spanish conquistadors. They take resources away from native animals and destroy native grasses. Wild horses are most common in the Virginia Range, particularly near Reno where naïve individuals feed them. The federal government, on the other hand, has taken steps to limit their population.

Piñon-Juniper Woodland

Utah juniper (*Juniperus osteosperma*) is a truly majestic plant, providing shade where no other trees seem to grow. No two junipers are alike, as some appear to be bushy shrubs while others are 30 feet tall with twisted, sprawling trunks. Two-thirds of the tree's total mass is made up of its extensive root system, which can be upwards of 25 feet down and 100 feet laterally. They are slow growing, and a 30-year-old tree may only be 5 feet tall. Junipers typically live between 350 and 700 years. The edible, though unpleasant, pea-sized blue "fruit" is actually a tiny cone covered in a waxy coating.

Like the juniper, the single-leaf piñon (*Pinus monophylla*) is a slow-growing wonder of the Great Basin Desert. It is the only single-needled pine tree in the world. Piñon trees may take 100 years to reach just 30 feet tall. They only begin to grow cones after 35 years.

Pink penstemon flowers (mountain pride)

These cones are quite sappy but house delicious pine nuts. Many birds and mammals feed off the piñon seeds. Historically, these seeds were an important winter food source for the local Washoe, Paiute, and Shoshone people. The best time to harvest them on the trail is in October. The dark pine nuts can be cracked open easily with your teeth and taste more buttery than dried store-bought ones. At 3,000 calories per pound, they are a good emergency food if you find yourself stranded. Current Bureau of Land Management rules allow you to collect up to 25 pounds of pine nuts per person per year.

Penstemons (*Penstemon* genus) are a broad genus of colorful, sculptural flowers, ranging from white to pink and purple to deep blue. The flower has five stamens and is tubular. With more than 250 penstemon species in the West, you will need to take accurate photographs and field notes if you wish to identify

Desert paintbrush between granite rocks

them. The Indian paintbrush or desert paintbrush (*Castilleja chromosa*) looks like a whimsical paintbrush dipped in the dyes of a sunset. Ranging in color from red to orange and yellow, these plants grow at all elevations in the Reno area.

Montane Forest

Jeffrey pines (*Pinus jeffreyi*) and ponderosa pines (*Pinus ponderosa*) are two of the most common pine trees surrounding Reno. For a while, botanists thought the two were the same species and referred to them as western yellow pine, due to the yellow "bellies" that the old-growth pine trees display. Today, both are sold as yellow pine because their wood is so similar. The bark of both trees smells amazing. Scratching it with your fingernail or crushing twigs in your hand, you will smell something like vanilla, lemon, or apple. Ponderosa pines generally have smaller, prickly pine cones and longer needles; they are often found at lower elevations. "Gentle Jeffrey" pine cones are twice the size and are comfortable to hold when fully open. Many of the Tahoe area hikes are through Jeffrey pine forests, though the two intermix.

Mule's ears (*Wyethia mollis*) look similar to arrowleaf balsamroot with their large leaves and vibrant yellow blooms. However, they can easily be distinguished by their multiple flower heads per stem. Mule's ears also tend to grow in wetter environments and higher elevations. Lupine (*Lupinus*) are another common flower both in the forest and sagebrush. They form lovely, dense, elongated clusters of blue or white flowers similar to that of a pea with palmate leaves. As nitrogen-fixing plants, they are useful for restoring soil conditions. Although it is tempting to pick wildflowers, please do not. Lupines are toxic. Fatalities have occurred in sheep and cattle that have grazed in meadows over several days. Keeping your dogs and children from ingesting lupine is the safest decision.

Manzanita (*Arctostaphylos*) are a genus of beautiful sculptural plants with smooth red gnarled bark and flat, rounded green leaves. The most common species in the Sierras is greenleaf manzanita (*Arctostaphylos patula*). In the spring, they produce pink globular flowers. The flowers and fruit are edible, supposedly tasting like a bitter green apple. *Manzanita* is the diminutive form of "apple" in Spanish.

If you see a grove of quaking aspen (*Populus tremuloides*) on a hike, you are close to water. Aspen require large amounts of water and are usually found along perennial springs, creeks, and lakes. The white bark and shimmering leaves are lovely to walk among. In the fall, the aspen leaves turn vibrant yellow. Aspen have an extensive interconnected root system. One grove of aspen is considered a single organism because of their connectedness, making them technically the largest living organism on earth.

Nothing quite welcomes you to the mountains like a sweet mountain chickadee (*Poecile gambeli*) song. These tiny gray birds flit through the tops of trees singing "ham-bur-ger" or "fe-fee-bee-bee." They sing year-round and provide welcome cheer in the dead of winter. They have black heads with white cheeks and white eyebrow stripes.

Montane forest with alpine lupine

Black bears (*Ursus americanus*), which can be black or brown, are mostly active at night, but they are common enough in Greater Reno that there is a fair chance you will see one while day hiking. They are less aggressive and smaller than grizzly bears, which are no longer in the area. Most black bears in the area weigh between 100 and 300 pounds, as opposed to the bears that are 600 pounds or greater found in other parts of North America. Black bears here are afraid of humans and will do what they can to avoid you. Unlike the bears in Yosemite, Greater Reno bears will not break into cars. Throughout California and Nevada, there have been no recorded fatalities from black bear attacks. Bear spray is not recommended and unnecessary. The best way to avoid surprise encounters with bears is to make noise. Talking or the click of your trekking poles will warn the bear that you are coming. In the rare event that a bear approaches you aggressively, do not run. Running unleashes the chase instinct in bears, and they can run at 30 miles per hour. Instead, look big and make loud noises. If the bear attacks, do not play dead. Fight back with rocks, sticks, trekking poles, or anything else that is handy. Many people have successfully fended off bear attacks this way.

Subalpine

The tree line in Mount Rose Wilderness is marked by whitebark pine (*Pinus albicaulis*). The gnarled trees are often stunted from exposure and grow close to the ground, a condition called krummholz. Whitebark pine is a primitive pine, meaning that its cones do not open on their own. Instead, it relies on the Clark's nutcracker (*Nucifraga columbiana*) to break them open. These gray-and-black birds swoop among the trees, collecting seeds in a pouch under their tongues. Each bird caches tens of thousands of seeds for winter feeding. Uneaten seed stores germinate and become new whitebark groves. Above 10,000 feet, listen for the grating, metallic *"kraas"* of the Clark's nutcracker.

Whitepark pine

Cultural History

ARCHAEOLOGICAL REMAINS INDICATE THAT ancient native peoples inhabited the Greater Reno area upwards of 10,000 years ago. For at least the last 1,000 years, the nomadic Paiute and Washoe tribes, and to a lesser extent, the Shoshone, have lived in the area. The Paiute fished in the Pyramid Lake area and ventured into the surrounding mountains to harvest pine nuts and hunt animals. The Washoe spent their summers fishing and hunting in the Lake Tahoe Basin, their autumns in the Virginia Range collecting pine nuts, and their winters and springs in valleys such as Truckee Meadows. It is no coincidence that this schedule is an excellent seasonal hiking itinerary as well.

In the 1840s, pioneers of European descent began traveling in wagon trains to California. One of the main arteries of the California Trail passed through present-day

Ancient petroglyph rock art

Reno and Donner Pass, named after the infamous band of settlers who were trapped in the Sierra Nevadas in the winter of 1846. Trails were later developed across other nearby Sierra Nevada passes, including Henness Pass and Beckwourth Pass, that helped connect the economy of California to the East. The discovery of gold in Virginia City in 1850 increased the number of Europeans to the Greater Reno area. However, it was the immense amount of silver of the Comstock Lode discovered there in 1859 that resulted in a population explosion. Reno started as a small toll town around this time for parties passing to California and held almost no significance compared to Virginia City. About 7 million tons of ore were processed in the Virginia City area during the bonanza years, which produced a quantity of gold and silver worth about $8 billion in today's dollars. Gold and silver mining in Nevada continues to be an important part of the state's economy. Most other towns in the Greater Reno area, such as Truckee, developed alongside the Transcontinental Railroad in the late 1860s. Now, despite a rapid growth rate throughout the area as a result of a burgeoning technology industry, the community still prioritizes outdoor recreation. By hiking the trails in this book, you will help keep this open space movement strong so future generations can enjoy this area's beauty.

Safety

Match Your Adventure with Your Skill and Experience

Compared to many common activities, like driving a car, hiking is extraordinarily safe. Nonetheless, because the possibility for serious injury exists, it is imperative to take necessary precautions. The number one rule is to not embark on adventures that are far beyond your skills and experience. For example, it would not be wise to attempt a 20-mile hike if the longest hike you have completed in recent memory is only 5 miles. Sure, it is nice to push yourself physically, but just like any other exercise, it is only safe to do so incrementally. Aside from the likelihood of physical injury, when you are exhausted on the trail, you are more likely to make poor decisions, like taking a risky shortcut.

Protective clothing and hydration are imperative for comfortable hiking.

Hydration

Staying hydrated during your hike is extremely important. An often cited guideline is to bring one liter of water for every two hours of hiking. However, the amount of water you need varies widely depending on the temperature, your exertion level, and your physiology. Err on the side of bringing more water, especially if you feel like you are guessing about how much water to carry.

Backpacks with an internal bladder and straw are useful because they allow you to drink water without stopping. For longer hikes, a water filter is a worthy investment. Many of the hikes described in this book take you along waterways, and the ability to refill your water bottles will allow you to cover long distances comfortably.

A common symptom of mild dehydration is headache. Signs of severe dehydration include dizziness, rapid breathing, uncontrollable heartbeat, dark urine, fainting, and sleepiness. Drink often, and you will never get to that point. If you are not urinating during a longer hike, you are not drinking enough. Bury any human waste in a 6-inch-deep hole at least 300 feet from any water sources. Heat stroke is common in the desert among inexperienced hikers. Take it easy in the heat, and hike somewhere with shade during hot summer days.

Overhydrating is possible and can be prevented by consuming sports drinks with electrolytes. However, if you are eating snacks and lunch during your hike, overhydrating is unlikely because almost all food contains ample electrolytes.

Getting Lost

Getting lost in the great outdoors is a big fear for many people. Being lost can range from temporarily drifting off trail to not knowing the direction of the trailhead to walking for hours without knowing you are going in the wrong direction. Before hiking, carefully read a map and plan your route. Take notice of any trail junctions or spots on the route that may cause confusion. If hiking in groups, at least two adults should review the route together. Always tell a friend or family member at home your plans before embarking.

Cell phone service is spotty on many of the hikes. Cell signal is usually stronger on top of a peak than in a canyon. GPS on your phone is an excellent tool for navigating, but do not rely on it exclusively. There is always the chance that your phone will run out of battery or stop working because you drop it in a creek.

While hiking, get a feel for the lay of the land. Note any obvious landmarks like buildings, lone trees, or water features. For desert hikes, you can often see for miles ahead of you, which is generally useful for navigating. However, be aware that it is impossible to estimate the distances of faraway rocky landscapes because rocks can be of any size. Estimating the distance of tree-covered landscapes is possible but takes practice. Dense forests increase your likelihood of getting off course. Fortunately, the densest forests in Greater Reno are still relatively open compared to other forests in the country. Practice looking through the trees for landmarks as you hike. Lastly, keep in mind that the chance of becoming disoriented is far greater on a loop hike than on an out-and-back hike.

Washoe Lake, Hike 91

Hypothermia and Heat Stroke

Hypothermia and heat stroke can occur when the body is excessively cold or hot, respectively. Because of the large temperature changes that occur during a hike, dressing in layers is instrumental in maintaining appropriate body temperature. Remember that bodies of water are often very cold because they are formed from snowmelt. Proper hydration is the key to preventing heat stroke. On hot days, keep in mind that weather forecasts indicate the temperature in the shade. Effective temperatures in the sun are typically 10–20°F higher.

Altitude Sickness

Altitude sickness is a discomfort and, in rare cases, serious illness that occurs when a person accustomed to lower elevations travels to a much higher elevation. The symptoms of altitude sickness are generally mild below elevations of 10,000 feet and include headache, shortness of breath, and nausea. Only a few hikes in the Carson Range in this book exceed 10,000 feet. If you are sensitive to altitude, the easiest way to overcome altitude sickness is to acclimatize by spending a day at higher elevation before doing any strenuous activity.

Other Dangers

Watch for old barbed wire on the ground if heading off trail. Never enter mine shafts because they could be unstable. Stay away from areas used for target shooting, which is allowed on most public lands. Do not approach wild animals. Most animals are skittish and will try to stay away from you. Check yourself for ticks after completing a hike through high brush.

Mount Houghton and Relay Peak, Hike 76

Clothing and Equipment

PROPER ATTIRE CAN MAKE THE DIFFERENCE BETWEEN AN ENJOYABLE ADVENTURE AND A miserable outing. Cotton is a poor fabric choice for shirts and socks because it absorbs a lot of water and dries slowly. Wool or any synthetic material is better. Regardless of the season, it is best to wear long sleeves and long pants. Being covered will protect you from the sun and brush.

Dress in layers because you will likely experience large swings in temperature on your trip. Wear sunglasses and a hat. The best hats are wide-brimmed desert hats that protect your face and neck. Wear sunscreen, regardless of the season and your skin type. Invest in durable hiking shoes with good soles and proper ankle support. Running shoes are less than ideal for most of the described hikes.

A hiking backpack with a chest strap and a hip belt is the best option for carrying supplies. The straps significantly reduce the weight load on your shoulders. Trekking poles are excellent pieces of equipment. They reduce strain on your knees and are instrumental when navigating through high brush. We have hiked thousands of miles, and the only times we have fallen were when we were not using our poles! Beginner

Marlette Lake, Hike 70

hikers will be happy with inexpensive, low-end trekking poles. More committed hikers should invest in more durable, expensive poles. We learned this lesson only after breaking many cheap hiking poles when traversing over difficult terrain. The one disadvantage of trekking poles is that they slow you down, especially on paved trails or well-maintained dirt trails; however, you will not have the discomfort of puffy hands if you hike with poles. Without poles, blood tends to accumulate in your hands from their extended time in a pendulum-like motion, which results in an uncomfortable puffy feeling for many hikers.

For snowy adventures, metal cleats and aluminum-framed snowshoes are the two best options. Winter traction devices are cleats that strap onto the bottom of your boots. They are ideal for walking on icy surfaces and in areas where there is less than 6 inches of snow. These traction devices are lightweight, so you can keep them in your backpack at lower elevations and put them on at higher snowy elevations. Snowshoes are necessary for traversing through snow deeper than 6 inches at any appreciable speed. Even modern snowshoes are relatively cumbersome to carry on your back, so it is best to pack cleats unless you are sure most of your route will be through deep snow.

Essentials for the Hike

- Plenty of water
- Lunch and snacks
- Layers of clothing
- Sunscreen
- Small first-aid kit containing tweezers, moleskin, adhesive bandages, antibiotic ointment, antihistamine, ibuprofen, emergency matches, whistle, small scissors or a pocket knife, duct tape (tape a piece of some to a water bottle)
- GPS/smartphone
- Flashlight

Extras for the Hike

- Water filter (for longer hikes only)
- Binoculars
- Camera
- Lightweight blanket for picnicking
- Bug spray (not needed for 95 percent of hikes)
- Notebook

Barile family

Final Words

HIKING IS A WONDERFUL ANTIDOTE TO THE HECTICNESS OF OUR MODERN LIFESTYLES. Spend a few hours in the great outdoors focusing on the beauty of your surroundings, and you will likely feel all your worries melt away. Additionally, the more you hike, the more you will appreciate the intricacies and interdependencies of the natural world. Nature never ceases to surprise, and as the eminent mountaineer and conservationist John Muir wrote, "In every walk with nature one receives far more than he seeks." It seems as if the deeper you delve, the more beauty and mysteries are revealed. Whether it is the delicate form of a flower, the silence of falling snow, the rush of a raging river, or the piercing scream of a red-tailed hawk, there are endless sources of inspiration. For us, hiking keeps our bodies, minds, and souls healthy. We hope you find the same joy out in the wilderness. Happy trails!

Christopher & Elizabeth Barile
November 2021

The Northeastern Sierra Nevadas

The Lesser Known Sierras

Overshadowed by the popularity of the Lake Tahoe region, the northeastern Sierra Nevadas are a hidden gem. With bountiful meadows filled with wildflowers, numerous streams cutting vast canyons, and verdant springs dotting gorgeous mountainsides, these lesser known Sierras provide ample hiking opportunities.

Explore pristine waterways with adventures to Badenough Waterfalls (Hike 5), the Little Truckee River (Hike 9), and the Truckee River Canyon (Hike 12). Gain a bird's-eye perspective of the sheer cliffs of the Truckee River with an ascent of Boca Ridge (Hike 11). Hikes to Frenchman Lake (Hike 1) and Stampede Overlook (Hike 8) provide trips to two of the many reservoirs in the region.

Expeditions to Babbitt Fire Tower (Hike 6), Sardine Peak (Hike 7), and Verdi Fire Tower (Hike 10) take you to three summits adorned with fire towers that afford spectacular views of the Sierra Nevadas to the west and the Great Basin to the east. Hike to four different lakes with a trip to gorgeous Lakes Basin (Hike 3). The most difficult hike in the region is an off-trail pursuit to the top of Adams Peak (Hike 2), which stands nearly a mile above the desert landscapes of Long Valley below to the east. For those looking for an easier climb, explore those same desert landscapes more closely with the Beckwourth Pass Loop (Hike 4).

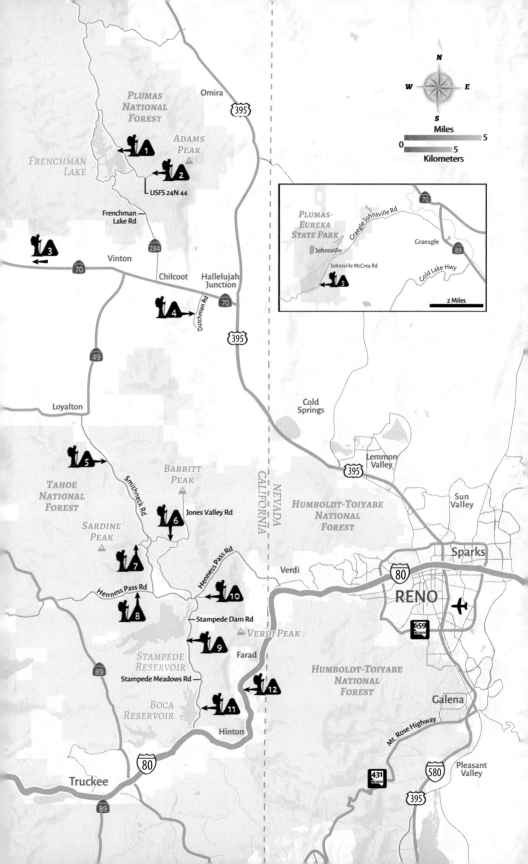

1 Frenchman Lake

TAKE AN EASY STROLL ALONG A SUBALPINE RESERVOIR WITH MYRIAD AQUATIC BIRDS AT the shore and eagles soaring above. This hike is perfect for all ages and skill levels.

At a Glance

DIFFICULTY	Very Easy	**DISTANCE/TIME**	1.6 miles/1 hour
ELEVATION GAIN	100 feet	**TRAIL TYPE**	Foot trail
SOLITUDE	Medium use	**USERS**	Hikers
BEST SEASON	May–November	**LAND OWNERSHIP**	National Forest
ANIMALS	Eagles, bears, deer	**FEATURES**	Lake, wildflowers

Deep in the Diamond Mountains, the headwaters of Little Last Chance Creek flow south to Sierra Valley. Frenchman Lake is a gorgeous reservoir formed by the damming of this creek a few miles north of Sierra Valley. Because it provides easy access to the Diamond Mountains wilderness, the Frenchman Lake area is popular with campers, anglers, birders, and hikers.

The hike is a short exploration of Crystal Vista, one of the most scenic of Frenchman Lake's many peninsulas. Walk past the parking area on a dirt foot trail that heads south. In 0.1 miles, you will be at the water's edge and have excellent views of the southern portion of the lake and surrounding mountains. Afterward, return to the parking area, and take the other foot trail that heads east. The trail

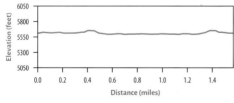

first passes a small cove, the shallow waters of which provide perfect recreating spots for families with young kids. Past the cove, you are granted larger views of the northern portion of the lake. As you hike, look for a wide variety of ducks, fish-loving birds of prey such as bald eagles and osprey, and shoreline birds such as avocets and sandpipers.

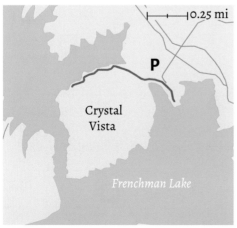

Frenchman Lake

After 0.6 miles, the trail gradually fades away. If desired, continue to explore the shoreline of Crystal Vista for as long as you like. Despite the lack of trail, the terrain is flat and open, making for easy navigation. An additional 1.7 miles is required to walk the entire perimeter of the peninsula. Otherwise, return to your car the way you came.

From Reno. Take Highway 395 north past the California state line for 23 miles. Take the exit for Highway 70 heading west toward Portola/Quincy. At the first stoplight in 5.7 miles, turn right onto Frenchman Lake Road. Take Frenchman Lake Road for 8.3 miles until it ends at the lake. Here at the T-junction, turn right, and drive for 1.9 miles until you reach a second T-junction. Turn left, and drive for an additional 2.0 miles. Following signs for Crystal Point, turn left, and drive for 0.1 miles to the large parking lot located at 39.9166, -120.1885. All dirt roads are suitable for low-clearance two-wheel-drive vehicles. *55 mins.*

One of many calm coves at Frenchman Lake

Frenchman Lake

2 Adams Peak

CLIMB TO THE BOULDER-CRESTED HIGH POINT OF THE DIAMOND MOUNTAINS, WHICH precipitously overhangs the Great Basin and affords spectacular views in all directions. This exhilarating hike is a strenuous off-trail adventure.

At a Glance

DIFFICULTY	Epic	DISTANCE/TIME	7.5 miles/7 hours
ELEVATION GAIN	2,500 feet	TRAIL TYPE	Dirt road, off trail
SOLITUDE	Complete solitude	USERS	Hikers, OHVs
BEST SEASON	July–November	LAND OWNERSHIP	National Forest
ANIMALS	Deer, bears	FEATURES	Expansive views, streams

After spanning 400 miles, the Sierra Nevada ridge makes its final stand in the Diamond Mountains before it gives way to the Cascades north of Susanville. As the northernmost range in the Sierra Nevadas, the Diamond Mountains lie at the interface between the volcanic Cascades to the north and the desert Great Basin peaks to the east. As a result, the flora and fauna of these mountains is incredibly diverse as it contains elements from all three regions. Towering above the surrounding valleys at 8,199 feet, Adams Peak invites adventurous hikers to boulder-strewn peaks with some of the best views in the Greater Reno area. Ex-

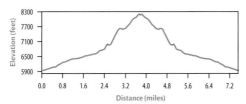

tensive off-trail climbing coupled with dense vegetation makes this hike particularly challenging.

The parking area is at the nexus of five dirt roads. Begin walking on the dirt road that

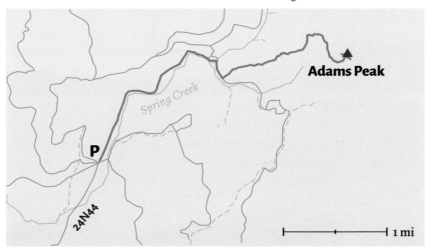

Looking up at Adams Peak from the first sandy plateau

heads north, which is labeled Snow Lake Road on some maps. Fortunately, a forest service sign at the parking area with an arrow pointing north toward Adams Peak eliminates any confusion as this is the direction to begin your hike. For the first 0.5 miles, the dirt road takes you through an open Jeffrey pine forest with a dense understory of sagebrush, bitterbrush, and manzanita. The road then follows Spring Creek, and water-loving aspens line your path. Willows, wild roses, and tobacco brush are also plentiful. In another 0.5 miles, the road climbs away from the creek as white fir and incense cedar intermix with large Jeffrey pines.

Although their exact number depends on the season, you will cross several small tributaries on the road. You will also pass a few junctions with poorly defined spur roads, but stay on the main path. In another 1.0 miles, the road will begin to level out as you reach a small meadow with a wooden fence and a house. Instead of continuing on the road past the house, turn left off the road, and begin your off-trail ascent to Adams Peak.

Your off-trail pursuit begins with a gradual ascent through a dry ravine over the first 0.3 miles as you head northeast. The next 0.2 miles are much steeper as you pass occasional granite outcroppings among the Jeffrey pine and fir forest. Head for the ridge above you. Once on top of the ridge, you can see into a ravine below you farther to the east. Fortunately, this ravine is only a couple of hundred feet below you, so you will not lose too much elevation before climbing again. The next 0.5 miles of climbing are the steepest of the hike. Hiking poles are highly

Rocky outcropping near the summit

recommended because the loose sandy soil here, blanketed with a layer of fallen pine needles, is especially slippery. The going will be particularly difficult if snow, which usually lingers until early summer, is on the ground. Although the terrain is steep, the groundcover vegetation is not dense, which makes finding your route easy.

After the steep climb, you will reach a flat sandy plateau filled with yellow mule's ears and pink Sierra beardtongues that bloom in the summer. As the eagle flies, Adams Peak is about 0.4 miles to the east. However, instead of climbing the steep cliff face in front of you, it is much easier to hike around it by going north. Avoid the densest groves of aspen and high brush as best you can. Here lies the spring-fed headwaters of Spring Creek, which give rise to the dense and verdant vegetation. After traveling north for 0.1 miles, turn right to head east for another 0.1 miles before climbing back south through a gently sloping ravine lined with Jeffrey pines. In about 0.3 miles, this ravine leads you to another sandy plateau with more wildflowers. This plateau sits at the base of Adams Peak.

Adams Peak consists of two summits that are only 0.1 miles apart. It is unclear which summit is higher, but both offer spectacular views and are exhilarating destinations. To climb the summits, hike to the sandy saddle point between the

Mixed pine forest off of the main ridge

two peaks. Both peaks are adorned with large, lichen-covered granite boulders. Stash your hiking poles at the saddle point, and use your hands and knees to climb the boulders. Although rock-climbing experience is not needed for these summits and the careful hiker can find straightforward paths, these final ascents are not recommended for those afraid of heights.

All of Frenchman Lake (Hike 1) is visible below you to the west. The Sierra Valley extends before you to the south with countless Sierra Nevada peaks fading away in the distance behind it. You will also have excellent views of Long Valley, particularly from the eastern summit, where you can watch cars drive on Highway 395 nearly a mile below you. After you have enjoyed the views from both summits, carefully return to your car the way you came.

From Reno. Take Highway 395 north past the California state line for 23 miles. Take the exit for Highway 70 heading west toward Portola/Quincy. At the first stoplight in 5.7 miles, turn right onto Frenchman Lake Road. In 4.6 miles, turn right on an unsigned forest service road (labeled 24N44 on maps). The road is the first main dirt road past the entrance sign to Plumas National Forest. 24N44 is a dirt road that is suitable for low-clearance two-wheel-drive vehicles under dry conditions. In 4.2 miles, park at a large five-way intersection at 39.8953, -120.1445. *1 hour.*

3 Lakes Basin

VISIT FOUR EXQUISITE BACKCOUNTRY LAKES CARVED IN SCENIC GRANITE BASINS ON THIS well-maintained trail in the Lost Sierras. Go fishing and swimming in the lakes, and enjoy the accompanying gold rush–era history.

At a Glance

DIFFICULTY	Hard	**DISTANCE/TIME**	7.9 miles/5 hours
ELEVATION GAIN	1,600 feet	**TRAIL TYPE**	Dirt trail
SOLITUDE	Heavy use	**USERS**	Hikers, bikers
BEST SEASON	June–October	**LAND OWNERSHIP**	State Park, National Forest
ANIMALS	Deer, bears	**FEATURES**	Lakes, streams, waterfalls, wildflowers

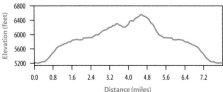

The portion of the northern Sierra Nevadas near the town of Graeagle has been dubbed the "Lost Sierras" because after California's gold rush era ended, it never received as much tourism as more popular Sierra destinations such as Lake Tahoe and Yosemite. Nevertheless, this portion of the Sierra Nevadas contains several spectacular hiking destinations. The centerpiece of the Lost Sierras is Lakes Basin, a collection of dozens of glacial-scoured lakes carved in rugged granite mountainsides. This gorgeous hike takes you to four pristine lakes along with 60-foot waterfalls. Because of heavy snow in the area, summer and early fall are the best times for this hike, which is also an excellent backpacking location.

From the parking area, walk through the campground to site number 54. Past this site, walk across the bridge that crosses Jamison Creek. A signed trailhead welcomes you to Jamison Creek Trail after a total distance of 0.4 miles.

At the beginning of the trail, you pass through the historic mining town of

Grass Lake

Manzanita along the trail from Grass Lake to the upper lakes

Jamison. Several nineteenth-century buildings still remain from bygone days of gold mining. You can learn more information about Jamison at the interpretative center that is at the entrance of Plumas-Eureka State Park, just up the road from the trailhead.

The first 0.5 miles of this trail are relatively steep, and a series of rocky steps have been constructed on the trail to aid you as you climb above the creek drainage. The creek supports a wide variety of tree species, including maples, alders, willows, pines, and firs. Past the steps, the trail continues to climb, albeit more gradually. In 0.2 miles, walk straight through the junction to continue on the main trail toward Grass Lake.

In another 0.2 miles, a sign pointing to the right leads you to Little Jamison Falls. The spur trail to the perennial waterfalls is well worth taking and only goes a few hundred feet off the main trail.

Back on the main trail, it is another 0.3 miles to Grass Lake. Grass Lake and

Jamison Lake

the subsequent three lakes on this hike are formed from snowmelt corralled in granite basins that were carved by an ancient glacier. This glacier eroded basins in the rock as it moved through the valley between Mount Washington to the west and Mount Elwell to the east. The steep walls of these two mountains give scenic backdrops to all four lakes.

Past Grass Lake, the trail continues to gradually climb and crosses over three intermittent streams. Previous hikers have strategically placed logs and rocks to help you with these stream crossings. Turn left at the junction 0.6 miles past the south end of Grass Lake to continue to Rock and Jamison Lakes. The trail terminates between the two lakes, but you can take several unofficial paths to explore the shores of both lakes. True to its name, Rock Lake contains the most boulders and least vegetation. Because of the lack of trees, it is the sunniest of the lakes and contains the least snow, making it a good spot to warm up on cold days. Jamison Lake is arguably the most beautiful of the four lakes, framed by dramatic

Heading down from Wades Lake with Grass Lake in the distance

granite cliffs. If you are feeling adventurous, you can swim out to its rocky island.

After you have enjoyed Rock and Jamison Lakes, head back to the main trail, and retrace your steps for 0.3 miles until you reach a junction. At the junction, turn left to climb up into the Wades Lake basin. Over the next 0.6 miles, the trail switchbacks steeply up a granite hillside before plateauing in a forest of lodgepole pine surrounding Wades Lake. The climb up to Wades Lake affords outstanding views of the lower lakes and the surrounding mountains. Beyond the mountainside that holds in Wades Lake lies the Sierra Nevada crest; these lakes truly lie deep in the center of the Sierras.

To return to the trailhead, walk through the forest away from Wades Lake, and in 0.3 miles, turn right at the junction to head back toward Jamison Creek Trail. During the next 0.5 miles, the trail descends steeply back to the junction south of Grass Lake. From here, retrace your steps for the remaining 2.6 miles to your car.

From Reno. Take Highway 395 north past the California state line for 23 miles. Take the exit for Highway 70 heading west toward Portola/Quincy. In 33.7 miles, turn left on Mohawk Highway Road. In 0.6 miles, turn right on Graeagle Johnsville Road. In 4.0 miles, turn left onto Johnsville McCrea Road, which takes you into Plumas-Eureka State Park. Park at the signed trailhead 1.2 miles down the road at 39.7423, -120.7075. *1 hour, 15 mins.*

4 Beckwourth Pass Loop

GET AWAY FROM CIVILIZATION ON DESERT HILLSIDES IN A REMOTE PORTION OF THE SIERRA Nevadas. Enjoy views of forested peaks above and expansive valleys below.

At a Glance

DIFFICULTY	Hard	DISTANCE/TIME	4.4 miles/3.5 hours
ELEVATION GAIN	1,900 feet	TRAIL TYPE	Off trail, dirt road
SOLITUDE	Complete solitude	USERS	Hikers
BEST SEASON	All	LAND OWNERSHIP	Bureau of Land Management
ANIMALS	Coyotes	FEATURES	Expansive views

Find solitude atop a pair of desert peaks in the northern Sierras located near Beckwourth Pass, the lowest-elevation pass in the Sierras. To begin your hike, walk 0.1 miles down the road, and turn right on a poorly defined trail that leads through a dry creek bed. The trail fades away as you continue to ascend Beckwourth Pass Benchmark, the first of the two peaks. Continue to stay close to the ravine, which will lead you all the way to the top. Some route finding is required to avoid the steepest portions. It is at least 1.0 miles to the top, but likely longer as you will be making your own switchbacks. The final summit block is not steep, and a relatively large sandy area sheltered with many rock outcroppings makes for an excellent break spot.

In August 2020, lightning in the area started a 47,000-acre fire that burned uncontrollably for nearly a month. The first-ever fire tornado warning was issued by the National Weather Service, and several tornadoes with fire-driven winds of 110 miles per hour touched down on these hills. Notice how new sagebrush and grasses have grown back among the charred vegetation. Low vegetation, like that found throughout this hike, recovers almost completely in a few years after a fire. Look for the once-forested taller mountains in the distance to the south. A conflagration of burning timber and dense brush there largely fueled the raging inferno that spread to surrounding sage steppes like Beckwourth Pass.

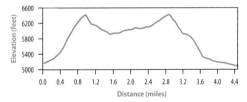

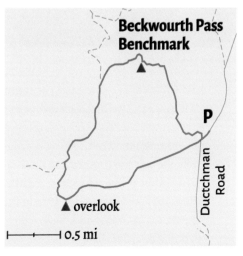

View from on top of Beckwourth Pass Benchmark

Return the way you came for a short trip. For a longer adventure, continue on to the next peak farther south. Walk to a jeep road on the west side of Beckwourth Pass Benchmark, which takes you through the saddle that connects to the second overlook. However, heading directly to the west is too steep, and the route is blocked by large boulders. Instead, go about 300 feet to the north before turning left to head west. This approach will take you through a ravine that although steep, is free from boulders.

From here, it is about 0.5 miles to the road, which is visible from the top of Beckwourth Pass Benchmark. Stay on the road, heading south for about 1.0 miles. The barren peak is visible from the jeep road. After about 1.0 miles, the jeep road begins to bend to the right and climb steeply. At this point, go off trail and continue south toward the peak. The ascent is gentle, and the summit consists of grasses scattered with low rocks. Enjoy the views of Sierra Valley to the west and Long Valley to the east. The return route to your car is mostly a direct northeast descent. Decline eastwardly down the peak via the least steep route, which is clearly visible. Trek through three ravines running east-west on your way back.

From Reno. Take Highway 395 north past the California state line for 23 miles. Take the exit for Highway 70 heading west toward Portola/Quincy. In 2.5 miles, turn left on Dutchman Road, a dirt road that is suitable for low-clearance two-wheel-drive vehicles under dry conditions. Drive on Dutchman Road for 1.5 miles, and park at 39.7673, -120.0905, which is near a ranch home. There is no formal parking area, but there is space for one car in the wide spots of the road. *35 mins.*

5 Badenough Waterfalls

THIS SECLUDED HIKE JUST OUTSIDE OF SIERRA VALLEY HAS A LITTLE BIT OF EVERYTHING and is accessible to everyone. Experience lovely landscapes, waterfalls, and Native American petroglyphs.

At a Glance

DIFFICULTY	Easy	**DISTANCE/TIME**	3.2 miles/1.5 hours
ELEVATION GAIN	500 feet	**TRAIL TYPE**	Dirt road
SOLITUDE	Light use	**USERS**	Hikers
BEST SEASON	All	**LAND OWNERSHIP**	National Forest
ANIMALS	Deer, cattle	**FEATURES**	Petroglyphs, waterfalls

Just outside of Sierra Valley in the foothills of the northern Bald Mountains, water from several springs trickles down gentle sloping canyons to form Badenough Creek. With the open grasslands of Sierra Valley below you, snow-capped mountains above you, and Jeffrey pine forest around you, this hike takes you through an idyllic corner of the eastern Sierra Nevadas. In addition to beautiful landscapes, you will be treated to Native American petroglyphs and secluded 10-foot waterfalls.

Out of the parking area, walk through the forest service gate. Follow the dirt road east, which takes you through scattered Jeffrey pines mixed with sagebrush and manzanita understory. In 0.2 miles, walk to a conspicuously large boulder about 100 feet off trail to the right. The 6-foot-tall and 10-foot-wide boulder is unsigned and unadvertised, but it is the only large rock in the area, making it easy to spot from the trail.

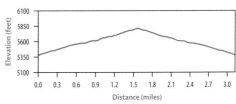

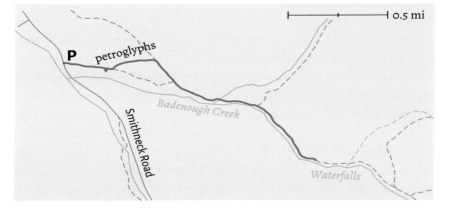

Ancient petroglyph rock art

The boulder is covered in Native American petroglyphs, likely created by ancient Washoe people. Most obvious are the numerous spiral patterns carved into the stone. There are also several small holes, or rock cupules, that were hammered into the rock. Cupules are the most common form of petroglyph and are found worldwide, and their meaning is not known. Please treat this special area with respect.

Return to the dirt road, and continue hiking east. In 0.1 miles, veer left at the junction, and in 0.2 miles, turn right at another junction to stay on the main road. Here, an intermittent tributary nourishes grasses in a small meadow, often frequented by grazing cattle. The road takes you to the edge of perennial Badenough Creek in 0.3 miles. Deer are common along with a plethora of birds such as sparrows, grosbeaks, woodpeckers, and warblers. Frogs croak along the banks in the evening, and fish dart in the cold water. Willows and aspen line the creek drainage and turn beautiful fall colors late in the year. After the leaves are gone and snow has fallen, the flat terrain is amenable to snowshoeing.

In 0.8 more miles, the waterfalls are visible from the road to the right. A short but steep foot trail leads to the base of the falls. In the late spring and early summer, a number of water-loving wildflowers add color to the area. After you have enjoyed the waterfalls, return to the road, and descend back to the trailhead.

Badenough Falls

From Reno. Take Highway 395 north past the California state line for 23 miles. Take the exit for Highway 70 heading west toward Portola/Quincy. In 7.8 miles, turn left on Highway 49 towards Loyalton. In 10.2 miles, just before the town of Loyalton, turn left onto Smithneck Road. Drive for 3.6 miles, and turn left onto unsigned Badenough Canyon Road. Park in the dirt area at the forest service gate at 39.6320, -120.1995. *50 mins.*

6 Babbitt Fire Tower

HIKE UP A LUSH CANYON WITH SUMMER WILDFLOWERS AND BEAUTIFUL FALL COLORS TO the top of Babbitt Peak, the highest point in the Bald Mountains.

At a Glance

DIFFICULTY	Hard	**DISTANCE/TIME**	8.7 miles/5 hours
ELEVATION GAIN	1,800 feet	**TRAIL TYPE**	Dirt road
SOLITUDE	Light use	**USERS**	Hikers, OHVs
BEST SEASON	June–November	**LAND OWNERSHIP**	National Forest
ANIMALS	Deer, bears	**FEATURES**	Expansive views, wildflowers, streams

Located near the Nevada-California border, Babbitt Peak is the highest point of the Bald Mountains at 8,760 feet. As the tallest peak within a 17-mile radius, the mountaintop affords outstanding views of the Sierra Nevadas to the west and the Great Basin to the east. Because a forest road leads to the top and the summit is part of a gentle sloping ridge, hiking Babbitt Peak is much easier than other mountains of similar grandeur in the Northeastern Sierras.

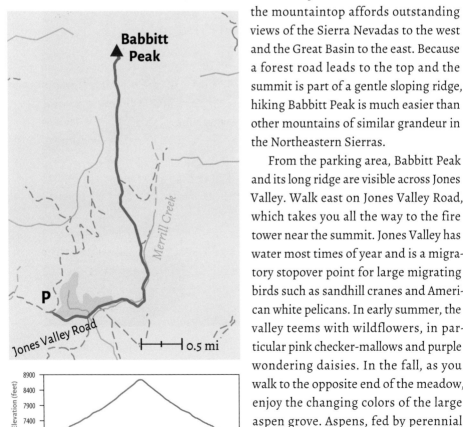

From the parking area, Babbitt Peak and its long ridge are visible across Jones Valley. Walk east on Jones Valley Road, which takes you all the way to the fire tower near the summit. Jones Valley has water most times of year and is a migratory stopover point for large migrating birds such as sandhill cranes and American white pelicans. In early summer, the valley teems with wildflowers, in particular pink checker-mallows and purple wondering daisies. In the fall, as you walk to the opposite end of the meadow, enjoy the changing colors of the large aspen grove. Aspens, fed by perennial Merrill Creek, are common throughout the hike. As their leaves transition from

Plenty of colorful aspens make this a beautiful fall hike.

green to yellow to orange to brown, the location of any one color shifts about 500 feet lower in elevation per week in the autumn due to colder temperatures at higher elevations. As a result, you have more than a month's window to view the fall colors on Babbitt Peak, with the peak viewing times typically during October.

Past Jones Valley, the trail steadily climbs. In 1.5 miles, the trail bends around some interesting rock formations, and a short spur trail to the left leads to a plateau. This area has nice views of the valley and is a good breaking spot. In the summer, look here for wild elderberries in the rocky drainages surrounding Merrill Creek.

As you climb farther, the forest ecosystem becomes increasingly diverse. The conifers include Jeffrey, lodgepole, and western white pines along with red and white firs. On the eastern slopes of Babbitt Peak near the summit, the rare Washoe pine grows. A 90-acre grove here is the only area in the world with pure stands of Washoe pine. This little-studied pine is also found in isolated pockets on Mount Rose (Hike 75).

Many large western junipers also line the trail, so look for nearby bear tracks. In the fall, when other food sources begin to dwindle, black bears rely heavily on juniper berries. Although the berries are edible for both bears and humans, their intense flavor will quickly teach you why these juicy berries are not an ursine delicacy.

While the conifers dominate the slopes, in flatter areas where snowmelt accumulates, large patches of mule's ears, which bloom yellow in the summer, are ubiquitous. In another 1.0 miles, spectacular views develop along the main ridge-line of Babbitt Peak. Behind you and to your left, Sardine Valley and Stampede Reservoir lie below you. Ahead of you, a large grove of aspens blankets the ravine that forms the headwaters of Rock Creek.

The end of the road leads you to the Babbitt Fire Tower. Unlike most fire towers in California, this tower is staffed during fire seasons. Despite increasing reliance on satellites, manned fire towers are still the most effective way to detect fires early. The true high point of Babbitt Peak, marked by a small rock pile, is located a few hundred feet north of the fire tower. On a clear day, Lassen Peak and Mount Shasta are visible to the north. The latter is 170 miles away. Cragged Sierra Buttes (Hike 51) is easily identified to the west, and Peavine Peak (Hike 40) dominates the foreground to the east. Sierra Nevada peaks as far as those on the south side of Lake Tahoe are also visible. Hike back down the way you came to return to the parking area.

From Reno. Take Highway 395 north past the California state line for 23 miles. Take the exit for Highway 70 heading west toward Portola/Quincy. In 7.8 miles, turn left on Highway 49 toward Loyalton. In 10.2 miles, just before the town of Loyalton, turn left onto Smithneck Road. Drive for 9.8 miles before turning left on Jones Valley Road at the sign for Jones Valley and Babbitt Peak. After 1.8 miles, park in a dirt turnout to the right of the road at 39.5589, -120.1212. Smithneck Road and Jones Valley Road are dirt roads suitable for low-clearance two-wheel-drive vehicles under dry conditions. *1 hour, 10 mins.*

The Babbitt fire tower

7 Sardine Peak

A KALEIDOSCOPE OF COLOR AWAITS YOU. LAKE BLUES, FOREST GREENS, AND SNOW whites mix with wildflower rainbows to give magical vistas during your climb to Sardine Peak.

At a Glance

DIFFICULTY	Hard	**DISTANCE/TIME**	8.5 miles/5 hours
ELEVATION GAIN	1,700 feet	**TRAIL TYPE**	Dirt road
SOLITUDE	Light use	**USERS**	Hikers, OHVs
BEST SEASON	July–November	**LAND OWNERSHIP**	National Forest
ANIMALS	Deer, bears	**FEATURES**	Expansive views

Tahoe National Forest in the area surrounding Stampede Reservoir is exquisite country. Within the National Forest, Sardine Peak is a wonderful destination north of Sardine Valley, a thousand-acre meadow that teems with purple and yellow wildflowers in early summer. Along with deer and bears, the forest here supports many different types of birds and trees.

From the parking area, cross the bridge over aspen-lined Smithneck Creek, and continue up the forest service road through mixed coniferous forest along the right side of the creek. In 1.5 miles, a meadow filled with summer wildflowers opens up to the left of the creek. Springs feed these wildflowers and form the headwaters of perennial Smithneck Creek.

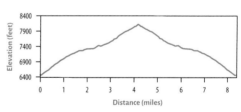

After 1.0 more miles of gentle climbing, you reach a ridge with

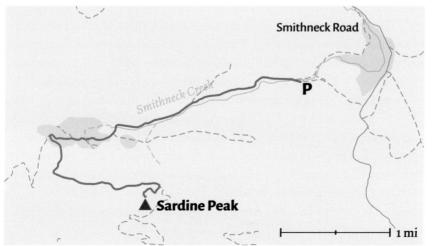

Mount Rose Wilderness with Boca Reservoir in the foreground from the top of Sardine Peak

views of the valleys to the west. At the dirt road junction, turn left to continue climbing the additional 1.7 miles to Sardine Peak. If hiking during spring, be prepared for significant amounts of snow on this shaded north side of the mountain.

A recently renovated fire tower sits on top of the summit. Two flights of stairs take you to a balcony with extraordinary wraparound views. Eat your lunch at the picnic table at the base of the fire tower. Enjoy exquisite views of the many meadows in the greater Stampede Reservoir area below you. To the south, there are outstanding views of Mount Rose Wilderness with, from left to right, Snowflower Mountain, Mount Rose (Hike 75), and Mount Houghton and Relay Peak (Hike 76) visible in all their glory. Behind these peaks, Mount Tallac and other peaks in the Desolation Wilderness stand tall. Many desert peaks of Nevada are visible to the east. Among the landmarks to the west, Sierra Buttes (Hike 51) draws attention, sticking out like a castle in the sky. Return the way you came to your car.

From Reno. Take Highway 395 north past the California state line for 23 miles. Take the exit for Highway 70 heading west toward Portola/Quincy. In 7.8 miles, turn left on Highway 49 toward Loyalton. In 10.2 miles, just before the town of Loyalton, turn left onto Smithneck Road. In 10.4 miles, just after Pat's Meadow, turn right on an unmarked forest service road. Park in a dirt turnout located at 39.5553, -120.1610. Smithneck Road and the forest service road are dirt roads suitable for low-clearance two-wheel-drive vehicles under dry conditions. *1 hour, 10 mins.*

Sunset at the headwaters of Smithneck Creek

8 Stampede Overlook

THIS SHORT OFF-TRAIL ASCENT CULMINATES IN OUTSTANDING VIEWS OF STAMPEDE
Reservoir. With nobody else in the area, the only chatter you will hear is that of
birds, chipmunks, and the cool lake-driven wind.

At a Glance

DIFFICULTY	Hard	DISTANCE/TIME	2.7 miles/2 hours
ELEVATION GAIN	1,200 feet	TRAIL TYPE	Off trail, dirt road
SOLITUDE	Complete solitude	USERS	Hikers
BEST SEASON	June–November	LAND OWNERSHIP	National Forest
ANIMALS	Deer, bears	FEATURES	Expansive views, streams, lakes

In the 1850s, a road through Henness Pass across the Sierras was the main
commercial supply route for Nevada silver and gold miners. Today, Henness Pass
Road, which stretches 88 miles from Verdi, Nevada, to Camptonville, California,
is a lightly used dirt recreational road that passes through beautiful landscapes.

This hike is a short off-trail climb to the top of a peak with excellent views of
Stampede Reservoir and Henness Pass. Once at the parking area, immediately
head south down the road cut and toward perennial Davies Creek. Be prepared

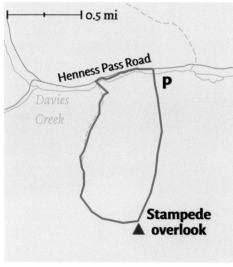
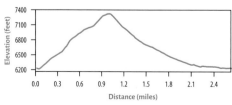

to get your feet and ankles wet if traversing in early spring. Once across the creek, continue heading south up the forested slopes. On your ascent, you will cross three faint logging roads. Your exact approach is unimportant because the ascent is not steep.

You will reach the summit after 1.1 miles of trekking across lightly vegetated forest. The only obstacles along the way are several dense patches of manzanita bushes, which can easily be avoided. Enjoy the out-

Willows and pines

standing summit views. In late spring and early summer, Sardine Valley below will be carpeted in brilliant wildflowers. The major peaks of Mount Rose Wilderness stretch majestically behind Stampede Reservoir.

You can return the way you came or take a different approach down and

Stampede Reservoir and the Sierra Nevadas

explore any of the numerous spring-fed tributaries on the mountain's north side.

From Reno. Take I-80 west for 24.2 miles to the Hirschdale Road exit. Turn left on Hirschdale Road/Stampede Meadows Road, and drive for 10.2 miles until you reach Henness Pass Road. Turn left on Henness Pass Road, a dirt road suitable for low-clearance two-wheel-drive vehicles under dry conditions. In 3.3 miles, turn left at a junction to stay on Henness Pass Road. Drive for 1.1 miles, and park at 39.5125, -120.1627 in a shoulder on the left side of the road. *1 hour, 10 mins.*

Uncovering one of many springs on the slopes

9 Little Truckee River

Hike along a meandering portion of the Little Truckee River in between Boca and Stampede Reservoirs. Look for wildlife and wildflowers during this flat adventure suitable for all ages.

At a Glance

DIFFICULTY	Easy	DISTANCE/TIME	2.1 miles/1 hour
ELEVATION GAIN	200 feet	TRAIL TYPE	Foot trail
SOLITUDE	Medium use	USERS	Hikers, anglers
BEST SEASON	All	LAND OWNERSHIP	National Forest
ANIMALS	Deer, bears	FEATURES	River, wildflowers

Enjoy a peaceful hike along an easily accessible portion of the Little Truckee River, the largest tributary of the Truckee River. The river provides habitat for a wide variety of birds, and the lush vegetation provides coverage for large mammals such as deer and black bears.

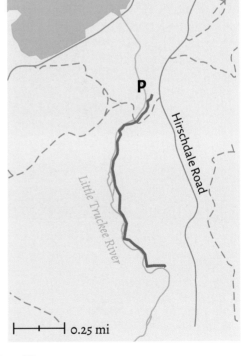

From the parking area, take the foot trail that follows the river downstream. Throughout the hike, several spur trails lead you to the water's edge. The trail alternates between the shade of lodgepole and Jeffrey pine trees and open riparian vegetation consisting of wildflowers and willows.

In 1.0 miles, the river bends sharply to the left. During periods of low flow, adventurous hikers can navigate across the steep rock wall and continue hiking downstream for several miles. Otherwise, the rock wall marks a good place to turn around and head back to the trailhead.

From Reno. Take I-80 west for 24.2 miles to the Hirschdale Road exit. Turn left on Hirschdale Road/Stampede Meadows Road, and drive for 7.0 miles. Turn left into a dirt parking area at 39.4675, -120.1024 just before Stampede Reservoir. *40 mins.*

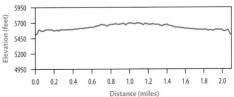

Enjoying the Little Truckee River

At the banks of the Little Truckee River

10 Verdi Fire Tower

FOR OUTSTANDING MOUNTAIN VIEWS, NOTHING BEATS A FIRE TOWER. MAKE THE challenging climb to the tower at the top of Verdi Peak for impressive panoramas of snow and desert.

At a Glance

DIFFICULTY	Epic	**DISTANCE/TIME**	11.3 miles/8 hours
ELEVATION GAIN	2,500 feet	**TRAIL TYPE**	Dirt road
SOLITUDE	Light use	**USERS**	Hikers, OHVs
BEST SEASON	July–November	**LAND OWNERSHIP**	National Forest
ANIMALS	Deer, bears	**FEATURES**	Expansive views, streams, wildflowers

The Verdi Range is a 12-mile stretch of beautiful wilderness in the northern Sierras. The range runs from the Truckee River to the south to Henness Pass to the north. It is home to the closest large swath of forested open space to downtown Reno and provides welcome respite from summer heat on the lightly shaded desert floor. Climb to Verdi Peak, both the highest point in the Verdi Range and a prominent point in the Reno skyline.

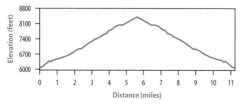

Verdi and the neighboring peaks in the range are uniquely two-faced. The western slopes are lush with pine trees, and snowmelt feeds nearby Stampede Reservoir. In contrast, the eastern slopes are classic desert with sagebrush on the lower slopes that is replaced by dense thickets of manzanita higher in elevation.

From the parking area, hike east past the campground and a small stream. Continue walking straight across the stream and up along the main road. The road narrows and becomes increasingly rough. On your right, you will soon pass a small grove of aspen trees fed by a branch of the stream you previously crossed. The road, now more like a foot trail, bends away from the stream until

View from atop the fire tower

it reaches a larger dirt road 0.6 miles from the trailhead. Turn left on this wider dirt road, and take it for 0.2 miles before turning right on an eastward, narrower dirt road. Follow this road all the way to Verdi Peak. After 4.6 miles of total hiking, a spur trail to the left (north) takes you to Ladybug if you desire.

An old fire tower on top of Verdi Peak makes for a good resting spot and offers exquisite views of Tahoe National Forest and the Greater Reno area. Marvel at the sheerness of the Truckee Canyon, the serenity of the northern Sierras, and the vastness of western Nevada in the distance.

Thousands of convergent ladybugs at the top of Ladybug Peak

Verdi Peak can easily be doubled with nearby Ladybug Peak, which is less than 1.0 miles away. Ladybug Peak is so named for the tens of thousands of colorful beetles that migrate to its mountaintop each autumn. As air temperatures cool in the fall, ladybugs fly to the top of peaks with the help of strong mountain wind currents. They then huddle together and hibernate while they are buried in feet of snow in the winter. It is a mystery why ladybugs congregate on some peaks and not others or why they even climb peaks at all. One theory is that they choose mountaintops because these remote hiding

Nearly all of Reno is visible from the top.

places are safe from predators. Ladybug colonies can be found on top of several peaks throughout the Greater Reno area, including Spanish Springs Peak (Hike 36) and Relay Peak (Hike 76).

If you choose to visit Ladybug Peak in addition to Verdi Peak, budget for an additional mile of hiking and 400 feet additional elevation gain. Return to the trailhead the way you came.

From Reno. Take I-80 west for 24.2 miles to the Hirschdale Road exit. Turn left on Hirschdale Road/Stampede Meadows Road, and drive for 10.2 miles until you reach Henness Pass Road. Turn right on Henness Pass Road, and in 0.1 miles turn right on a dirt road leading to a campground. Drive for 0.3 miles to the opposite side of the campground, and park near 39.5081, -120.0798. The dirt roads on this route, which begin with Henness Pass Road, are suitable for low-clearance two-wheel-drive vehicles under dry conditions. *50 mins.*

11 Boca Ridge

WITH LAKE VIEWS TO THE WEST AND SHEER CANYON VIEWS TO THE EAST, THERE IS PLENTY to look at on this hike. Halfway through, break at a series of springs among birds and butterflies.

At a Glance

DIFFICULTY	Hard	**DISTANCE/TIME**	9.0 miles/5 hours
ELEVATION GAIN	1,800 feet	**TRAIL TYPE**	Dirt road, off trail
SOLITUDE	Light use	**USERS**	Hikers, OHVs
BEST SEASON	March–November	**LAND OWNERSHIP**	National Forest
ANIMALS	Deer, bears	**FEATURES**	Expansive views, lakes, springs

Boca Ridge is the high point of the sheer cliffs on the west side of the Truckee River near the Nevada-California border. This hike reaches Boca Ridge from the more gentle slopes starting from Boca Reservoir. It features charm, shade, and water while still allowing hikers to appreciate the rugged terrain on the opposite side of the ridge.

After hiking up the dirt road on which you parked, you will reach your first junction in 0.1 miles. Turn left at the junction, and in 0.7 miles turn right at another junction to begin your ascent westward.

After 2.1 miles of additional climbing, the relatively sparse

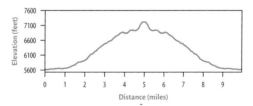

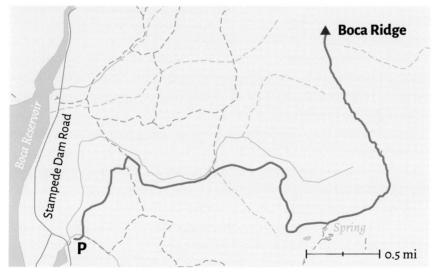

Above: At its beginning, the trail leads you through Jeffrey pine forest.   *Below: Boca Springs*

Jeffrey pine forest transitions to a dense, more diverse forest, which includes incense cedars, firs, and several species of deciduous trees. This area of biodiversity is made possible by a series of springs in the area. Birds and deer abound, and the springs, which are only a few hundred feet to the right of the main road, can be visited via a spur road.

Farther up the road, excellent views of Boca, Stampede, and Prosser Reservoirs open up to the east. Simultaneously, you will appreciate steep Truckee Canyon below you to the west. You will pass an enormous timber cross somebody erected on the right. When you reach the end of the road after 1.4 additional miles, continue to ascend off trail. The vegetation here is relatively open, and you will reach the summit after 0.2 miles of gentle bushwhacking. The flat ridge is sheltered by a few Jeffrey pines and large manzanita bushes. Views of the Truckee River canyon and overhanging Mount Rose Wilderness are stunning. Return the way you came.

From Reno. Take I-80 west for 24.2 miles to the Hirschdale Road exit. Turn left on Hirschdale Road/Stampede Meadows Road, and drive for 1.9 miles. Turn right onto an unmarked dirt road, and park in the dirt turnout on the left immediately off of Stampede Meadows Road at 39.4053, -120.0848. *30 mins.*

12 Truckee River Canyon

FOLLOW THE ROARING TRUCKEE RIVER THROUGH A DIVERSE ARRAY OF VEGETATION AND wildlife habitats. Marvel at the steep canyon walls while enjoying the flat riverside trail.

At a Glance

DIFFICULTY	Easy	DISTANCE/TIME	4.7 miles/2 hours
ELEVATION GAIN	400 feet	TRAIL TYPE	Foot trail
SOLITUDE	Heavy use	USERS	Hikers, bikers
BEST SEASON	All	LAND OWNERSHIP	Wildlife area
ANIMALS	Deer, bears	FEATURES	River, wildflowers

Hike along a rugged portion of the Truckee River, where the canyon walls rise steeply above you on both sides. The hike follows a portion of the Tahoe-Pyramid Trail, which when its construction is complete will follow the entire course of the river from Lake Tahoe to Pyramid Lake.

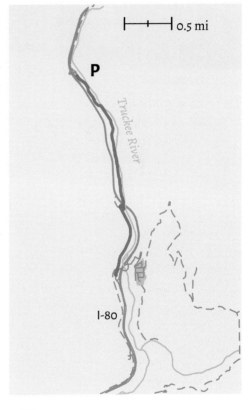

From the parking area, head to the right and follow the wide gravel trail upstream. In 0.2 miles, stairs take you over the Farad hydroelectric power plant. Built in 1899, this power plant is not operational, but three similar power plants downstream still power Reno today. Past the power plant, notice the flume structure to your right, which consists of an elevated wooden platform. Some flumes were used to manage water for hydroelectric power plants, while others were used to transport logs to saw mills or bring ice to Reno and Virginia City.

As you continue walking along the Truckee River, some of the trail takes you through dry vegetation consisting of Jeffrey pines, mountain mahogany, sagebrush, bitterbrush, and rabbitbrush.

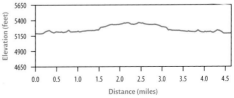

A beaver's work

When the trail veers closer to the river, the diversity of the vegetation increases to include willows, bitter cherries, chokecherries, and serviceberries. These large bushes are also interspersed with stinging nettle, primroses, larkspurs, and many other wildflowers. Look also for gnawed trees along the river bank, which are the work of resident beavers.

You can continue hiking along the river for another 2.1 miles until you reach the Floriston exit on I-80. Arrange for a second car to pick you up here, or enjoy the easy downhill hike back to the trailhead.

From Reno. Take I-80 west for 17.0 miles to the Farad exit. Park at 39.4223, -120.0344 in the parking area immediately following the off-ramp. *20 mins.*

Looking down the canyon

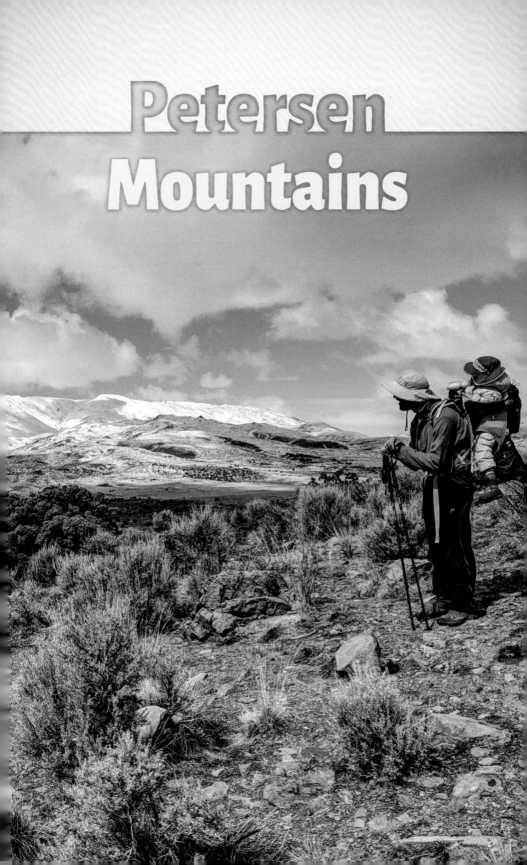

Petersen
Mountains

The Great Basin Desert with a Sierra Nevada Twist

The seven hikes in this chapter span the Petersen Range, the Little Petersen Range, and the surrounding foothills. Although these mountain ranges are in the Great Basin Desert, their proximity to the Sierra Nevadas causes them to receive more precipitation than typical desert locales. As a result, hikers can enjoy excellent hiking opportunities across ecological zones that are a lovely mixture of those found in the Sierra Nevadas and Great Basin.

Little Petersen (Hike 16), Goldstone Loop (Hike 17), and Silver Knolls (Hike 19) are easier and shorter hikes that take you through lower sage-juniper woodlands and wildflowers. Choose Sand Hills (Hike 14) for a longer outing that is still relatively flat. Red Rock Cliffs (Hike 13) is a short but adventurous scramble through exquisitely vibrant rock formations. Cold Springs (Hike 18) is a great introductory hike in the Petersen Range for those craving grand mountaintop views. The most difficult hike in this chapter is Petersen Springs (Hike 15), which is an off-trail journey that takes you not only to numerous springs on steep slopes but to the highest point in the Petersen Range. It is among the authors' favorite hikes in the Greater Reno area.

All of the hikes with the exception of Cold Springs (Hike 18) begin off of Red Rock Road. This 25-mile scenic country road runs from Silver Lake in North Reno to just past the California state line.

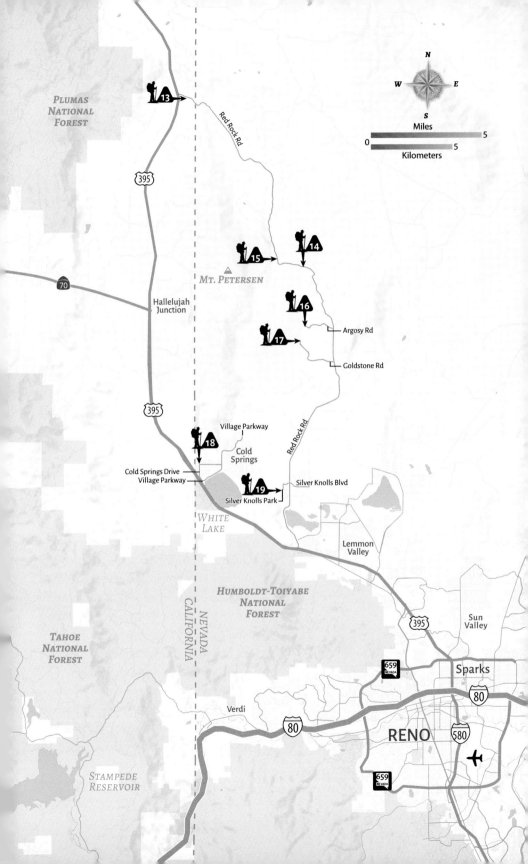

13 Red Rock Cliffs

SCRAMBLE AMONG GORGEOUS OUTCROPPINGS OF VIBRANT RED, WHITE, PURPLE, AND yellow rocks. A trail takes you to the base of the rocks, but from there explore the steep colorful cliffs as much as you please.

At a Glance

DIFFICULTY	Hard	DISTANCE/TIME	1.5 miles/1.5 hours
ELEVATION GAIN	800 feet	TRAIL TYPE	Foot trail, off trail
SOLITUDE	Light use	USERS	Hikers
BEST SEASON	September–June	LAND OWNERSHIP	Bureau of Land Management
ANIMALS	Jackrabbits	FEATURES	Colorful rock formations

Near the California-Nevada state line you will find the brilliantly colored outcroppings of Red Rock Cliffs. Here, towers of brick red, chalk white, lavender, and yellow-green rise above the sage and juniper vegetation. The rocks were formed about 25 million years ago from the ash of an ancient volcano. The ash was buried, and the resulting pressure caused it to accumulate into masses of soft rock. Today, erosion has revealed the rock in what are called volcanic tuffs. The tuffs at Red Rock Cliffs consist of a mixture of several minerals including quartz, feldspars, and biotite. Slight variations in mineral composition differentiate the red, white,

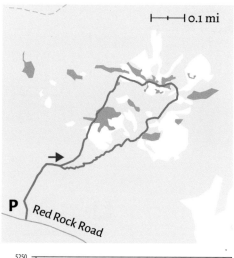

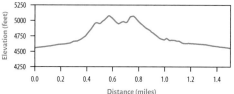

and purple rocks. Higher concentrations of iron give rise to the red rocks for the same reason that our blood is red.

The hike is a short but challenging adventure into the rock formations. From the parking area, head north out of a small stand of juniper trees and onto a well-defined dirt road. The tuffs are immediately visible. After 0.3 miles, you will find yourself at the base of a large mass of red and white outcroppings, and the road will lose definition. From here, you can choose from several poorly defined foot trails that enable you to explore the area. To immerse yourself in the rocks, follow the trail that heads straight up into the lower white outcropping. It is easiest to scramble up this outcropping along its west side because the east side is

The western red and white rock outcroppings

Taking a break under a Utah juniper

quite steep. Be sure to wear shoes with good traction, and hiking poles are recommended. Soft, crumbly pebbles from the tuffs make for very slippery terrain.

Once atop the first red rock outcropping, you can stop and savor the views on the flatter ground of the sage and juniper. To the south, the Petersen Range extends ahead of you. Look below you to the west at sinuous Long Valley Creek running parallel to Highway 395. Behind the creek lies heavily forested Adams Peak, which rises 3,000 feet above you. Adams Peak (Hike 2) is snow-capped half the year and is the highest point of the Diamond Mountains. These mountains are the northernmost in the Sierra Nevada with peaks farther north belonging to the Cascades. Your vantage point, however, lies in the Great Basin, plac-

Sheer red cliffs

ing you at the intersection of three large geographical locales. The result is that the area boasts wonderful geological and ecological variety.

If after enjoying the views you are inspired to hike deeper into this country, open Bureau of Land Management space abounds. You can head off trail farther north 2.0 miles to summit Seven Lakes Mountain for an even grander vista. Just do not be fooled by the name. The seven "lakes" are merely seven ponds that hold water only in the winter. Otherwise, begin the loop plotted on the included map by heading east for 0.2 miles across more colorful outcroppings. Notice below you to the east the large, highly corrugated white outcropping. The beautifully symmetric corrugations are the result of years of erosion by snowmelt slowly percolating through the soft tuffs. Head south along the west side of this rock network, finding your way to a sandy ravine. The ravine makes for easy downhill hiking that allows you to still enjoy the colorful outcroppings without worrying as much about slipping down them. You can take the ravine all the way back to the parking area or cut over to the starting dirt road when the ravine widens out and its walls become less steep.

From Reno. Take Highway 395 north past the California state line for 33 miles. Turn right on Red Rock Road. In 0.5 miles, an unlabeled dirt parking area among juniper trees is visible to your left at 39.9077, -120.0052. *35 mins.*

Above the canyon with spectacular rock outcroppings

14 Sand Hills

HIKE THE GENTLE ROLLING TERRAIN OF THE LARGE SAND HILLS EXPANSE. THE TRAIL IS FLAT and wide, making this an excellent outing for hikers of all age groups.

At a Glance

DIFFICULTY	Easy	**DISTANCE/TIME**	6.8 miles/3 hours
ELEVATION GAIN	600 feet	**TRAIL TYPE**	Dirt road
SOLITUDE	Medium use	**USERS**	Hikers, equestrians, OHVs
BEST SEASON	September–June	**LAND OWNERSHIP**	Bureau of Land Management
ANIMALS	Deer, antelope	**FEATURES**	Rock formations

Just east of the Petersen Range, the Sand Hills stretch for 10,000 acres as an array of rolling knolls topped with pink granite lined with white sandy quartz-rich valleys. The entire area is open space actively managed by the Bureau of Land Management as an antelope and deer migration area. Because of the migrations, motorized vehicles are forbidden in the Sand Hills from December to April, making this period an excellent time for hikers seeking extra solitude. Regardless of when you visit, this relatively flat hike is a great introduction to the wide swath of desert open space north of Reno.

Begin your hike by walking over the cattle guard at the trail's entrance and onto the sandy road. The light green sage and white sand characteristic of most of the hike are immediately striking and contrast with the tan mountaintops covered with juniper in the surrounding taller mountains. After 1.0 miles of traveling straight on this gentle and wide road, you will pass a large corral for equestrians. On a typical summer day, you are likely to see several horseback riders because the area is popular with beginner equestrians. At the corral, head mostly straight but veer to the right to stay on the main road. After an additional 0.9 miles, you will reach a junction and need to turn right on another sandy road. This road will gradually descend 150 feet over the next 0.8 miles. The main road then begins to climb, and near the

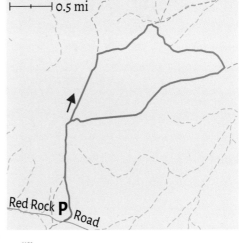

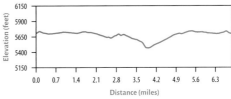

Sandy trail with Mt. Petersen views

Serpentine trail heading back to the trailhead

inflection point, you will pass a small water tank, presumably built to fill nearby horse troughs.

Climb on the main road, which is a straight shot, for the next 0.6 miles. After a gentle climb, the road bends to the right and ends its ascent as it wraps around Granite Peak, visible in front of you. Keep your eyes open for deer and antelope, which are abundant here and browse on vast quantities of sage and bitterbrush. Each year, approximately 3,000 mule deer that make up the so-called Truckee-Loyalton herd, migrate from the Sierra Nevadas to the Sand Hills and surrounding desert areas to spend the winter. In a typical year, the herd will leave the Sierras in October and return in May to browse on more nutritious upper montane vegetation. Antelope are common too and can be distinguished from mule deer by their black faces and distinct horns.

As you traipse by Granite Peak, you will soon pass a strange rusty tanker of a bygone era on the side of the road. The route then descends nearly 300 feet over the next mile. At the low point, you will reach a junction. Take a right to head west back toward your original route. This stretch is a gentle climb up for 1.5 miles to regain the elevation you just lost. Back at the large horse corral, retrace your steps the last mile back to the car.

From Reno. Take Highway 395 north for 9.5 miles to the Red Rock Road exit in Nevada. Drive for 14 miles on scenic Red Rock Road. Park at 39.8023, -119.9102 in a large Bureau of Land Management dirt parking area on the right side of the road. *30 mins.*

15 Petersen Springs

EMBARK ON AN EPIC OFF-TRAIL ASCENT TO THE HIGHEST POINT IN THE PETERSEN RANGE.
Hike through remote wetlands teeming with wildlife, and discover the many
surprises of the desert.

At a Glance

DIFFICULTY	Epic	**DISTANCE/TIME**	6.8 miles/8 hours
ELEVATION GAIN	2,900 feet	**TRAIL TYPE**	Off trail, dirt road
SOLITUDE	Complete solitude	**USERS**	Hikers
BEST SEASON	March–June, September–November	**LAND OWNERSHIP**	Bureau of Land Management
ANIMALS	Deer, antelope	**FEATURES**	Springs, expansive views, wildflowers, rock outcroppings

To the flippant highway passenger, many of the mountains in Nevada are mere
brown hills with low shrubs and an occasional tree. Hikers who have ventured
into these desert mountains know, however, that life is much more vibrant than
it may seem from the road. Green, deciduous trees cluster around wet canyons,
secret valleys filled with wildflowers hide behind roadside ridges, and wildlife
congregates near verdant springs. Songbirds chatter in meadows, water fowl
play in ponds, and birds of prey soar above as guardians of these hidden lands.

Nowhere, perhaps, is the lifeless archetype of the desert demolished more
evidently than on Petersen Moun-
tain. The ridgeline of the Petersen
Range extends for 14 miles in
an almost straight north-south
line near the California-Nevada
border north of Reno. From either

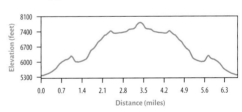

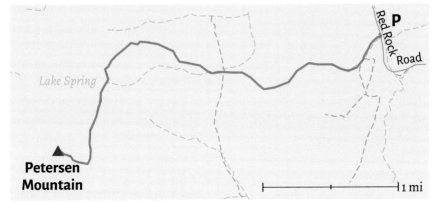

Amphitheater filled with arrowleaf balsamroot flowers

Highway 395 to the west or Red Rock Road to the east, the mountains dominate the local landscape. The high point of the range sits at 7,857 feet and rises steeply more than 2,700 feet above the valley floors only 2.5 miles away. Snow, spilling over from the nearby Sierra Nevadas, blankets the ridgeline more often than not.

This hike is an adventurous off-trail pursuit to the top of the Petersen Range and a plethora of springs on its steep eastern slopes. The Bureau of Land Management recognizes the biodiversity of the Petersens and the important habitats these mountains host for migrating animal populations, particularly mule deer. For this reason, the Bureau of Land Management seeks to keep this area as roadless as possible, and indeed there are few roads or even trails in these mountains.

Out of the parking area off Red Rock Road, you will begin your trek on one of these rare roads. Hike along the dirt road, however, for only 0.2 miles. At this point, the road will begin to bend back toward Red Rock Road. This bend is your cue to begin your off-trail expedition up the east-trending canyon in front of you. In early spring, a small creek flows through the canyon, but by late spring, the ravine is carpeted with lavender-colored thread-leaved phacelia flowers. In addition to sage, bitterbrush, and rabbitbrush, the upper portion of the canyon contains several large boulders of granodiorite, a rock consisting of minerals that are darker in color than granite.

After 0.6 miles of climbing, you will reach the top of the canyon, already having climbed nearly 700 feet. Here, you enter the first of many beautiful meadows on the hike. This one is filled with equal parts yellow arrowleaf balsamroot, light green sage, and pink-red grasses.

Head farther east for an additional 0.2 miles to reach the top of the small ridge in front of you. On top of this ridge, the high point of Petersen Mountain with its verdant rocky top confronts you in the distance. Note the scattered deep green pockets of deciduous trees across Petersen's slopes. Each of these forests is fed by a perennial spring. Take some time at this ridge to visualize your route. First, you will descend into Little Valley and head toward a pocket of aspen trees at the base of the mountain. Then you will take the ridge to the north of the aspen grove up Mount Petersen. Although walking in the stream up the canyon may sound tempting, notice how steep the canyon becomes. The ridgeline ascent is safer and more beautiful.

To reach the springs, you must first descend 300 feet into Little Valley. Your approach is generally due east, toward the lowest of the forest patches on Petersen. Across Little Valley, there is a barbed wire fence that is the Bureau of Land Management's attempt to keep cattle away from the upper slopes of the Petersen Range. Hike along the barbed wire fence heading north toward the creek. A few hundred feet south of the creek, someone has constructed a wooden cattle guard that you should use to safely cross to the other side of the fence.

Lake Valley Springs

Soon after this crossing, a north-south trending broad dirt road will become visible. Take this road north toward the creek. At the creek bank, you will reach a junction. Lush vegetation abounds here. Look for huge bushes of wild roses along the creek edge and cattails and tules growing in the wetlands.

Turn left at the junction onto another dirt road, which in 0.1 miles will take you to a small grove of aspen trees on your right. This grove of aspen makes for an outstanding shaded break spot. Take your shoes off and cool your feet in a small waterfall, or filter and drink the spring-fed water. This spring and others nearby combine with local snowmelt to form Ross Creek, which is used by downstream ranchers on Red Rock Road. If desired, you can continue up the dirt road another 0.1 miles to visit a much larger grove of aspen. This grove, however, is on much steeper terrain and makes for a less ideal break spot.

After enjoying the shady respite of the lower aspen grove, cross over the creek and ascend the hills to the north. You will find yourself on the bottom portions of a west-east ridgeline after about 0.1 miles hiking off trail to the north through open sage steppe. Head west up the ridgeline for the start of the most difficult portion of the hike. During your ascent, stay away from the steeper, more southerly or more northerly sections of the mountainside that form two canyons above Little Valley Spring. Walking along the ridge's spine will generally be the safest and easiest.

After 0.1 miles of heading west, you will reach a small grove of mountain mahogany atop a rocky outcropping. Next, ascend 600 feet over 0.4 miles of travel, and keep your eyes open for colorful desert flowers such as blue Anderson's larkspur and purple Royal penstemons. At this stage, you will reach another rocky outcropping with a larger grove of mountain mahogany. An additional 0.5 miles of climbing west will take you through a gorgeously dense field of arrowleaf balsamroot to yet another grove of mountain mahogany. Break in the shade of the mahogany, and congratulate yourself for making it to more than 7,000 feet above sea level. Enjoy the spectacular views east. Among the many landmarks, a discerning eye will be able to see a small portion of Pyramid Lake to the northwest.

The greater precipitation at these higher elevations results in dense shrubbery of manzanita, sage, and bitterbrush. Meander your way through this high brush for 0.4 miles heading southwest. Fortunately, this portion of the route is not steep.

The first aspen grove

Follow narrow deer trails to avoid the highest brush.

Soon the terrain becomes rockier once again, but the mahogany here is less dense, and views of the surprisingly flat Lake Springs area open up. Head south straight toward the green springs. Depending on the time of year and how wet it is, you can walk in the middle of this riparian area or along its banks. Notice the beautiful gold-colored pyrite shimmering at the bottom of the spring-fed creek. The aspen groves at the south end of Lake Springs make for an excellent breaking spot. Although you have hiked fewer than 3 miles, the large elevation gain and difficult off-trailing will make you feel as if you have traveled many more.

In May and June, look for wild onions growing in the fertile ground along the perimeter of the aspen groves. These delicious plants are easily identified by their pink flowers and white underground bulbs. Eat wild onions only when they can be positively identified by their pink flowers. Onions can easily be confused with poisonous death camas, which looks very similar but has white flowers.

After visiting Lake Springs, climb up a gentle ravine following a foot path that becomes visible to the south. In 0.2 miles, you will pass another wetlands area with a pipe tapped into it feeding an old cattle trough. Around this area, you may also see several old wooden birdhouses on the ground amid fields of red, orange, and yellow desert paintbrush and purple and white phlox.

Straight ahead of you to the south lies an exquisite 1.5-mile-long valley, completely untouched by man and isolated from all of his urban pursuits. Surprises in this valley include a few lone fir trees and ponderosa pines, presumably left over from larger groves that existed when this area was much wetter. Explore this valley if you wish, but make sure to reach the high point of Mount Petersen, only 0.2 miles to your right and 300 feet above you. The rocky summit, located at 39.7959, -119.9762, is visible from this lonely valley.

Views atop Mount Petersen are stunning and grand. All of Long Valley below you and the Bald Mountain Range across from it are visible to the west. The snow-capped Mount Rose Wilderness area is glorious to the south. To the north, you will see large and muddy Honey Lake and towering State Line and Tule Peak (Hike 30). To the east, the long ridges of the Pah Rah and Virginia Ranges are visible as well as many desert peaks farther east in central Nevada.

After savoring the views, spend the night at one of Petersen's many springs, or return to your car the same way you came.

From Reno. Take Highway 395 north for 9.5 miles to the Red Rock Road exit in Nevada. Drive 15.4 miles on scenic Red Rock Road. Park at 39.8073, -119.9318 in a small dirt parking area on the left side of the road. *35 mins.*

16 Little Petersen

EXPLORE THE FOOTHILLS OF THE PETERSEN RANGE, AND CLIMB TO THE TOP OF A ROCKY outcropping with local views of Reno's North Valleys. This short hike provides an excellent introduction to the Petersen Range.

At a Glance

DIFFICULTY	Easy	DISTANCE/TIME	2.1 miles/2 hours
ELEVATION GAIN	600 feet	TRAIL TYPE	Dirt road, off trail
SOLITUDE	Light use	USERS	Hikers, OHVs
BEST SEASON	All	LAND OWNERSHIP	Bureau of Land Management
ANIMALS	Deer, desert cottontails	FEATURES	Expansive views, wildflowers, rock outcroppings

The Little Petersens are a small 5-mile-long mountain range that are separated from their larger counterparts by an unnamed valley less than a mile to the east. Take a short excursion to the highest point of the Little Petersen Range. This short hike on sandy trails to massive boulders makes for impressive photographs without a full day of effort. Enjoy several nearby rock-scrambling opportunities and excellent local views of the area. Snow in the winter adds charm to this hike, but it is short enough to complete even in the heat of the summer.

From the parking area, start your hike by walking west, the direction that you were driving up Argosy Road. A road blocked by a gate heading downhill and to

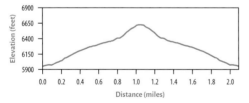

the left of the parking area goes toward private land. Although there are no signs indicating the Bureau of Land Management boundary, walking on Argosy

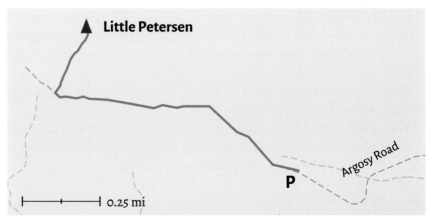

Road will take you to Bureau of Land Management land within 0.3 miles. With an additional 0.2 miles, three rocky peaks to your right become visible. The middle peak is the highest point and your target. Although it is possible to approach this high point from Argosy Road, it is easier and more enjoyable to continue hiking on Argosy Road for 0.4 miles more, at which point you will reach a junction. At the junction you will see a rocky outcropping with foot trails to the south. This area is fun to explore if you wish to make your hike longer. Otherwise, turn right at the junction onto another dirt road, and climb this steep road for another 0.1 miles. Arrowleaf balsamroot, desert paintbrushes, desert buckwheat, and several other species of wildflowers bloom here in the early summer.

Southern rocky outcropping near junction

During your short ascent on this unnamed road, the prominent rocky outcropping to your right marks the high point of the Little Petersen Range at 39.7712, -119.9216. After 0.1 miles of travel, veer to the right on a small worn foot trail to the highest summit. Although its slopes are gradual, the peak itself consists of a rocky outcropping, which may require some light scrambling, depending on your exact route. The northwestern rock face,

Round-headed desert buckwheat

View of Peavine Peak and Mount Rose from Little Petersen

which you will not need to traverse, is particularly rocky.

A cluster of Utah juniper trees grow in piles of dirt caught by the boulders on the summit. Find a comfortable spot to sit in the shade of these trees, and enjoy the views. Hundreds of clustered upright rock outcroppings are visible in the foreground to the west. Mountain landmarks include Peavine Mountain (Hike 40), the Petersen Range, and Freds Mountain (Hike 23).

For a much longer trek, it is possible to combine this hike with Mount Petersen, which lies more than 1,000 feet above you and 3.4 miles to the northwest. Otherwise, savor the views, and return the way you came.

From Reno. Take Highway 395 north for 9.5 miles to the Red Rock Road exit in Nevada. Drive 10.7 miles on scenic Red Rock Road. Turn left on Argosy Road, a well-compacted dirt road suitable for low-clearance two-wheel-drive vehicles. Drive for 1.4 miles, and park at 39.7652, -119.9086, coordinates that mark a good parking spot at a wide three-way intersection. The last house on the edge of Bureau of Land Management land is visible 0.3 miles up the hill to the north. *35 mins.*

17 Goldstone Loop

TAKE A CASUAL VENTURE IN THE LITTLE PETERSEN RANGE. ALTHOUGH IN THE LATE SPRING and early summer desert wildflowers are in bloom, this easy hike is enjoyable anytime of the year.

At a Glance

DIFFICULTY	Easy	DISTANCE/TIME	3.2 miles/1.5 hours
ELEVATION GAIN	700 feet	TRAIL TYPE	Dirt road, foot trail
SOLITUDE	Medium use	USERS	Hikers, OHVs
BEST SEASON	All	LAND OWNERSHIP	Bureau of Land Management
ANIMALS	Deer	FEATURES	Wildflowers

Residents of Reno-Sparks are fortunate to have large swaths of public land so close to home. An outstanding example is a roughly 30,000-acre swath of land protected by the Bureau of Land Management that encompasses the Petersen and Little Petersen mountain ranges in their entirety. The Little Petersen Range is a small cordillera spanning 5 miles north-south that runs parallel just east of the larger and longer Petersen Range. During most months, it is covered by dry and low vegetation, although several springs in the area give rise to unexpected pockets of moisture.

Begin your excursion by walking on the jeep road to the left that heads west out of the parking area. Hike for 0.4 miles, during which you will descend 100 feet. At the T-junction, turn right onto another jeep road. Walk another 0.4 miles on this road, at which point you will pass

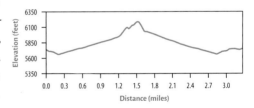

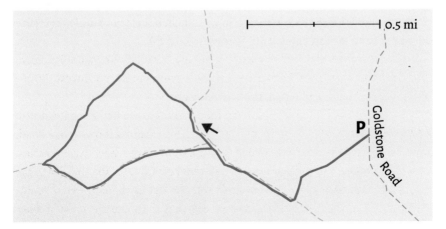

Arrowleaf balsamroot flowers

several old cattle troughs in the area. Continue walking straight as the road gently climbs for another 0.4 miles until you reach a junction.

Turn left at the junction onto another dirt road. In the next 0.4 miles, you will climb 300 feet and reach the top of the ridge. From this ridge, you have excellent views to the east across the sparsely populated North Valleys of Reno with the Pah Rah Mountains behind them.

Over the next 0.1 miles, follow the steep road as it heads to the bottom of the ravine. In the early spring, this ravine hosts a snow-fed creek, but most of the year it is dry. Instead of continuing up the steep jeep road, turn left, and follow a very faint OHV track that leads you down the ravine. The extra moisture accumulated in this ravine during the spring makes it an excellent spot to view wildflowers, such as purple lupines and yellow arrowleaf balsamroots.

Follow the gradual contours of the west-trending canyon for 0.7 miles until you reach the jeep road with the cattle troughs. At the cattle troughs, turn right, and retrace your steps for 0.8 miles back to your car.

From Reno. Take Highway 395 north for 9.5 miles to the Red Rock Road exit in Nevada. Drive for 9.3 miles on scenic Red Rock Road. Turn left on Goldstone Road. This road is formed from well-compacted dirt and is generally plowed by the locals after snowstorms. After 1.9 miles, the well-compacted dirt turns into a rougher dirt jeep road past the final house in the area. Unless there is snow on the ground, low-clearance two-wheel-drive vehicles can easily make it to 39.7557, -119.9132, which is 0.2 miles up the jeep road. The coordinates are at an intersection with another jeep road, which gives you some room to park and gets you on Bureau of Land Management land. *35 mins.*

Desert view from the upper portion of Goldstone Loop

18 Cold Springs

SOAK IN VALLEY AND LAKE VIEWS ABOVE THE COMMUNITY OF COLD SPRINGS WITH THIS exhilarating peak summiting adventure.

At a Glance

DIFFICULTY	Hard	DISTANCE/TIME	7.0 miles/4 hours
ELEVATION GAIN	2,000 feet	TRAIL TYPE	Dirt road, off trail
SOLITUDE	Light use	USERS	Hikers, OHVs
BEST SEASON	September–June	LAND OWNERSHIP	Bureau of Land Management
ANIMALS	Deer, antelope	FEATURES	Expansive views

The Petersen Mountains stretch gorgeously for 14 miles directly along the Nevada-California border. The many surprises of these desert mountains include numerous springs, a large mule deer population, and interesting rock formations. This hike is a nice introduction to the Petersens and takes you to the lowest and southernmost peak in the range.

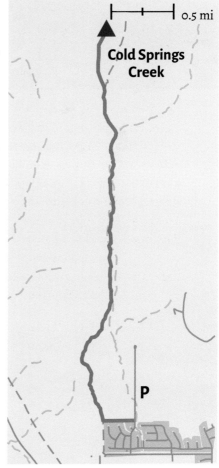

Out of the parking area, begin hiking west on the wide dirt road that runs along the subdivision. The hike takes place entirely on public Bureau of Land Management land, although early on there are some fenced parcels of private property that are easily avoided. In 0.3 miles, the subdivision ends. Turn right and take the main dirt road that goes up into the hills.

Over the next 0.5 miles, you will gain 300 feet, but you will then lose almost all of that elevation in the next 0.5 miles as you descend into a valley. The road takes you alongside some private land in the valley, which is clearly fenced. Continue hiking north on the

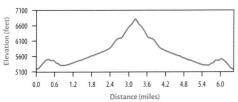

main jeep road as the valley narrows into a wash with steep, rocky slopes emerging to your left. In the spring, keep your eyes open for mule deer, which enjoy browsing grasses that grow on these rocky slopes.

After 1.4 miles of additional hiking, you will reach a junction at the fork of two ravines. Take a left, and head up the jeep road, which steeply climbs up the ravine before flattening out. The base of Cold Springs Peak and its summit are visible in front of you.

Hike an additional 0.3 miles on relatively flat terrain before reaching another junction. The easiest approach from this point is to take neither the road to the left nor to the right but to continue straight off trail up the peak's gradual south slope. Continue about 0.6 miles straight ahead until you reach the rounded summit at 39.7256, -119.9972. A small wooden cross adorns the summit.

View from Cold Springs Peak overlooking Long Valley and the Bald Mountain Range

Enjoy outstanding views of White Lake and Long Valley below you and Peavine Peak (Hike 40), Babbitt Peak (Hike 6), Mount Ina Coolbrith, and Mount Petersen (Hike 15) above you. Return the way you came.

Canyon approach to Cold Springs Peak

From Reno. Take Highway 395 north for 14.7 miles to the Village Parkway exit in Nevada toward the community of Bordertown. Once off the highway, immediately turn left on Cold Springs Drive. In 0.9 miles, turn left on Little Valley Road. The parking area is in 0.3 miles at 39.6828, -119.9927 just before the pavement ends. *25 mins.*

Peavine Mountain and White Lake from the trail

19 Silver Knolls

WARM UP YOUR LEGS IN SAGEBRUSH FOOTHILLS ON THIS FLAT HIKE WITH SCENIC VIEWS
of the Petersen Mountains and lightly populated valleys north of Reno.

At a Glance

DIFFICULTY	Very easy	**DISTANCE/TIME**	2.0 miles/1 hour
ELEVATION GAIN	300 feet	**TRAIL TYPE**	Dirt road
SOLITUDE	Medium use	**USERS**	Hikers, equestrians, OHVs
BEST SEASON	All year	**LAND OWNERSHIP**	County park
ANIMALS	Coyotes	**FEATURES**	Wildflowers

There is no shortage of open space west of Red Rock Road in the foothills
north of Reno. Hike this short, flat loop through the sagebrush ecosystem on a
peaceful, dog-friendly trail.

From the parking area, walk past the playground and onto the wide dirt trail
heading north. In 0.1 miles, the path passes an equestrian area. Turn left at the
junction here.

The sandy road gradually climbs into the hills. The sage steppe vegetation
around you provides excellent coverage for the two types of quail, the more
common California quail and the rarer mountain quail, found in the Greater

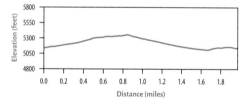

Reno area. The mountain quail can be
differentiated from the California quail
by looking at the feather cluster on top
of the bird's head, which is known as the
plume. The plume of the mountain quail
is longer and narrower than that of the
California quail.

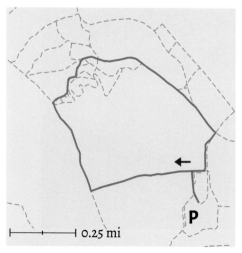

After 0.4 miles, the road terminates at
a junction. Turn right, and hike another
0.4 miles toward the light, sandy hillside
before making a second right. There
are two parallel paths here, but the one
farther to the left is less circuitous. The
road bends back down the hillside and
reaches the main park road in 0.8 miles.
Turn right on the main park road to
return to the equestrian area in 0.1 miles.
There is a parallel jeep road to the right
of the main road you can take if desired

instead of walking on the main road. From the equestrian area, it is only 0.2 miles back to your car.

From Reno. Take Highway 395 north for 9.5 miles to the Red Rock Road exit in Nevada. Drive for 3.1 miles on Red Rock Road. Turn left on Silver Knolls Road, which is a dirt road suitable for low-clearance two-wheel-drive vehicles. In 0.6 miles, enter Silver Knolls Park, and park in the main parking lot at 39.6634, -119.9285. The park is open from 8 a.m. to sunset. *25 mins.*

The flat, wide trail makes for easy hiking.

Looking towards Peavine Mountain from Silver Knolls

The North Valleys

Desert Islands in the Sky

Most of the valleys north of Reno are lightly populated, and there is plenty of public land open to hiking. Each of the valleys is interrupted by rugged desert mountains that afford excellent panoramas to those who climb them.

To warm up your legs with easy desert ascents, climb to the top of Warm Springs Mountain (Hike 22) and Granite Hills (Hike 26). Trips to Hungry Valley (Hike 24) and the summits of Freds Mountain (Hike 23), Hungry Ridge (Hike 25), and Spanish Benchmark (Hike 28) are more challenging adventures that offer outstanding views along with opportunities to see deer and antelope herds. The ascent to Dogskin Mountain (Hike 20) is the most strenuous hike in the North Valleys and requires significant orienteering off trail.

To complement these summiting experiences, explore the otherworldly geologic formations at Moon Rocks (Hike 21), and see how many different bird species you can count at Swan Lake (Hike 27).

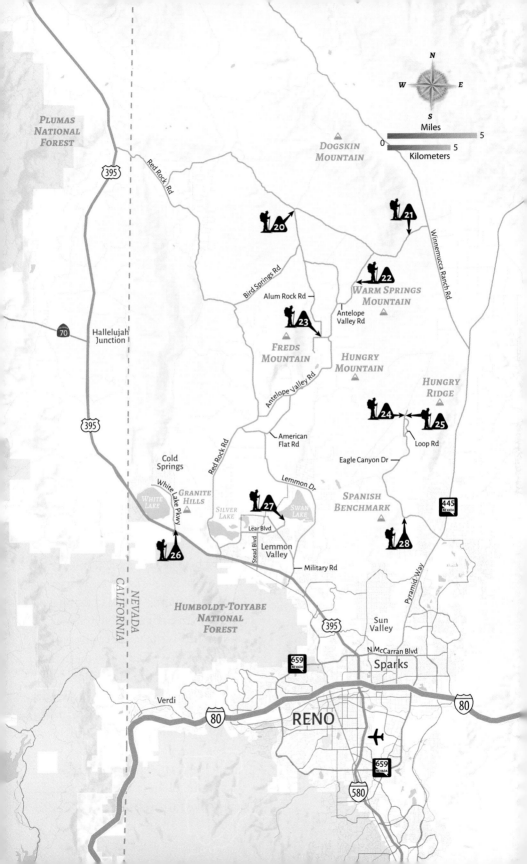

20 Dogskin Mountain

THIS STRENUOUS HIKE TO DOGSKIN MOUNTAIN PROVIDES SOME OF THE BEST DESERT VIEWS described in this book. From the top, enjoy a magnificent panorama of Pyramid Lake, red rocks, and dozens of snow-capped mountain ranges.

At a Glance

DIFFICULTY	Epic	DISTANCE/TIME	8.7 miles/6 hours
ELEVATION GAIN	2,700 feet	TRAIL TYPE	Dirt road, off trail
SOLITUDE	Light use	USERS	Hikers, OHVs
BEST SEASON	March–June, September–November	LAND OWNERSHIP	Bureau of Land Management
ANIMALS	Deer, antelope, wild horses, raptors	FEATURES	Expansive views, wildflowers

The Dogskin Mountains are a narrow mountain range that rises over 2,500 feet above both Winnemucca Valley to the east and Bedell Flat to the west. The proximity of the range to Pyramid Lakes gives rise to lake-effect snow, and as a result, the crest of the Dogskin Mountains will often be snow-capped in the late fall, winter, and early spring.

On this hike, you will follow a seldom-used dirt road up to the ridge of the mountains before heading off trail to reach the high point of the range. Because the summit block is always in view and the off-trail portion is fairly short, this hike is a great adventure for orienteering novices. The remoteness of the region and the spectacular civilization-free views from the top provide added exhilaration.

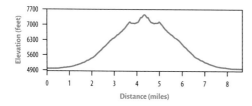

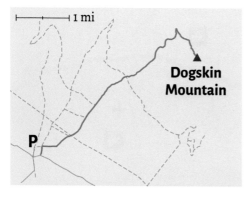

The hike begins in the sage-covered lowlands of Bedell Flat. From the parking area, walk on the dirt road that heads north. Turn right at the junction in 0.2 miles. This is the primary dirt road of the hike, and it takes you to the highest ridge of the Dogskin Mountains.

After 1.6 miles, the sandy trail leads you past the first Utah juniper trees, which coincide with a significant steepening of the path. Fantastic views of the Petersen Range, Warm Springs Mountain (Hike 22), and Freds Mountain (Hike 23) develop behind you. After

Summit views of Pyramid Lake and beyond

an additional 2.0 miles and a total of 2,200 feet of climbing, you will reach the final summit ridge. At this point, the main dirt road begins to level out as it veers to the left. Instead of following the main road, turn sharply right onto a narrow sandy trail.

View of Dogskin Mountain from the trailhead

You now will walk among the rocky outcroppings of the final ridgeline. The flat path disappears in 0.3 miles at a saddle between two shoulders of the mountain. Climb along the narrow ridge to the summit over the next 0.3 miles. During this final ascent, be sure to avoid straying too far to the east. The east side of Dogskin Mountain is very steep, and this portion of the mountain is perilous if snow is on the ground.

Large granite boulders adorn the summit, but it is relatively easy to navigate across them. The views from the top are downright stunning. Tule Peak (Hike 30) and the red hills of Incandescent Rocks (Hike 31) form a lovely foreground to Pyramid Lake to the northeast. To the northwest, in between Stateline Peak and Adams Peak (Hike 2), snowy Lassen Peak can be seen 100 miles away on a clear day. Sierra Buttes (Hike 51) and many other landmarks of the Sierra Nevadas stretch out before you to the west. After you have enjoyed the magnificent views, return to the car the way you came.

From Reno. Take I-80 east 3.2 miles to the Pyramid Way (NV-445) exit. After the off-ramp, turn left to head north on Pyramid Way. In 16.8 miles, turn left onto Winnemucca Ranch Road. In 6.3 miles, turn left onto a dirt road that is marked with a brown Bureau of Land Management sign. Stay straight on this road for 7.9 miles, and park on the right side of the road at a junction at 39.8668, -119.8452. There are many unlabeled crisscrossing dirt roads in this area, so it is best to navigate using the GPS coordinates. The dirt roads on this route are suitable for low-clearance two-wheel-drive vehicles under dry conditions. *55 mins.*

View of Tule Peak from the summit

21 Moon Rocks

EXPLORE A STRANGE DESERT LANDSCAPE COVERED WITH HUGE GRANITE SPHERES. THIS outing is great for all ages because the boulders can be appreciated from their bases or climbed by more adventurous hikers.

At a Glance

DIFFICULTY	Very easy or easy	**DISTANCE/TIME**	0.7 miles/1 hour or 2.7 miles/2 hours
ELEVATION GAIN	200 feet or 900 feet	**TRAIL TYPE**	Dirt road, off trail
SOLITUDE	Heavy use	**USERS**	Hikers, OHVs
BEST SEASON	All	**LAND OWNERSHIP**	Bureau of Land Management
ANIMALS	Deer, coyotes	**FEATURES**	Interesting rock formations, expansive views

In a small pass connecting the Winnemucca and Hungry Valleys, percolating water has eroded granite over thousands of years to create a strange and beautiful landscape that looks out of this world. This hike is a short exploration of Moon Rocks with an optional side trip to a nearby peak with excellent views of the surrounding valleys.

The impressive spherical boulders of weathered granite are visible from the parking area. Numerous OHV trails traverse the area, and you can follow any of them to explore the rocks. Most of the interesting rocks are concentrated in a 0.2 by 0.2 mile area. While most hikers will be satisfied viewing the rocks from their bases, enthusiastic teenagers will be entertained for hours by climbing higher. The Moon Rocks are very popular with dirt bikers and riders of other OHVs, particularly on the weekends, so explore the rocks carefully. The area is most enjoyable during weekdays when there are fewer of these vehicles.

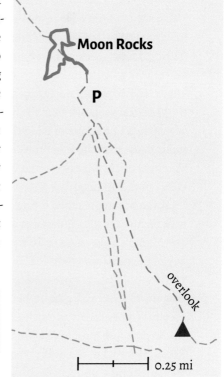

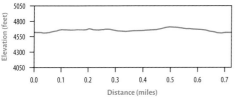

One of the many outcroppings at Moon Rocks

The Moon Rocks began as normal slabs of granite with sets of crisscrossing linear cracks. Flowing water from snowmelt off of nearby Dogskin Mountain (Hike 20) slowly caused these boulders to erode. Because more water flows where two cracks meet to make a corner, the corners erode faster, creating rounded edges. The accumulation of many rounded corners over millennia resulted in the spherical shapes seen in the rocks today. If you look carefully, you will notice several sets of red-brown and yellow-brown rings on the boulders. These bands indicate the path the water took to erode the rocks. As the water passed through the rocks, it chemically reacted with minerals in the granite and changed their colors in the process.

If you are in the mood for more hiking after exploring Moon Rocks, you can walk 1.0 miles to the southeast to reach a peak with excellent views of Winnemucca and Hungry Valleys. Cross to the opposite side of the parking area, and follow any of the dirt roads that lead into the sage-dotted hills. The summit, located at 39.8366, -119.7349, requires you to climb about 700 feet from the trailhead. These hills are adorned with granite, but because their higher location collects less water, they have not eroded as much as the Moon Rocks. These granite slabs are how the Moon Rocks must have looked many moons ago! Enjoy views of Incandescent Rocks (Hike 31) to the north. From the summit, return to the parking area the way you came.

From Reno. Take I-80 east 3.2 miles to the Pyramid Way (NV-445) exit. After the off-ramp, turn left to head north on Pyramid Way. In 16.8 miles, turn left onto Winnemucca Ranch Road. In 6.3 miles, turn left onto a dirt road that is marked with a brown Bureau of Land Management sign. In 1.0 miles, park in a large dirt area on the right side of the road at 39.8487, -119.7412. The dirt roads on this route are suitable for low-clearance two-wheel-drive vehicles under dry conditions. *40 mins.*

The Moon Rocks are great for bouldering.

---

22 Warm Springs Mountain

WARM UP YOUR LEGS WITH THIS SHORT EXCURSION TO THE TOP OF WARM SPRINGS MOUNTAIN. Enjoy scenic desert views with sagebrush steppe in the foreground and the silhouettes of mountains in the background.

At a Glance

DIFFICULTY	Easy	DISTANCE/TIME	4.7 miles/2.5 hours
ELEVATION GAIN	900 feet	TRAIL TYPE	Dirt road
SOLITUDE	Medium use	USERS	Hikers, OHVs
BEST SEASON	All	LAND OWNERSHIP	Bureau of Land Management
ANIMALS	Deer, antelope, coyotes	FEATURES	Expansive views

Warm Springs Mountain, named for a series of springs on its eastern slopes, is one of many Great Basin peaks in a large swath of open space managed by the Bureau of Land Management in the North Valleys outside of Reno.

From the parking area, hike the sandy dirt road that takes you to the hills below Warm Springs Mountain. This road very gradually climbs for the first 0.8 miles, which makes for rapid trekking. Over the next 1.0 miles, you will climb 500 feet before dipping down slightly over a small rocky ridge. You will then enter a relatively flat saddle filled with juniper trees, mountain mahoganies, and sagebrush, habitat for a variety of birds such as spotted towhees and red-tailed hawks.

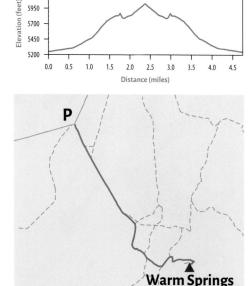

The peak is visible to you on the right and is adorned with cellular towers. Another 0.6 miles on the road takes you to the top. Views to the north are excellent, and even a portion of Pyramid Lake, which is about 14 miles away, is visible on a clear day. After visiting the summit, return to your car the way you came.

From Reno. Take Highway 395 for 5.8 miles to the Lemmon Drive exit. Turn right at the off-ramp onto Lemmon Drive. In 4.6 miles, turn right onto Waterash Street. In 0.2 miles, turn right onto Tulepo Street, and in an additional 0.2 miles, turn left onto

Matterhorn Boulevard. In 5.4 miles, turn right onto Antelope Valley Road, which transitions from pavement to well-graded dirt. In 5.3 miles, turn right onto an unlabeled dirt road. Drive for 0.9 miles, and park near a large Bureau of Land Management information sign at 39.8160, -119.7906. *35 mins.*

Mountain views from the flat beginnings of the trail

23 Freds Mountain

WITH ITS DRAMATIC DESERT SLOPES, FREDS MOUNTAIN RISES FROM THE SURROUNDING valleys like an island in the sky. This strenuous hike to the summit culminates in extraordinary views of the Greater Reno area.

At a Glance

DIFFICULTY	Hard	DISTANCE/TIME	6.9 miles/4.5 hours
ELEVATION GAIN	2,200 feet	TRAIL TYPE	Dirt road
SOLITUDE	Light use	USERS	Hikers, OHVs
BEST SEASON	March–November	LAND OWNERSHIP	Bureau of Land Management
ANIMALS	Deer, antelope, wild horses	FEATURES	Expansive views, colorful rock formations

Freds Mountain is the centerpiece of the North Valleys of Reno, rising steeply in all directions from its surroundings. In this hike, climb more than 2,000 feet from the floor of Antelope Valley to the rocky summit for outstanding desert views.

From the parking area, Freds Mountain is visible directly in front of you with its precipitous slopes dotted with juniper trees. Immediately take the lesser traveled jeep road that heads toward the mountain and diverges from the road on which you parked. This dirt road switchbacks up Freds Mountain with a consistent slope.

After 1.0 miles of hiking, you will find the road makes its first major bend as it

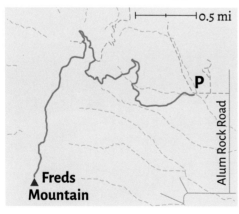

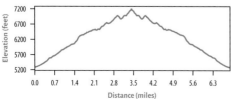

curves through a ravine. Look for bright green-colored rocks among the hillside outcroppings. These rocks contain copper minerals and have a color that is uncoincidentally similar to the Statue of Liberty. As you continue to climb the mountain, increasingly impressive views of Antelope Valley develop below you.

In 0.8 miles, veer left at the junction to continue on the main road, which in 0.2 miles bends south to the final ridgeline. The dirt road continues traveling south for 1.4 miles and terminates a few hundred feet from the top of the mountain.

The rock-adorned summit consists of

a closely spaced triple-pronged crest and can easily be reached from the end of the road. At the top, there are excellent views, including a portion of Pyramid Lake to the east, the Petersen Range to the west, and Mount Rose Wilderness to the south. This trip makes for good hiking spring through fall. Winter ascents are possible, but be prepared for significant snow depths, especially after winter storms. After you have enjoyed the views, retrace your footprints back to the trailhead.

From Reno. Take Highway 395 for 5.8 miles to the Lemmon Drive exit. Turn right at the off-ramp onto Lemmon Drive. In 4.6 miles, turn right onto Waterash Street. In 0.2 miles, turn right onto Tupelo Street, and in an additional 0.2 miles, turn left onto Matterhorn Boulevard. In 5.4 miles, turn right onto Antelope Valley Road. In 2.7 miles, turn left onto Serpentine Road. In 0.4 miles, turn right onto Alum Rock Road, and in 0.8 miles, turn left to stay on the same road. Drive for 0.3 miles, and park on a dirt shoulder on the right side of the road at 39.7885, -119.8283 just past a Bureau of Land Management sign. The dirt roads on this route are suitable for low-clearance two-wheel-drive vehicles. *35 mins.*

Colorful copper ore along the trail

On the final summit block looking east with endless desert ranges

24 Hungry Valley

A HIKE THROUGH HUNGRY VALLEY IS AN OPPORTUNITY TO EXPLORE UNSPOILED GREAT Basin scenery just north of Reno, and the climb to Hungry Mountain culminates in outstanding views.

At a Glance

DIFFICULTY	Hard	**DISTANCE/TIME**	7.7 miles/4 hours
ELEVATION GAIN	1,200 feet	**TRAIL TYPE**	Dirt road
SOLITUDE	Light use	**USERS**	Hikers, OHVs
BEST SEASON	All	**LAND OWNERSHIP**	Bureau of Land Management
ANIMALS	Deer, antelope, coyotes	**FEATURES**	Expansive views

Hungry Valley and the surrounding peaks provide tranquil desert scenery. Enjoy a gradual ascent and straightforward hike to Hungry Mountain, and be treated to excellent views of the surrounding valleys.

Start your hike by entering the gate at the parking area, and walk straight up the wide sandy road for 0.4 miles before taking a narrower, but equally well-defined, dirt road to the left. This road gently takes you westward up the slopes of Hungry Mountain. After about 2.0 miles, the road loses definition, and you will find yourself in a sandy wash, which during wet parts of the year will contain water or snow.

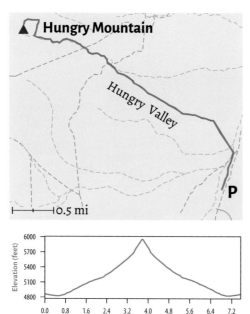

Continue hiking up through the pleasant wash. The wash provides excellent habitat for upland ground birds such as quail, and deer and antelope frequently graze on the grasses here in the spring. After you have hiked up the wash for 1.0 miles, you will find a well-worn jeep road running perpendicular to you. Take a right on this road, which leads up to the final summit block of Hungry Mountain.

In 0.2 miles, you will reach the top of a ridge and spot another junction. Turn left at this junction, and hike another 0.2 miles, this time to the west and farther up.

Climbing through sagebrush vegetation

The summit of Hungry Mountain, adorned with a small rocky outcropping, will now be visible to you. Go a few hundred feet off trail to reach the top. Some light rock scrambling is required to reach the true summit. Views of the surrounding valleys and mountains are excellent in all directions, and a small portion of Pyramid Lake is visible. When you are finished savoring the views, return the way you came back to the trailhead.

From Reno. Take I-80 east 3.2 miles to the Pyramid Way (NV-445) exit. After the off-ramp, turn left to head north on Pyramid Way. In 7.6 miles, turn left onto Eagle Canyon Drive. In 7.4 miles, turn right onto Loop Road. Loop Road is unsigned, but it is across the street from signed Fancy Dance Drive. Drive for 1.3 miles on Loop Road until you reach a green Bureau of Land Management gate. Park in the dirt area near the gate at 39.7238, -119.7443. Loop Road is a dirt road suitable for low-clearance two-wheel-drive vehicles. *35 mins.*

On top of the rocky summit

25 Hungry Ridge Loop

THIS DESERT ADVENTURE BEGINS WITH AN EXPLORATION OF A COLORFUL CANYON BEFORE a venture along Hungry Ridge leads to gorgeous views of the surrounding valleys.

At a Glance

DIFFICULTY	Hard	**DISTANCE/TIME**	7.2 miles/4 hours
ELEVATION GAIN	1,800 feet	**TRAIL TYPE**	Dirt road, off trail
SOLITUDE	Light use	**USERS**	Hikers, OHVs
BEST SEASON	All	**LAND OWNERSHIP**	Bureau of Land Management
ANIMALS	Deer, antelope, coyotes	**FEATURES**	Expansive views, colorful rock formations

The Hungry Valley is a restful pocket of open space. Whereas Antelope Valley to the west is dotted with ranch-style homes and Spanish Springs Valley to the east is heavily populated, Hungry Valley is isolated. The valley receives a little more moisture than typical valleys in the Great Basin thanks to precipitation spillover from the Sierras and a few springs. For these reasons, under the right conditions, wildlife such as deer, antelope, and numerous bird species can be quite plentiful. One early spring morning, the authors hiked alongside a herd of more than 30 antelope!

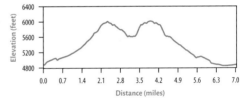

Hungry Ridge runs for 3.0 miles in a north-south orientation. Its straight and spiny appearance catches the eye when you are driving on the Pyramid Highway (NV 445) parallel to the ridge's east side. This scenic hike explores the two peaks on the ridge and begins from Hungry Valley to the west.

Start your hike by entering the gate at the parking area. On the other side of the gate, immediately turn right on a dirt jeep road that ascends steeply

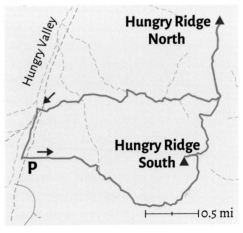

during the first several hundred feet. This road takes you directly east and runs parallel to a fence that borders the Reno-Sparks Indian Colony. Continue on this main path, which begins to veer southeast after 0.5 miles. The terrain becomes sandy, and soon you will enter a canyon adorned with yellow and pink rock

View of Hungry Ridge from Hungry Valley

formations on the hillsides to your left. Several large basalt rock fields above you are also impressive.

Hiking through the canyon is straightforward, and after 1.5 miles, you will reach the top of the canyon. Here, the terrain flattens considerably, and the vegetation abruptly becomes treeless. Another jeep road above you and to your right becomes visible. Your path and that road become one on top of Hungry Ridge. The final summit block of the southern summit becomes apparent to your left, and a quick 0.2-mile diversion from the jeep road takes you there. The total one-way distance to the southern peak is about 2.5 miles. Views from the southern peak's rocky summit are open and grand.

To reach the northern summit, retrace the 0.2 miles back to the jeep road that runs along the ridge. Stay straight on this road for about 1.3 miles as it takes you down and up the saddle between South and North Hungry Ridges. The ascent up the saddle is very steep, and depending on the road conditions, it is easier to ascend through the sagebrush alongside the road and avoid the loose rocks (and possibly mud) on the road itself.

After climbing, the road will reach a maximum in height and begin to veer to the right and head downwards. At this point, leave the road behind and continue to hike straight north through open sage-juniper forest. It is an additional 0.2 miles of hiking through a lovely juniper forest to the northern peak. The top is very flat, and the trees make a great shaded spot for lunch. The trees obscure 360° views from any one spot, but views in any one direction between the trees can be had.

To return to your car, the most direct route is to return to the jeep road and walk back down to the saddle. From the saddle, head west down the ridge, following one of a few poorly defined jeep roads. These roads all connect a little farther down the mountainside and lead you through an unnamed canyon. The canyon loses definition after about 1.0 miles, giving way to more open country. A maze of poorly defined roads crisscrosses this area. The exact approach you pursue is not important. Just walk southwest on roads or through sagebrush toward the main dirt road on which you parked. The distance from the canyon mouth to your car is roughly 1.5 miles.

From Reno. Take I-80 east 3.2 miles to the Pyramid Way (NV-445) exit. After the off-ramp, turn left to head north on Pyramid Way. In 7.6 miles, turn left onto Eagle Canyon Drive. In 7.4 miles, turn right onto Loop Road. Loop Road is unsigned, but it is across the street from signed

The rocky canyon

Fancy Dance Drive. Drive for 1.3 miles on Loop Road until you reach a green Bureau of Land Management gate. Park in the dirt area near the gate at 39.7238, -119.7443. Loop Road is a dirt road suitable for low-clearance two-wheel-drive vehicles. *35 mins.*

26 Granite Hills

CLIMB TO THE TOP OF GRANITE HILLS FOR A QUICK WORKOUT NOT FAR FROM DOWNTOWN
Reno. Enjoy views of Peavine Mountain and three lakes from the summit.

At a Glance

DIFFICULTY	Easy	DISTANCE/TIME	3.7 miles/2 hours
ELEVATION GAIN	1,000 feet	TRAIL TYPE	Dirt road
SOLITUDE	Light use	USERS	Hikers, OHVs
BEST SEASON	All	LAND OWNERSHIP	Bureau of Land Management
ANIMALS	Coyotes	FEATURES	Expansive views

Just north of Peavine Mountain, take a short hike into desert hills laden with granite. From the parking area, walk on the jeep road into the hills. Early on in your adventure, you will pass several large dirt mounds. These tailings are evidence of past copper mining in the area. For the first 1.0 miles, stay on the main path through a few junctions as the road gains 700 feet.

After the first mile, the trail levels out as you enter a grassy plateau. To the right, gorgeous views of Peavine Mountain (Hike 40) are visible, and all signs of developments are hidden below the hills you just climbed. Once at the plateau, turn left at the junction. In an additional 0.1 miles, turn right at another junction to continue hiking to the high point.

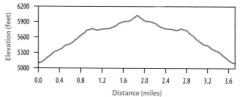

Over the final 0.6 miles, keep climbing through any subsequent junctions to reach the summit. From the top, views of the surrounding valleys are excellent.

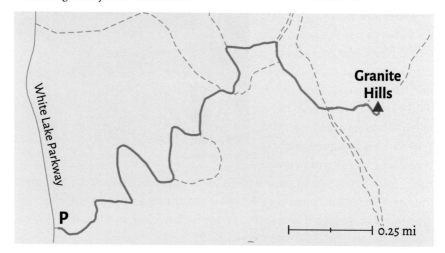

White Lake is visible to the west, and the blue waters of both Silver and Swan Lakes (Hike 27) contrast nicely with the desert landscapes to the east. Bald eagles and other water-loving raptors are often spotted soaring above Granite Hills due to the proximity of these three lakes. To return to the trailhead, follow your footsteps back the way you came.

From Reno. Take Highway 395 for 12.1 miles to the Cold Springs Valley exit. At the off-ramp, turn right on White Lake Parkway. In 0.1 miles, turn right onto the first dirt road, and park immediately on the nearby shoulder at 39.6459, -119.9572. 20 mins.

Peavine Mountain from the plateau

Granite outcroppings with White Lake in the background

27 Swan Lake

SWAN LAKE IS A DESERT OASIS THAT HOSTS HUNDREDS OF TUNDRA SWANS ALONG WITH many other bird species. This easy exploration of the lake is suitable for all ages. Bring your birding binoculars!

At a Glance

DIFFICULTY	Very easy	**DISTANCE/TIME**	2.0 miles/1 hour
ELEVATION GAIN	100 feet	**TRAIL TYPE**	Foot trail
SOLITUDE	Medium use	**USERS**	Hikers
BEST SEASON	All	**LAND OWNERSHIP**	Bureau of Land Management
ANIMALS	Birds, jackrabbits	**FEATURES**	Lake

Although Swan Lake lies right in the middle of suburban development, the 1,800 acres of preserved land set aside nearly pristine desert wetland habitat. Water in the desert is crucial for migrating birds, and more than 150 species of birds call the lake home for at least part of the year.

From the parking area, walk on the levee toward the lake. No matter the time of year, the marshes here will be alive with chattering birds. Look for red-winged and yellow-headed blackbirds, several varieties of sparrows, and rails in the reeds. After 0.1 miles, the levee ends at a junction. To the right, you can explore additional marshy habitat with several footbridges that lead over small creeks. This area also contains a shaded pavilion where you can eat your lunch while birding.

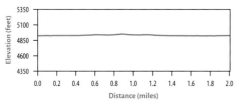

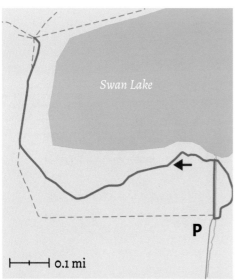

To continue on the main path, however, turn left at the junction at the end of the levee. The path first takes you through some high grasses with open views of the drier terrain away from the lake. Here is a good place to scan for hawks, falcons, and other birds of prey as they hunt for rodents. Watch also for nesting burrowing owls, which unlike most owls are active during the day.

As the trail nears the lake, look for shore birds such as American avocets,

Swan Lake at sunset

dunlins, herons, and stilts. Farther out in the water, there are always a large variety of ducks and related birds. Hundreds of large white tundra swans, for which the lake is named, enjoy the waters in the winter.

Birding at Swan Lake

On the far side of the bay, the trail merges with a dirt road at a junction after 1.0 miles of hiking. You can continue to explore these roads if you want, but otherwise turn around and return to the trailhead the way you came. Swan Lake is a particularly wonderful place to visit at sunset when the sky is aflame with color and the birds are giddy with excitement.

From Reno. Take Highway 395 for 5.8 miles to the Lemmon Drive exit. Turn right at the off-ramp onto Lemmon Drive. In 0.8 miles, turn left onto Military Road. In 1.7 miles, turn right onto Lear Boulevard. In 0.4 miles, turn left onto Swan Lake Natural Study Area Driveway. Drive for 0.2 miles, and park at the end of the road at 39.6504, -119.8565. *20 mins.*

28 Spanish Benchmark

IF YOU ARE LOOKING FOR A SHORT, LEG-BURNING ASCENT CLOSE TO RENO, CLIMB SPANISH Benchmark. The desert views at the summit are well worth the calories burned.

At a Glance

DIFFICULTY	Hard	**DISTANCE/TIME**	3.1 miles/2 hours
ELEVATION GAIN	1,300 feet	**TRAIL TYPE**	Dirt road
SOLITUDE	Light use	**USERS**	Hikers, OHVs
BEST SEASON	March–November	**LAND OWNERSHIP**	Bureau of Land Management
ANIMALS	Deer, coyotes	**FEATURES**	Expansive views

Climb to the top of Spanish Benchmark for a quick workout with a trailhead that is easily accessible from downtown Reno. Standing at 6,161 feet, Spanish Benchmark is not tall compared to other peaks in the Greater Reno area. However, what Spanish Benchmark lacks in elevation, it makes up for in prominence, which is a measure of how high a mountain rises above its surroundings. Spanish Benchmark has a prominence of more than 1,000 feet, which means that to reach a higher mountain starting from its top, you would have to first descend at least 1,000 feet. As a result, the views from the top are outstanding in all directions.

From the parking area, the ridge of Spanish Benchmark towers above you. Begin your hike on the dirt road that goes up the mountain. Over the first 1.0 miles, you relentlessly climb 900 feet through sagebrush and juniper trees complemented by the occasional Mormon tea plant. During this climb, pass straight through any junctions. Notice how the landscape to the left with low grasses and

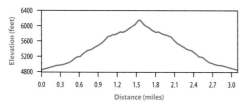

charred juniper trees differs from the greener scenery to the right. A fire in 2019 burned the hillsides here with this dirt road serving as a barricade and assembly point for fire crews.

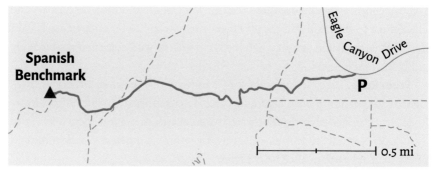

After the first mile, you reach the top of the first ridge, at which point the terrain levels out. Turn left at the junction. Snowmelt accumulates here as is evidenced by the denser vegetation. Canyon wrens and bushtits play among the rocks and juniper trees. Great Basin collared lizards with their iconic neck pattern bask in the sun on granite outcroppings. If snow is still on the ground, you may realize that you are following the footprints of a mountain lion that was out hunting at dawn.

A Great Basin collared lizard sunbathing

In 0.2 miles, veer right, and take the steep road that goes out of the ravine and to the top of Spanish Benchmark. From this point, it is 0.3 miles to the top. The summit is adorned with a few small slabs of weathered granite and is easily accessible. After you have savored the excellent views, return to your car the way you came.

From Reno. Take I-80 east 3.2 miles to the Pyramid Way (NV-445) exit. After the off-ramp, turn left to head north on Pyramid Way. In 7.6 miles, turn left onto Eagle Canyon Drive. In 2.3 miles, park in a dirt parking area on the left side of the road located at 39.6520, -119.7452. *25 mins.*

Spanish Benchmark rises above the sagebrush lowlands.

Looking down towards Spanish Springs Valley

Rock climbing at the summit

The Pah Rah Range

Home on the Basin and Range

The Pah Rah Range forms the northeastern boundary of the Reno metropolitan area and consists mostly of open desert landscapes that are devoid of development and excellent for hiking. Gorgeous and grand Pyramid Lake (Hike 29), the desert counterpart of Lake Tahoe, is a must-see attraction. Many hikes in the region offer elevated views of Pyramid Lake, including Tule Peak (Hike 30), Incandescent Rocks (Hike 31), and Seagull Point (Hike 32).

Also featured are several challenging hikes to the top of peaks such as Virginia Peak (Hike 33), Spanish Springs Peak (Hike 36), Olinghouse (Hike 37), and Airway Beacon (Hike 38), which collectively reflect the steep topography of the region. These summits all afford outstanding views of the Great Basin and Sierra Nevadas. For an easier summiting experience suitable for children, journey to the top of Sugarloaf (Hike 34).

The most popular hike in the region is a short excursion in Griffith Canyon (Hike 35), which features dozens of ancient petroglyphs. Because the Pah Rah Range is little explored compared to well-known hiking areas in the Greater Reno area such as Lake Tahoe, "popular" in regard to Griffith Canyon means you will see a handful of other hikers, whereas on most of the other outings described in this chapter, you are likely to be completely alone!

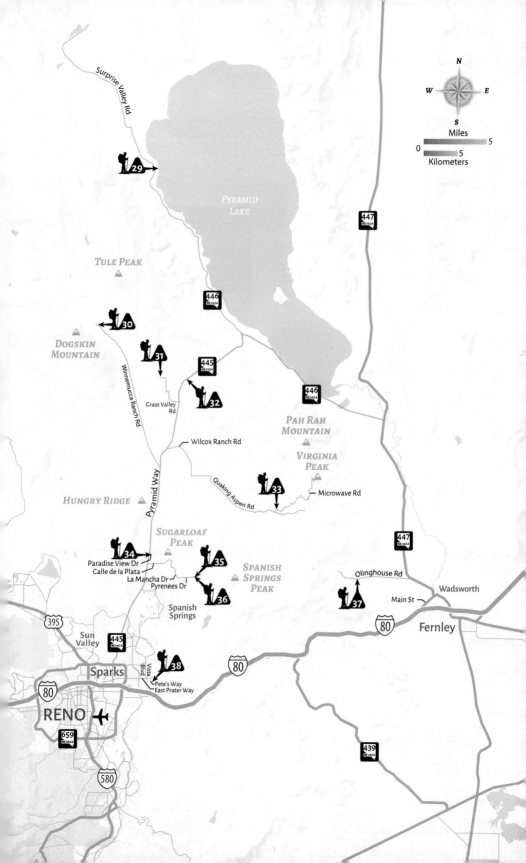

29 Pyramid Lake

WALK ALONG PYRAMID LAKE, AND ENJOY SPECTACULAR TUFA FORMATIONS, THOUSANDS of birds, and brilliant blue shores. This oasis is among the country's largest desert lakes and is a memorable destination for all ages.

At a Glance

DIFFICULTY	Very easy	**DISTANCE/TIME**	2.1 miles/1.5 hours
ELEVATION GAIN	100 feet	**TRAIL TYPE**	Off trail
SOLITUDE	Light use	**USERS**	Hikers, anglers
BEST SEASON	All	**LAND OWNERSHIP**	Pyramid Lake Indian Reservation
ANIMALS	Birds, coyotes, jackrabbits	**FEATURES**	Lake, tufas

While visitors to Reno make sure to visit Lake Tahoe, most people have never heard of Pyramid Lake, the Truckee River's outlet and a desert lake that is nearly the same area as its more popular counterpart. Named for the spectacular pyramidal tufa formations along its shores, Pyramid Lake impresses with its stark desert landscapes and electric blue water. While thousands of people congregate at Lake Tahoe's shores, there is plenty of room to spread out and enjoy the sandy shores at Pyramid Lake. The cool refreshing water is ideal for swimming in the summer, and the large Lahontan cutthroat trout offer world-class fishing opportunities.

There are no official trails along Pyramid Lake, but the lake can easily be hiked along its shores and adjacent unofficial paths. This hike is an easy exploration of the shore near the Monument Rock area. From the parking area, first walk to the pair of large tufa formations straight ahead.

Tufa formation on the shores of Pyramid Lake

Tufas are rock formations composed primarily of calcium carbonate, an insoluble mineral that forms in alkaline lakes with fluctuating water levels. As you look at the shores of Pyramid Lake, notice the striations in different shades of brown, which are indicative of the various previous lake levels. The towering tufas were formed over the last 30,000 years, which in geological time is like a blink of an eye, when the lake level was much higher. Before then, the water level was even higher, and the lake was part of ancient Lake Lahontan, which covered the lowlands across all of western and central Nevada.

From the tufas at Monument Rock, look to the left toward the north end of the lake. In the distance are dozens of enormous tufas called "The Needles," several of which protrude from the water. Understandably, these spectacular formations are sacred to the local Paiute, but unfortunately, they have been closed to the public since 1980 due to problems with vandalism.

After you have enjoyed the tufas at Monument Rock, head to the right toward the shore. Follow the treeless shoreline for 1.0 miles until you reach a riparian area. This lush location, containing green grasses and deciduous trees, is fed by an intermittent creek that originates on the

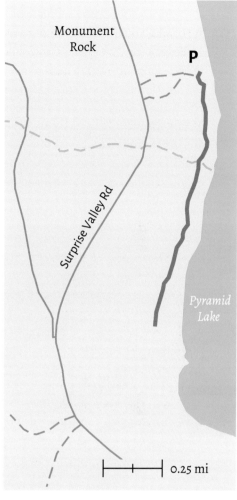

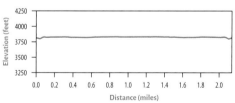

slopes of Tule Peak (Hike 30). This area provides excellent habitat for a wide variety of bird species. In the trees, look for songbirds such as sparrows, kinglets, and the western meadowlark. Along the shore, water birds are plentiful. Common species include buffleheads, coots, grebes, mergansers, cormorants, and several types of ducks. In the spring and summer, be sure to look for the magnificent American White pelican, which nests on Anaho Island in numbers upward of 10,000.

If you wish, you may continue exploring the shores of Pyramid Lake for as long as you like. Otherwise, return to your car the way you came.

From Reno. Take I-80 east 3.2 miles to the Pyramid Way (NV-445) exit. After the off-ramp, turn left to head north on Pyramid Way. In 30.0 miles, veer left at the junction near the Pyramid Lake shoreline to stay on Pyramid Way, which eventually becomes Surprise Valley Road. In 11.7 miles, turn right at signed Monument Rock into a dirt parking area at 40.0904, -119.6897. The last 3.5 miles of travel are unpaved but suitable for low-clearance two-wheel-drive vehicles under dry conditions. A $22 day use permit is required to enter Pyramid Lake and can be obtained online or at the ranger station in Sutcliffe. *1 hour.*

Tufas are made of the white mineral, calcium carbonate.

30 Tule Peak

SOAR LIKE A GOLDEN EAGLE 5,000 FEET ABOVE PYRAMID LAKE ON TULE PEAK'S GLISTENING slopes. The steep route to the top is largely off trail, making this hike the most strenuous in the book.

At a Glance

DIFFICULTY	Epic	**DISTANCE/TIME**	10.0 miles/8 hours
ELEVATION GAIN	4,000 feet	**TRAIL TYPE**	Off trail, dirt road
SOLITUDE	Complete solitude	**USERS**	Hikers
BEST SEASON	March–June, September–November	**LAND OWNERSHIP**	Bureau of Land Management
ANIMALS	Deer, antelope, wild horses, raptors	**FEATURES**	Expansive views, wildflowers

The large massif of Tule Peak, with a high point of 8,723 feet, rises almost a mile above Pyramid Lake's western shores. As the highest desert peak in the Greater Reno area, this remote area of open space encompasses several ecological zones of the Great Basin, including grasslands, sagebrush steppe, spring-fed creeks, and steep rocky outcroppings. In the winter and spring, the Tule Peak ridge is white from lake-effect snow and contrasts gorgeously with the green and brown hills and brilliant blue waters of Pyramid Lake.

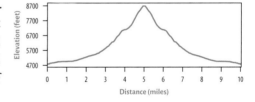

This largely off-trail climb to the top of Tule Peak is the most strenuous hike in the book. Those who make it to the summit will be treated to stunning views of Pyramid Lake below, accompanied by a panorama of countless mountains that extends more than 100 miles in all directions.

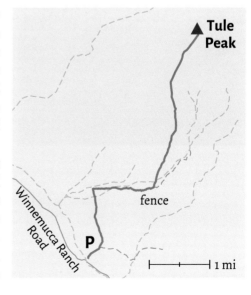

To begin your adventure, walk east on the dirt road on which you parked that heads into the mountains. In 0.3 miles, the road reaches a junction at the mouth of a spring. The green grasses here provide excellent habitat for upland ground birds. Listen here for species

Huge clumps of rabbitbursh adorn the slopes.

such as California quail, mountain quail, and, if you are lucky, the increasingly rare greater sage-grouse. At the junction, take the road to the left, and follow its sandy path for 1.0 miles until you reach a fence that forms the boundary of public land and ranchland. Turn right at the fence, and walk along the road that parallels it for the next 0.3 miles.

Past the ranch fence, another fence, this one in poorer condition and on public land, appears near the road. In 0.7 miles, the road passes through an opening in this second fence before bending away from Tule Peak. Here is a good place to initiate your off-trail adventure and is where the climbing begins.

Although the hiking is strenuous because of the large elevation gain, reaching the top of Tule Peak is fairly straightforward. For one, the vegetation is low throughout the hike and, outside of the winter months, snow cover will be sporadic on the exposed slopes. Secondly, you can almost always see massive Tule Peak towering above you, which makes it difficult to get lost.

Your general off-trail approach is a northerly ascent that spans 2.7 miles to the summit. After the first 0.1 miles, you must cross a gentle spring-fed ravine that in wetter months will have a small amount of water in it. Open-range cattle often graze here along with wild horses, migrating antelope, and deer.

Over the next 1.6 miles, ascend the open grassy mountainside in front of you, gaining about 2,300 feet in the process. In the late spring and early summer, yellow mule's ears, arrowleaf balsamroot, and buckwheat accompany purple lupine. Increasingly vast views of long and narrow Winnemucca Valley develop behind you with the rugged slopes of Dogskin Mountain (Hike 20) as a backdrop.

Make sure to avoid the steep and rocky ravine to your right. Raptors nest in the treacherous outcroppings here, and you are almost certain to spot a golden eagle or a red-tailed hawk.

Take refuge from the sun under one of the few juniper trees that grow on the plateau here, and prepare yourself for steeper climbing. The peak is only 1.0 miles away now, but 1,600 feet of climbing still remain. As you get closer to the summit, a small white pole sticking above the lichen-covered basalt guides you toward the high point.

The ridge at the summit is remarkably flat and expansive, offering you many excellent places to cool off in the thin high-elevation air. All of magnificent Pyramid Lake is visible below you. On the opposite side of the lake, you can see the cliffs of the Lake Range that rise precipitously from the shore. From this high vantage point, your view to the south now extends beyond the Dogskin Mountains, which have a lovely backdrop of the snow-capped Sierra Nevadas. Isolated State Line Peak is a recognizable landmark in the west, and mountains stretch far into central Nevada to the east.

The Tule ridgeline extends northward for several miles without losing much elevation, so if you are in the mood for more hiking, you can explore the northern ridge and enjoy varying vantages of Pyramid Lake. Otherwise, descend back to your car the way you came.

Looking back towards Dogskin Mountain

From Reno. Take I-80 east 3.2 miles to the Pyramid Way (NV-445) exit. After the off-ramp, turn left to head north on Pyramid Way. In 16.8 miles, turn left onto Winnemucca Ranch Road. In 12.2 miles, turn right onto an unlabeled dirt road, and in 0.1 miles, park in a dirt shoulder on the left side of the road at 39.9241, -119.7787. Winnemucca Ranch Road is an unpaved road suitable for low-clearance two-wheel-drive vehicles. *50 mins.*

Visit Tule Peak for guaranteed solitude.

Climbing the summit rock cairn

31 Incandescent Rocks

THE VIBRANT RED ROCKS ON THIS HIKE ARE REMINISCENT OF THOSE FOUND IN UTAH'S famous national parks. Bonuses of this hike are a hidden waterfall and a gorgeous view of Pyramid Lake.

At a Glance

DIFFICULTY	Hard	DISTANCE/TIME	5.1 miles/3 hours
ELEVATION GAIN	1,300 feet	TRAIL TYPE	Dirt road, foot trail
SOLITUDE	Light use	USERS	Hikers
BEST SEASON	All	LAND OWNERSHIP	Bureau of Land Management
ANIMALS	Deer, antelope, coyotes	FEATURES	Colorful rock formations, waterfalls

East of Pyramid Lake, Incandescent Rocks is a little known scenic area with some of the most colorful rock formations in northern Nevada. Ancient volcanism in the area produced the bands of brilliantly colored red, orange, and yellow rocks, and the action of water over the millennia has carved many different interesting formations such as small caverns and arches.

From the parking area, walk up the dirt road for 0.1 miles until you see the signed and gated entrance to the Incandescent Rocks area to your right. Past the gate, the painted hills are ahead of you, and after 0.8 miles of walking on the gently ascending dirt road, you reach the colored rocks. Continue following the main road, and in an additional 0.3 miles some of the more interesting red rock formations are visible on the opposite side of the ravine to the right. These dark red rocks are heavily eroded and contain numerous cubbyholes. Locals call rock formations like these "monkey condos," envisioning that small primates would enjoy living there.

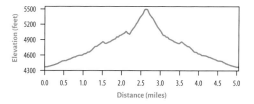

After an additional 1.0 miles, the main trail bends to the left and takes you to the base of a 40-foot waterfall, which contains water in the winter and early spring. The soft sand here makes for an enjoyable and secluded picnic spot. The trail then becomes fainter as it climbs

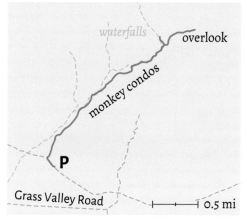

"Monkey condos" are common in the area.

above the waterfall and higher into the mountains. Instead of taking this poorly defined trail, turn around at the waterfall. Retrace your steps for 0.1 miles back to where the trail first began to bend. Turn left onto a narrow and well-defined trail that heads up the mountainside. Usually, this trail is unofficially marked by rock cairns.

This trail climbs 500 feet over 0.5 miles to a plateau above the rock outcroppings. Atop the plateau, you can enjoy a gorgeous view of the rock outcroppings behind you and the bright blue waters of Pyramid Lake ahead of you. You can explore farther out into the colored rocks beyond this plateau if you like, but there are no trails in the immediate vicinity. When you are ready to return to the trailhead, retrace your steps back down to the main dirt road, and follow its sandy path for 2.0 miles back to your car.

From Reno. Take I-80 east 3.2 miles to the Pyramid Way (NV-445) exit. After the off-ramp, turn left to head north on Pyramid Way. In 22.1 miles, turn left onto Grass Valley Road. For the next 2.8 miles to stay on Grass Valley Road; continue

The red rock towers are reminiscent of those in Utah's national parks.

on the main road as it turns several times. Turn left onto an unlabeled dirt road, and in 0.7 miles, park in a dirt shoulder on the right side of the road at 39.8717, -119.6878. Grass Valley Road is unpaved but suitable for low-clearance two-wheel-drive vehicles under dry conditions. *40 mins.*

Bands of colors

32 Seagull Point

An ancient volcano rises sharply from the floor of Palomino Valley. Join the nesting seagulls atop the volcano, and experience gull's-eye views of the valley and Pyramid Lake.

At a Glance

Difficulty	Hard	Distance/Time	2.1 miles/1.5 hours
Elevation gain	700 feet	Trail type	Dirt road, off trail
Solitude	Complete solitude	Users	Hikers
Best season	All	Land ownership	Bureau of Land Management
Animals	Wild horses, coyotes	Features	Expansive views

The landscape of Palomino Valley features sweeping vistas, red rocks, and wild horses. Take a short hike to the top of an impressive volcanic plug that steeply rises out of the northern part of the valley for outstanding local views.

From the parking area, walk on the dirt jeep road that heads east. The peak is immediately visible, but a direct approach is far too steep. Continue hiking this jeep road for 0.8 miles until you arrive at the southeast side of the peak. On your way, you will pass several mounds of excavated yellow dirt on the sides of the road,

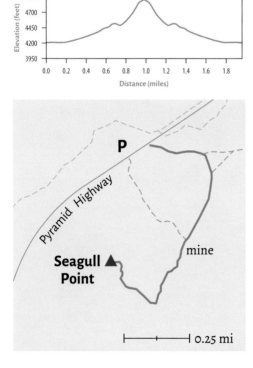

which are remnants of past mining activity.

Once on the southeast side of the peak, hike off trail to the summit. A broad open canyon offers an approach that is not exceptionally steep. The final summit block is relatively flat, although a small rocky outcropping adorns the actual summit. Enjoy the partial views of Pyramid Lake from the top and of the Palomino Valley all around you. Nesting seagulls, who fish at the lake, are likely to greet you there as well. Return the way you came, being particularly careful to avoid sections of the hillside that are loose.

From Reno. Take I-80 east 3.2 miles to the Pyramid Way (NV-445) exit. After the off-ramp, turn left to head north on Pyramid Way. In 24.2 miles, park on the right side of the highway at a junction with a dirt road at 39.8654, -119.6445. *35 mins.*

Although this portion of the hike is off trail, it is easy to navigate through the open sagebrush.

Rock outcroppings on the slopes of the ancient volcano

33 Virginia Peak

IN THIS CHALLENGING DESERT ADVENTURE, CLIMB TO THE TOP OF VIRGINIA PEAK, AND revel in the outstanding summit views, which extend for more than 120 miles in all directions.

At a Glance

DIFFICULTY	Epic	DISTANCE/TIME	12.0 miles/6 hours
ELEVATION GAIN	2,900 feet	TRAIL TYPE	Dirt road
SOLITUDE	Medium use	USERS	Hikers, OHVs
BEST SEASON	March–June, September–November	LAND OWNERSHIP	Bureau of Land Management
ANIMALS	Wild horses, deer, coyotes	FEATURES	Expansive views, wildflowers

Virginia Peak, the high point of the Pah Rah Range, offers sweeping panoramas of northern Nevada and California. A dirt road that leads all the way to the summit makes this a readily accessible hiking destination. In the late spring and early summer, the open hillsides on Virginia Peak burst into color with green grasses and vibrant wildflowers.

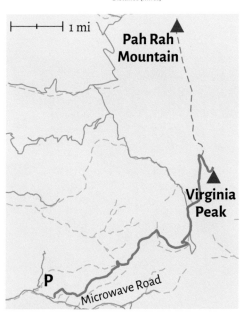

Begin your hike by walking up Microwave Road on which you parked. Although the climb is long, the road leads to the summit gradually the entire way. As you ascend, views to your left of the northern valleys of Reno open up below you. After 2.0 miles, charred mountain mahoganies dot the landscape from a fire that burned through the area in 2018. Wildflowers such as blue penstemons, purple lupines, and pink desert peach are particularly abundant. They likely thrive here as a result of the nutrients returned to the soil during the fire.

In another 2.4 miles, you reach a large plateau at the base of the final summit block. Lines of dark brown volcanic rocks are visible in the distance above you, while the foreground is filled with

A wide and smooth trail leads to the top of Virginia Peak

a huge field of yellow arrowleaf balsamroot flowers. At the plateau, turn right at the junction to remain on the same dirt road and to continue to the summit.

In 1.0 miles, turn right and walk toward the Virginia Peak high point, which is adorned with a National Weather Service radar tower, easily identified by its huge white dome. This radar tower is one of 160 in the United States, which together form a principal component of our weather forecasting system. However, this tower is one of only three in Nevada, which leaves a large swath of central Nevada uncovered, resulting in notoriously poor weather forecasts in much of the state.

From this junction, it is only 0.6 miles farther to the summit. Despite the radar towers, views from the top are outstanding. If you look toward the Sierra Nevadas to the west, a noticeable landmark is cragged Sierra Buttes (Hike 51). Lassen Peak, which is snow-capped almost all year, is visible to the northwest 120 miles away. To the east, numerous ranges in central Nevada present themselves. Perhaps the most striking are the Shoshone Mountains, which are also about 120 miles away. These snowy peaks in the heart of the Great Basin make up one of the longest ranges in Nevada, and the 66 mile ridgeline is almost entirely visible from this vantage.

Slightly lower mountains to the north block most of your views of nearby Pyramid Lake. If you are looking for spectacular views of Pyramid Lake and the salt flats of dry Winnemucca Lake behind it, return down to the junction that is

0.6 miles away. From here, head off trail north along the ridge for an additional 2.5 miles until you reach a high point at Pah Rah Mountain. Although the trail is rocky in places, it is relatively straightforward to navigate along the ridge, and you will only have to endure 500 additional feet of elevation change. Budget for an additional two hours of hiking if you choose to visit Pah Rah Mountain. In addition to Tule Peak (Hike 30), the top of Pah Rah Mountain affords some of the best all-encompassing views of Pyramid Lake.

Regardless of whether you decide to take a side trip to Pah Rah Mountain, return to the main dirt road and descend nearly 3,000 feet back to the trailhead by retracing your steps.

From Reno. Take I-80 east 3.2 miles to the Pyramid Way (NV-445) exit. After the off-ramp, turn left to head north on Pyramid Way. In 18.5 miles, turn right onto Iron Wood. In 4.9 miles, turn right onto Amy Road, and in 0.4 miles, turn left onto Wilcox Ranch Road. In 2.4 miles, turn left onto Quaking Aspen Road. In 3.4 miles, veer left onto Microwave Road. In 0.2 miles, park on a shoulder on the right side of the road at 39.7217, -119.5184. The dirt roads on this route are suitable for low-clearance two-wheel-drive vehicles under dry conditions. Vehicles with suitable clearance can climb farther up the road to decrease the hiking mileage to the summit. *35 mins.*

Looking north from the top across Pyramid Lake and the dry Winnemucca Lake bed

34 Sugarloaf

WITH A FLAT INITIAL STRETCH FOLLOWED BY A GENTLE CLIMB CULMINATING IN GRAND views, this hike to the top of Sugarloaf is an excellent family destination.

At a Glance

DIFFICULTY	Easy	**DISTANCE/TIME**	5.3 miles/2.5 hours
ELEVATION GAIN	800 feet	**TRAIL TYPE**	Dirt road, foot trail
SOLITUDE	Medium use	**USERS**	Hikers
BEST SEASON	All	**LAND OWNERSHIP**	County park
ANIMALS	Deer, coyotes	**FEATURES**	Expansive views

A hike to the top of Sugarloaf Peak is a quaint destination in a parcel of preserved space in the otherwise built-up Spanish Springs Valley. The beginning of the trail is flat and suitable for toddlers, while the short climb to the peak affords excellent views of the valley and surrounding mountains and can be a satisfying accomplishment for older children.

From the parking area, follow the well-signed trail as it passes along a subdivision and through an open section of sagebrush scrub. In 1.2 miles, the trail passes through a marked gate and turns to the left as you begin the ascent up Sugarloaf Peak. Over the next 0.6 miles, the wide trail takes you to the north side of the peak.

During business hours, you will notice the sights and sounds of a quarry operation to your left. The quarry is only a slight bother to most hikers, but the digging machines are a source of endless entertainment to toddlers. Once while on this hike, our ears perked up when we heard a bird with the strangest mechanical call we had ever heard. We followed

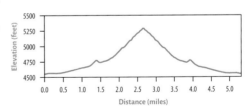

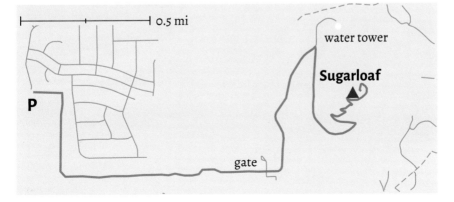

the bird's call and eventually found that it originated from two crows nesting on top of a nearby water tower. We realized that the crows had learned to imitate the sounds of the digging machines!

In 0.6 miles, turn right at the trail junction to continue your climb to avoid going to the water tower. From this point, it takes 0.9 miles and 500 feet of climbing to reach the top. Sugarloaf Peak consists of a granite base adorned with brown basalt formations at its summit. Views of Peavine Peak (Hike 40), Spanish Benchmark (Hike 28), Hungry Ridge (Hike 25), the Mount Rose (Hike 75) Wilderness, and Spanish Springs Peak (Hike 36) are all excellent. After you have enjoyed the views, return the way you come.

From Reno. Take I-80 east 3.2 miles to the Pyramid Way (NV-445) exit. After the off-ramp, turn left to head north on Pyramid Way. In 10.4 miles, turn right onto Horizon View Avenue. In 0.1 miles, turn right onto Paradise View Drive. Park at the end of the cul-de-sac at 39.6753, -119.6983. *25 mins.*

Strolling at the base of Sugarloaf

A rocky, but well-maintained ascent

Sign your name in the registry at the top.

35 Griffith Canyon Petroglyphs

AN EASY HIKE THROUGH GRIFFITH CANYON LEADS TO DOZENS OF PANELS OF PETROGLYPHS. Children and adults alike can have fun guessing the meaning behind these ancient rock carvings.

At a Glance

DIFFICULTY	Easy	DISTANCE/TIME	2.0 miles/1.5 hours
ELEVATION GAIN	400 feet	TRAIL TYPE	Foot trail
SOLITUDE	Medium use	USERS	Hikers
BEST SEASON	All	LAND OWNERSHIP	Bureau of Land Management
ANIMALS	Coyotes	FEATURES	Petroglyphs

An archeological treasure hides in Griffith Canyon at the base of the Pah Rah Range. When looking at the desert surroundings, it is hard to image that several thousand years ago this rocky landscape was much wetter, and the river running through Griffith Canyon attracted wildlife and people to its banks. While ancient peoples hunted and foraged here, they also carved their stories into the basalt canyon walls. Luckily for us, several dozens of these drawings remain preserved, etched into the patina of the sun-scorched basalt. We will never know for certain, but perhaps these petroglyphs tell stories about these people's daily experiences with the animals and the weather, or perhaps they depict something much more spiritual.

To visit the petroglyphs, head west into the canyon off of the road on which

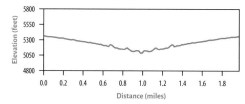

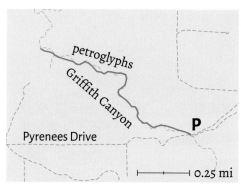

you parked. A faint trail leads you the entire way through the canyon. Although the hike is relatively flat, it is a good idea to wear sturdy shoes because loose rocks are scattered throughout the hike.

The first petroglyphs are visible on the left side of the canyon in 0.3 miles. The petroglyphs consist of anthropomorphic forms and several different kinds of animals along with spirals and other abstract drawings. Farther down the canyon, just past the first petroglyphs, a huge Utah juniper tree grows in the middle of the ravine. Junipers grow very slowly, and based on its diameter, we estimate that the tree is 500 years old,

The rocky terrain necessitates sturdy footwear.

ancient for a tree, but young compared to the accompanying rock art.

Look for more petroglyphs as you continue hiking through the canyon. The highest concentration of drawings is difficult to miss and appears at eye level on a large rock wall on the right side of the canyon in an additional 0.5 miles. Please respect this special area. Leave only footprints, and take with you only photo-

A stunning wall of ancient petroglyph art

graphs. Past this spectacular mural, a few more petroglyphs are visible over the next 0.2 miles, but the steep terrain here is a bit treacherous, so the casual hiker may want to turn around at the rock wall. Regardless of where you turn around, retrace your steps back up the canyon to return to the parking area.

From Reno. Take I-80 east 3.2 miles to the Pyramid Way (NV-445) exit. After the off-ramp, turn left to head north on Pyramid Way. In 9.6 miles, turn right onto Calle De La Plata. In 1.8 miles, turn right onto Valle Verde Drive. In 0.2 miles, turn right onto Agua Fria Drive. In 0.5 miles, turn left onto El Molino Drive. In 0.2 miles, turn right onto La Mancha Drive, which eventually becomes unlabeled Pyrenees Drive. In 2.3 miles, park in a dirt shoulder on the right side of the road at the bottom of a ravine at 39.6514, -119.6348. *35 mins.*

Is it a turtle? Thousands of years ago, this area was wetter..

Enormous Utah juniper

36 Spanish Springs Peak

ENJOY A REMOTE CORNER OF RENO DURING A LONG ASCENT TO SPANISH SPRINGS PEAK.
Enjoy classic Great Basin vegetation and spectacular views throughout the entire
hike.

At a Glance

DIFFICULTY	Epic	DISTANCE/TIME	8.2 miles/6 hours
ELEVATION GAIN	2,200 feet	TRAIL TYPE	Dirt road, off trail
SOLITUDE	Light use	USERS	Hikers, OHVs
BEST SEASON	September–June	LAND OWNERSHIP	Bureau of Land Management
ANIMALS	Wild horses, foxes, coyotes	FEATURES	Expansive views

Above the community of Spanish Springs, the scenic desert landscapes of the
Pah Rah Range disappear into the undeveloped distance of Reno's mountainous
eastern frontier. Here lies a large swath of open space little known to the average
hiker. Here you can take an adventurous outing up Spanish Springs Peak, and
hike the vast desert in solitude while enjoying spectacular views of the Greater
Reno area.

From the parking area, two parallel roads begin ascending into the mountains.
You can walk on either road, and you will pass an abandoned car in a gully between
the two roads. In 0.4 miles, turn right at a junction to continue on the main road.
The vegetation here is classically high desert, with sagebrush complemented
by Mormon tea, bitterbrush, rabbitbrush, and the occasional clusters of Utah juniper trees. In the spring, yellow buckwheat and arrowleaf balsamroot dot the landscape as well.

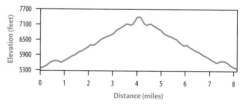

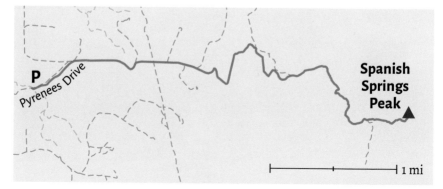

For the next 3.3 miles, follow the main dirt road, and stay straight through several junctions. Many of the junctions are spur roads for a planned housing development that never materialized. The main road becomes increasingly rocky and narrow, it but remains well-defined throughout its course. Over these 3.3 miles, you will climb 1,500 feet and have increasingly spectacular views of the valley below you. This ascent is treeless and can be very windy, so it is best to do this hike on calm days.

At the top of a hill, the road bends to the right and begins losing altitude. When you notice that the road is descending, continue hiking up toward Spanish Springs Peak off trail. The summit is visible 0.4 miles away and lies above a small valley, directly to the east. Cross the valley, and gain the last 400 feet of elevation by climbing the mountainside to the top. This eastwardly approach is not overbearingly steep, although there are several large rock fields that should be avoided to make the hiking as easy as possible.

From the top, enjoy spectacular views of the surrounding valleys and mountains. To the east, envision the difficult task early pioneers had in crossing the Great Basin. The seemingly endless ups and downs of these desert mountains were daunting to traverse even for the heartiest of travelers. To the west, desert peaks in the foreground are framed by the snowy Sierra Nevadas in the background. In the fall, look for thousands of convergent ladybugs congregating on the rocks at the high point. Each year, these ladybugs migrate to certain mountain

Wild horses on the slopes of Spanish Springs Peak

peaks to hibernate underneath snow in the winter and are also often found on Ladybug Peak (Hike 10). When you are done enjoying the views and the ladybugs, return to the trailhead the way you came.

From Reno. Take I-80 east 3.2 miles to the Pyramid Way (NV-445) exit. After the off-ramp, turn left to head north on Pyramid Way. In 9.6 miles, turn right onto Calle De La Plata. In 1.8 miles, turn right onto Valle Verde Drive. In 0.2 miles, turn right onto Agua Fria Drive. In 0.5 miles, turn left onto El Molino Drive. In 0.2 miles, turn right onto La Mancha Drive. In 2.3 miles, park in a dirt shoulder on the right side of the road at the bottom of a ravine at 39.6514, -119.6348. *35 mins.*

The summit ridge has extraordinary views.

37 Olinghouse

WITH CATTLE GRAZING IN REMOTE FIELDS AND GOLD FLOWING IN CREEKS, THIS DESERT hike outside the ghost town of Olinghouse embodies the spirit of the old west.

At a Glance

DIFFICULTY	Hard	**DISTANCE/TIME**	6.1 miles/4 hours
ELEVATION GAIN	1,300 feet	**TRAIL TYPE**	Dirt road, off trail
SOLITUDE	Complete solitude	**USERS**	Hikers
BEST SEASON	September–June	**LAND OWNERSHIP**	Bureau of Land Management
ANIMALS	Wild horses, coyotes	**FEATURES**	Expansive views

Spanning about 20 miles from the Truckee River in Sparks, Nevada, to Pyramid Lake, the Pah Rah Range is a classic desert range with plenty of interesting features to explore. The range's southwestern slopes are a dominant landmark for hundreds of thousands of people in the Reno-Sparks area. This pleasant hike to Olinghouse Peak is a great introduction to the range as seen from the almost entirely uninhabited eastern slopes. The large valley east of the ghost town of Olinghouse is lightly used for grazing by local ranchers. It seems that the cows here have to avoid at least one tumbleweed for every bunch of grass they eat. You will be hard pressed to find a larger density of these spiny yellow plants anywhere in Nevada. During one spring afternoon, in addition to navigating around tumbleweed, the authors were treated to views of a cattle drive by a group of three cowboys on horseback. It certainly felt like a scene straight out of an old western!

To begin your own western adventure, start hiking down the jeep road that leads out of the parking area and heads south. Notice your position between two sets of power lines. In less than 0.2 miles, cross Millers Creek,

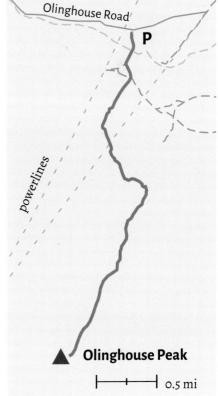

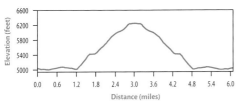

Looking towards the Sierra Nevadas from the top

which has a small amount of flowing water in the spring. One hundred years ago, prospectors panned for gold in this creek upstream a few miles in Olinghouse. According to local geologists, people still can find small gold nuggets in the area with enough perseverance and luck.

After an additional 0.6 miles past the creek, continue heading south off trail and head toward the well-defined mountains in that direction. This off-trail pursuit across open country will quickly lead you past one set of power lines, the ones that were to your left when you first started. You will cross several washes during this stretch. Thousands of tumbleweeds, corralled by the wind, accumulate in these washes. Choose your crossings wisely, lest you find yourself waist-deep in these mildly thorny plants.

After about a mile of off-trail traversing and a modest climb, you will reach a plateau on top of the first ridgeline. Relatively steep terrain surrounds you to the southeast and southwest. Instead, proceed due south up the large canyon that is plainly in view. The route up this canyon is not very steep, and there are a good number of flat rocks that serve as stepping stones that can keep you above the tumbleweeds.

After you exit the canyon, you will reach another plateau. Continue hiking another 0.7 miles across low-sloping open hills to reach the summit. The top of the summit is flat but marked with a large cairn. Views from the top are excellent. Pond Peak and a green-colored hill carved away by gold mining are in view above

Olinghouse to the north. To the south is the Virginia Range, and to the west, the snowy tops of Mount Rose Wilderness are visible. Return the way you came.

From Reno. Take I-80 east 29.9 miles to the Wadsworth/Pyramid Lake (NV-447) exit, and turn left at the off-ramp. In 3.6 miles, turn left onto Olinghouse Road. In 4.4 miles, park in a dirt shoulder at the junction with a jeep road at 39.6491, -119.4015. Olinghouse Road is a dirt road suitable for low-clearance two-wheel-drive vehicles under dry conditions. *45 mins.*

Beware of tumbleweeds on this walk.

Cattle often graze in the plateau below Olinghouse Peak.

38 Airway Loop

HIKE THROUGH GRASSY FIELDS AND AROUND A STEEP CANYON IN THE FOOTHILLS OF THE Pah Rah Range for outstanding views of Reno and the surrounding mountains.

At a Glance

DIFFICULTY	Hard	DISTANCE/TIME	5.0 miles/3 hours
ELEVATION GAIN	1,300 feet	TRAIL TYPE	Dirt road, off trail
SOLITUDE	Light use	USERS	Hikers
BEST SEASON	September–June	LAND OWNERSHIP	Bureau of Land Management
ANIMALS	Wild horses, coyotes	FEATURES	Expansive views

Take a hike in the open space surrounding Airway Beacon, the southernmost peak of the Pah Rah Range. The peak is so named because it has several large light towers at its top to help navigate incoming air traffic to the Reno Airport.

From the parking area, walk east along a jeep road. In 0.2 miles, turn left at the T-junction. The road quickly climbs and takes you into the uninhabited, lightly vegetated hills that rise above Sparks, Nevada. After you travel about 1.5 miles, the terrain flattens out, and you enter a large grassy plateau that sits atop a large unnamed canyon. Open range cattle sometimes graze here, and wild horses are common.

In 0.7 additional miles, you will reach a junction with three tall antennae visible in the distance. Here, turn right away from the antennae to continue on the main route.

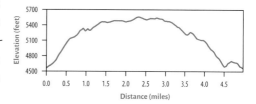

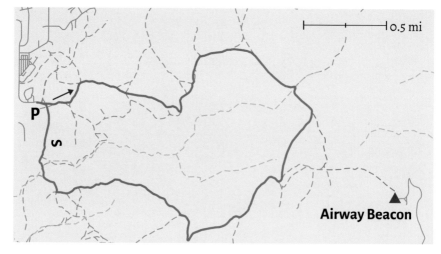

Climbing up the first hill

Alternatively, for those wanting to climb Airway Beacon, continue straight through the junction towards the antennae until the road ends in 0.4 miles. Airway Beacon towers above you as a brown, rocky massif still farther to the east. Several jeep roads unite from all directions in this area, but there is no road to the top,

Reno from the Sparks "S"

so you must travel off trail. The route is direct and very steep. You will gain 250 feet of elevation in 750 feet of lateral distance with some spots having greater than 30° slopes. The climb to the summit is not recommended for those with a fear of heights. The relatively steep drop-offs on both the north and south faces, though, make the views outstanding. Eventually, you will reach a fence, which is essentially at the top of the peak. The fence surrounds the light towers that sit on a large graded swath of land. If desired, you may hike about 0.3 miles farther to reach the opposite side of the fenced area and enter the graded land via a dirt road. Regardless of what you choose, savor the views of the Pah Rah Range to the north, the Virginia Range to the south, Clark Mountain to the east, and the Truckee River and Truckee Meadows below you. Descend carefully down Airway Beacon, and return to the junction.

Whether or not you choose to climb the summit, return to your car by hiking about 2.5 miles in the southern portion of the loop. There are several poorly defined junctions, but stay on the main dirt road as it takes you past the opposite side of the canyon. Near the end of this portion of the trail, you will pass hundreds of rocks on the hillside painted white to form the letter "S" for Sparks.

From Reno. Take I-80 east 5.7 miles to the Vista Boulevard exit. At the off-ramp, turn left onto Vista Boulevard. In 1.2 miles, turn right onto E. Prater Way. In 0.3 miles, turn right onto Pete's Way. Over the next 0.4 miles, drive to the back of the hospital, and park in the farthest parking lot at the end of the complex at 39.5384, -119.6967. *15 mins.*

Cows graze below Airway Beacon.

Truckee Meadows

Urban Escape

Whether you are looking for a quick place to exercise or an all-day escapade, you do not need to travel far from Reno to access outstanding hiking trails. Although the valley of Truckee Meadows is largely developed, the outskirts of the metropolitan area quickly give way to wilderness.

Five of the hikes described take place on Peavine Mountain, the most prominent desert backdrop to the Reno skyline that interfaces with the Sierra Nevadas to the west. Enjoy easy pursuits through the Peavine foothills with hikes up Keystone Canyon (Hike 41) and Evans Canyon (Hike 42). Venture to the wilder and wetter half of the mountain with a strenuous hike at West Peavine (Hike 44), or marvel at magnificent wildflowers in nearby Dog Valley (Hike 43).

For the best views in Reno, climb nearly 3,000 feet to the top of Peavine Peak (Hike 40). The foothills of the Carson Range provide hikers with excellent views of snow-capped peaks at Steamboat Ditch (Hike 46) and Steamboat Hills (Hike 50) along with an adventure to gorgeous Hunter Creek Falls (Hike 47). For shorter excursions within the city limits, visit Sun Valley Park (Hike 39), Oxbow Park (Hike 45), Rattlesnake (Hike 48), and Huffaker Hills (Hike 49), all of which reside in lovely pockets of open space.

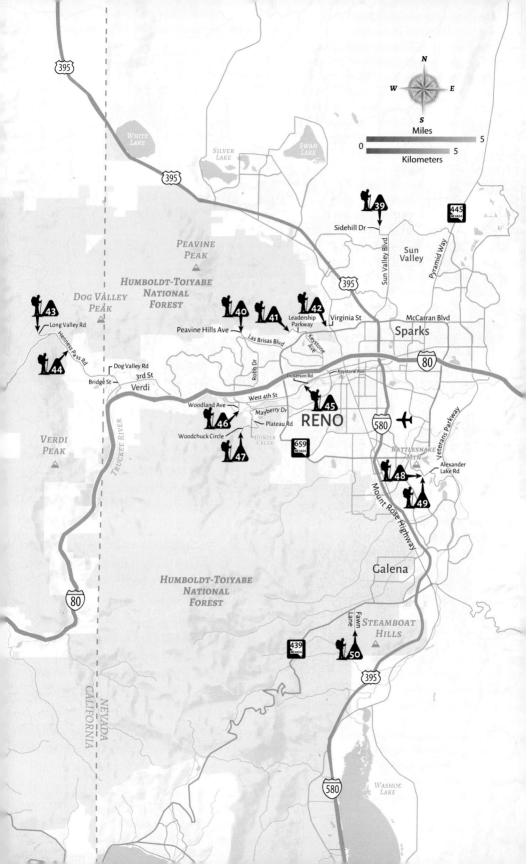

39 Sun Valley Park

SUN VALLEY PARK PROVIDES SCENIC DESERT VIEWS WITHOUT MUCH CLIMBING, MAKING it suitable for hikers of all abilities who want a quick outing near downtown.

At a Glance

DIFFICULTY	Very Easy	**DISTANCE/TIME**	1.4 miles/1 hour
ELEVATION GAIN	400 feet	**TRAIL TYPE**	Foot trail, dirt road
SOLITUDE	Heavy use	**USERS**	Hikers, OHVs
BEST SEASON	All	**LAND OWNERSHIP**	County park, Bureau of Land Management
ANIMALS	Deer, coyotes	**FEATURES**	Expansive views

Nestled among suburbs north of downtown Reno, Sun Valley Park protects a charming pocket of open desert space. From the park entrance, walk up the foot trail that meanders past several large granite outcroppings. The landscape here is typical of the Great Basin at around 5,000 feet above sea level. The vegetation, which is dominated by sagebrush, rabbitbrush, and Mormon tea, is punctuated with Utah juniper trees. Many of these trees are covered with pale blue juniper berries, which are not true berries but the tree's female cones.

After 0.2 miles of gentle climbing, turn left at a junction onto a dirt road. In 0.1 miles, turn right at a second junction. As you ascend the hillside, expansive views of the city open up below you to the south. After 0.1 miles of additional climbing, you reach the top of the hike, as the main road continues north but now approaches a sandy ravine. Moisture that accumulates here nourishes a denser stand of juniper trees.

In 0.2 miles, past the ravine, turn right at a prominent junction to continue your loop hike. The path descends gently, and in an additional 0.2 miles, make a sharp right at the next junction to head south. Continue heading south on the main path. Past a fence, the dirt road will merge into the park proper, and a foot trail will lead you back to your car.

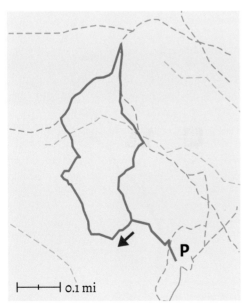

Rocks demarcate the trail.

From Reno. Take Highway 395 north for 1.0 miles to the Clear Acre Lane exit. Drive on Clear Acre Lane for 1.1 miles, at which point it turns into Sun Valley Boulevard. In 2.2 miles, turn left onto Quartz Lane. After 0.2 miles, turn right onto Sidehill Drive. In 0.1 miles, turn left to enter Sun Valley Park, and park at the main entrance at 39.6119, -119.7871. The park is open from 8 a.m. to sunset. *15 mins.*

An expansive view of Reno

Hiking through sagebrush steppe

40 Peavine Peak

CLIMB NEARLY 3,000 FEET TO THE TOP OF PEAVINE MOUNTAIN FOR THE BEST VIEWS IN
Reno. In addition to the summit panorama, this desert mountain holds many
surprises, including gorgeous fall colors and historic arborglyphs.

At a Glance

DIFFICULTY	Epic	DISTANCE/TIME	9.5 miles/6 hours
ELEVATION GAIN	2,900 feet	TRAIL TYPE	Dirt road, foot trail
SOLITUDE	Heavy use	USERS	Hikers, OHVs, bikers
BEST SEASON	April–November	LAND OWNERSHIP	National Forest
ANIMALS	Deer, coyotes	FEATURES	Expansive views, streams, arborglyphs

Situated at the northwest edge of Truckee Meadows, Peavine Mountain is
perhaps the most recognizable landscape to Reno residents. Peavine Peak rises
more than 3,000 feet from the valley floor as a singular isolated mass that is
independent from any larger mountain range. Because Peavine is located at the
interface of the Sierra Nevadas to the west and the Great Basin Desert to the east,

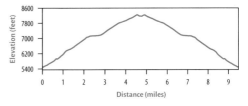

its western slopes contain pine forests,
while the rest of the mountain is mostly
treeless. Although a number of hikes
explore the lower foothills of Peavine
Mountain (Hikes 41, 42, and 44), this
strenuous hike to the mountain's high
point offers unparalleled views of the
Greater Reno area.

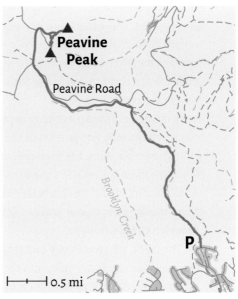

From the parking area, walk past the
National Forest gate and the highest
house of the suburbs. Follow the main
foot trail north up into the hills. Immediately obvious is the green band of
vegetation along your path. The willows
and other deciduous plants in this ravine
are watered by a spring, one of many
that dot the slopes of Peavine Mountain.
Quail and a wide variety of songbirds
make their homes here.

As the trail steadily climbs, south-
ward views of Reno become grander. The
vegetation here is typical of the Great

View looking north from the summit

Basin and contains sagebrush, rabbitbrush, bitterbrush, and Mormon tea. In 0.9 miles, veer right at the junction to stay on the main trail and follow the ravine. In 0.5 additional miles, you reach the top of the ravine and a small grove of ponderosa pines. These trees thrive on acidic soil created through ancient geothermal activity. Notice throughout the hike that the patches of ponderosa pines reside near the mountain's most interesting rock outcroppings, complex aggregates of multicolored rocks that give rise to the acidic soils. Turn left at the junction at the base of the ponderosa pines.

Continue climbing as the main trail leads you northwest. After 0.8 miles, you reach the only flat portion of the hike, a large plateau covered in mountain mahogany trees. Here lies the nexus of a large number of trails including Peavine Road, the main route OHVs use to reach the top of the mountain. Turn left onto a narrow dirt road 0.1 miles before Peavine Road. This road is the preferred option for hikers because it avoids OHV traffic and takes you through the scenic Brooklyn Creek drainage.

The creek, which typically contains water until midsummer, nourishes a large grove of aspen trees 0.9 miles into the drainage. Several stands of aspens line the upper slopes of Peavine Mountain in brilliant gold in October. Venture into the

Hunting for arboglyphs among the colored aspens

An undated arboglyph

groves to respite from the desert sun, and hunt for arborglyphs on the larger aspen trees. These tree carvings were carved by Basque sheepherders who called Peavine Mountain their home in the late 1800s and early 1900s. In most cases, the Basque arborglyphs are easy to distinguish from more recent vandalism.

Your path intersects with Peavine Road 0.6 miles past the aspen grove. Turn left on Peavine Road to continue your climb. In 0.7 miles, the road reaches a saddle point between the two peaks of Peavine, which are adorned with cell phone towers. The southeastern peak is the higher of the two and is easily accessed via a narrower service road. The two peaks are only 0.3 miles apart, though, and both are worthwhile destinations.

Views from the top are extraordinary. To the south, Mount Rose (Hike 75) and the surrounding wilderness impress. To the left of Mount Rose, Mount Davidson (Hike 90) and the Pine Nut Mountains behind it contribute to the beautiful horizon. To the east, the long line of peaks in the desert Virginia and Pah Rah Mountains are visible. To the north, the blue waters of Swan Lake (Hike 27) and Silver Lake contrast gorgeously with the desert mountains farther in the distance. Lastly, the westward perspective contains countless Sierra Nevada peaks. After you have savored the views, return to the trailhead the way you came.

From Reno. Take I-80 west for 2.1 miles to the McCarran Boulevard exit. Drive on McCarran Boulevard for 1.4 miles, and turn left onto Las Brisas Boulevard. In 1.8 miles, turn right onto Robb Drive. In 0.4 miles, turn left onto Peavine Hills Avenue. Park at the top of the street near the National Forest gate at 39.5516, -119.8963. *15 mins.*

Down the final canyon

41 Keystone Canyon

WARM UP YOUR LEGS WITH A GENTLE CLIMB THROUGH KEYSTONE CANYON, LOCATED minutes from downtown. Enjoy the contrast of the desert landscapes with the riparian vegetation lining the canyon.

At a Glance

DIFFICULTY	Easy	**DISTANCE/TIME**	4.4 miles/2.5 hours
ELEVATION GAIN	700 feet	**TRAIL TYPE**	Foot trail
SOLITUDE	Heavy use	**USERS**	Hikers, bikers
BEST SEASON	All	**LAND OWNERSHIP**	National Forest
ANIMALS	Coyotes	**FEATURES**	Streams, wildflowers

Just minutes from downtown, the southern slopes of Peavine Mountain are a popular play space for Reno residents. Take a short hike in and around Keystone Canyon, and enjoy the contrast of the moist interior of the ravine with the drier vegetation outside the canyon walls.

From the parking area, follow the main foot path along the **Keystone Canyon Trail**. A plethora of foot and mountain biking trails crisscross the area, but motorized vehicles are forbidden here. The archetypal Great Basin sage steppe plants, which include rabbitbrush, bitterbrush, Mormon tea, and sagebrush, grow on the canyon walls and on the surrounding hillsides. In the canyon, though, cottonwood and willow trees are nourished by the water of the ravine. The canyon receives water from snowmelt and an intermittent spring, and it holds moisture until early summer. During hot days, the hike is best done in the morning or evening when the tall canyon walls shade hikers from the sun.

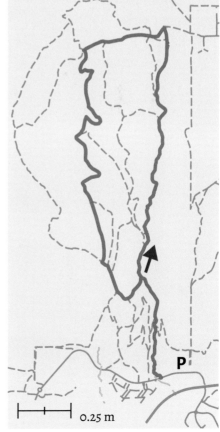

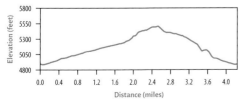

After 1.8 miles of hiking, you exit the canyon and reach a dirt road with a radio tower. Turn left on this road, and in 0.4 miles, turn left again to begin your return on the western slopes of the canyon. The trail here is called **Rabbitman Blast**, which climbs out of an auxiliary ravine over the course of 0.3 miles. At the high point, turn left at the junction to take the **Poedunk Trail**. This trail steadily descends back into the lower portion of Keystone Canyon. In 1.3 miles, turn right to regain the **Keystone Canyon Trail**. Retrace your footsteps over the 0.5 miles to reach your car.

From Reno. Drive on Virginia Street toward I-80. Past the interstate, continue on Virginia Street for 1.1 miles. Turn left on McCarran Boulevard, and in an additional 1.1 miles, turn right on Leadership Parkway. In 0.2 miles, park on the shoulder on the right side of the road located at 39.5504, -119.8477. *10 mins.*

Looking up Keystone Canyon

The canyon interior is surprisingly green.

42 Evans Canyon

HIKE IN A DESERT OASIS. COVERED BY THE SHADE OF TREES AND LINED WITH WILD ROSES, this easy hike through Evans Canyon is excellent for all age groups any time of year.

At a Glance

DIFFICULTY	Easy	**DISTANCE/TIME**	3.6 miles/1.5 hours
ELEVATION GAIN	600 feet	**TRAIL TYPE**	Foot trail
SOLITUDE	Heavy use	**USERS**	Hikers, bikers
BEST SEASON	All	**LAND OWNERSHIP**	County park
ANIMALS	Coyotes	**FEATURES**	Streams, wildflowers

With water present most of the year, Evans Canyon is the most luscious ravine on the Reno side of Peavine Mountain. The easily accessible trail gets you away from the bustle of downtown and into a slice of peaceful open space.

From the parking area, walk toward the tall bronze statue with a green patina.

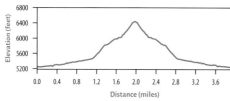

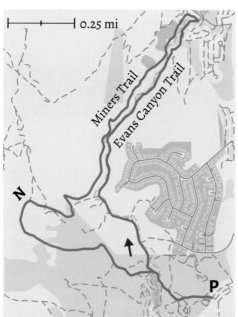

The monument commemorates the lives of Basque sheepherders in Reno and the Interior West. From the statue, you can see all of Truckee Meadows with the open lawns of Rancho San Rafael Park in the foreground. Every September, more than 100 hot air balloons launch from these lawns as part of the spectacular weekend-long Great Reno Balloon Race.

In 0.2 miles, you reach shady Evans Creek, lined with dense thickets of willows, cottonwoods, and grasses. Under normal circumstances, some quick rock hopping will get you across the creek, but during wet years the creek floods in the winter and early spring. On the other side of the creek, turn right at the trail junction to join the **Evans Canyon Trail**.

For the next 1.3 miles as you hike through the canyon, enjoy the gurgling sounds of the creek and reeds rustling in the wind. Dense thickets of wild roses line a significant portion of the trail

Walking alongisde Evans Creek

along with several other species of wildflowers. To the right, houses from the subdivision above you come in and out of view, while open National Forest land stretches before you to the left.

The trail reaches its northern limit at Vista Rafael Parkway. Turn left before the stairs to the street to turn around, and begin your southerly return on **Miners Trail**. Here a cluster of ponderosa pines grows on the red and orange soil. You will also pass by several conspicuous mounds of colored dirt, which are mining tailings created by nineteenth-century prospectors who hoped to strike it rich like their compatriots in Virginia City.

In 1.0 miles, a large "N" painted and maintained by University of Nevada students is visible on the hillside to the right. Take the **"N" Trail** to travel up to

Upper Evans Creek

this marker, and in 0.2 miles, turn left at the junction to head back down to Evans Creek, which is 0.5 miles away and close to the parking area.

From Reno. Drive on Virginia Street toward I-80. Past the interstate, continue on Virginia Street for 1.5 miles. Turn left into the parking lot, located at 39.5539, -119.8295, past a large softball complex. *10 mins.*

Evans creek drainage and the "N"

43 Dog Valley

IN A SECLUDED VALLEY, ENJOY ONE OF THE BEST WILDFLOWER SHOWS IN THE SIERRA Nevadas. Along with many other species, look for the rare Dog Valley ivesia, which can only be found here.

At a Glance

DIFFICULTY	Very easy	**DISTANCE/TIME**	1.4 miles/1 hour
ELEVATION GAIN	200 feet	**TRAIL TYPE**	Off trail
SOLITUDE	Light use	**USERS**	Hikers
BEST SEASON	June–August	**LAND OWNERSHIP**	National Forest
ANIMALS	Coyotes, deer	**FEATURES**	Wildflowers

Outside the town of Verdi on the Nevada-California state line, Dog Valley is a scenic 400 acre plateau that offers some of the best wildflower viewing opportunities in the northern Sierra Nevadas. The flowers are at their peak in late June and early July, and during these times, the casual observer can easily see several dozen species of wildflowers, especially after a wet winter.

The hike is a relaxing exploration of Dog Valley with no trail. From the parking area, head east through the Jeffrey pine forest. Clumps of yellow flowers containing mule's ears or arrowleaf balsamroot are common in the understory in patches of sunlight. Low creeping displays of mahala mat, which display their small lavender flowers in the spring, grow in shadier areas. Look also for the American vetch in the shade, a pink flower with a

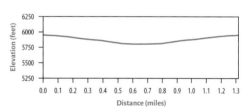

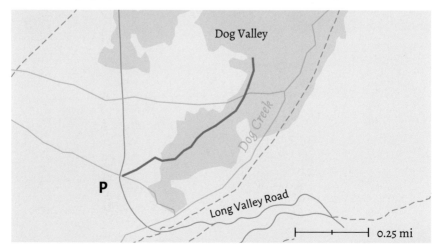

Colorful wildflowers are the highlight of this hike.

long vine-like stem that grows in singular blossoms. Silvery lupines with their blue or purple pea-shaped petals are also common.

After 0.2 miles of hiking east, the forest gives way to open meadow, and the wildflower hunting begins in earnest. You can follow the boundary between the trees and the meadow for another 0.5 miles to gain access to the larger, upper portion of the meadow. The rare Dog Valley ivesia can be found here, a delicate flower with yellow petals found only in Dog Valley and the surrounding area. Many other more common species fill the meadow. In drier areas, you will see various buckwheats, paintbrushes, yampahs, and desert parsleys. Larkspurs, checker-mallows, shooting stars, delphiniums, and blue-eyed Marys populate the wetter areas. See how long it takes you to spot a flower of every color of the rainbow!

In addition to satisfying flower lovers, the Dog Valley area is also a place of interest for history buffs. Dog Valley via Henness Pass Road from 1845 to the 1920s was a highly trafficked route for pioneers and their wagons traveling across the Sierra Nevadas. Its popularity stemmed from its avoidance of the treacherous terrain of the Truckee River Canyon and Donner Pass. Several historical markers in the vicinity indicate the location of the original road. Once you have enjoyed your stay in the meadow, return to the forest and to your car the way you came.

Enjoying the Dog Valley meadow

The rare Dog Valley ivesia is found nowhere else in the world.

From Reno. Take I-80 west for 7.4 miles to the East Verdi exit. Past the off-ramp, stay straight to drive on 3rd Street. In 2.4 miles, turn right on Bridge Street. In 0.6 miles, turn right on Dog Valley Road, just past the Truckee River. In 0.3 miles, Dog Valley Road turns into Henness Pass Road at the California state line. In 3.0 miles, stay straight to continue on Long Valley Road. In 0.9 miles, park in a dirt parking area to the left at 39.5510, -120.0533. Henness Pass and Long Valley Roads are dirt roads suitable for low-clearance two-wheel-drive vehicles under dry conditions. *35 mins.*

A view of the valley from up high

44 West Peavine

VENTURE THROUGH STEEP CANYONS AND ALONG SECLUDED STREAMS IN THIS EPIC adventure on the western slopes of Peavine Mountain. Despite being close to downtown Reno, you will have this beautiful country all to yourself!

At a Glance

DIFFICULTY	Epic	DISTANCE/TIME	6.2 miles/7 hours
ELEVATION GAIN	2,600 feet	TRAIL TYPE	Off trail, foot trail, dirt road
SOLITUDE	Complete solitude	USERS	Hikers
BEST SEASON	May–November	LAND OWNERSHIP	National Forest
ANIMALS	Bears, deer, coyotes	FEATURES	Expansive views, streams, wildflowers

Hike off the beaten path amid stately forests, magnificent wildflowers, luscious wetlands, and refreshing streams in a secluded world only 10 miles from downtown Reno. A peak we have dubbed Dog Valley Peak lies on the western slopes of Peavine Peak in California only 750 feet west of the Nevada border.

While the south and east slopes of Peavine that dominate the skyline from downtown Reno are quite barren and exhibit typical high desert vegetation, the western slopes receive far more snow and are surprisingly lush. The greener vegetation is also enabled by a multitude of tributaries and springs that combine forces to yield peaceful and perennial Dog Creek.

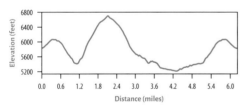

Dog Valley (Hike 43), which is visible from the peak, contains a large meadow that is carpeted with wildflowers in the summer. At the right time of year, hikers encounter dozens of species of wildflowers on the hike. Tree species are also quite variable and include large stands of Jeffrey pines, sugar pines, and mountain mahoganies together with aspen, willows, and alders along streams.

The parking area is located at the edge of the forest surrounding Dog Valley. Walk around the forest service gate that blocks vehicle access on a dilapidated forest service road that is often

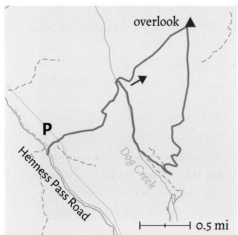

For being only a few miles outside of Reno, this landscape sure feels remote.

flooded by a south branch of Dog Creek. Unless it is late summer or fall, expect to get your feet wet as you pass through several tributaries. Outside of the stream bed, the road quickly leaves the forest as it climbs up exposed terrain.

After 0.2 miles, you will reach a junction, and the main road sharply bends right. Instead of turning right, hike on the less well-defined trail heading straight. In another 0.1 miles, you reach a T-shaped junction. The intersecting trail is a remnant of the Emigrant Trail. Starting in the 1840s, hundreds of wagons successfully used this route to traverse the Sierra Nevadas, but it is best known for being the route of the ill-fated Donner Party.

Instead of following in the wagon wheel tracks of the Donners, cross straight over their trail and into the brush. The terrain here is strikingly flat for what is otherwise such a mountainous locale. In the summer, this plateau is blanketed by the yellow flowers of mule's ears. Hike across the plateau, heading northeast, toward the pine trees 0.2 miles away. Once you reach the forest, the terrain becomes increasingly steep as you descend toward the main Dog Creek drainage, 0.7 miles away.

To reach the creek, the easiest route is to enter a northeast-southwest trending dry ravine. You will need to walk around the back side of some steep rock outcroppings at 39.5460, -120.0193 to enter this ravine. The boulder-strewn ravine will lead you to one of the few flat areas at the banks of Dog Creek. The wetlands here make for a lovely and hidden backpacking spot with year-round water. If camping, you may be awoken by a band of coyotes in the middle of the night; these are the dogs of the valley!

This area is also the best place to cross the creek, which can be several feet deep during periods of high flow. Regardless of the time of year, be prepared to get wet. After carefully performing the stream crossing, ascend the steep hills on the other side of the creek. The peak is only about 0.9 miles away to the northeast, and the route is direct, but relatively steep. You will need to climb approximately 1,200 feet to reach the mostly treeless summit. Enjoy excellent views of Dog Valley (Hike 43), Babbitt Peak (Hike 6), and Verdi Peak (Hike 10) to the west, views of Truckee Meadows to the south, and a unique perspective of Peavine Mountain (Hike 40) to the east.

To return to your car, it is possible to return the way you came, although the descent, especially near Dog Creek, is steep. Instead, you can return down the south side of Dog Valley Peak. Although this route is twice as long (about four miles instead of about two miles), it makes for faster travel because it is both less steep and mostly on a trail and road. It also gives you more mileage to enjoy the wetland scenery alongside Dog Creek.

Mixed pine forest and bitterbrush

For this approach, head south down the peak for 1.0 miles. The vegetation on this side of the mountain is substantially more open than the partially forested western slopes, and in late spring, the area is dotted with wildflowers such as lupine and desert paintbrush. Be on the lookout for a faint narrow bike trail after you have traveled about 1.8 miles and the terrain has leveled out some. Follow the zigzagging trail for another 1.0 miles until you reach a wide dirt road that runs along the north side of Dog Creek. Hike on the road upstream for about 1.0 miles to reach the wide part of the creek you crossed previously. From the other side of the creek, hike the same 1.2 miles back to your car.

From Reno. Take I-80 west for 7.4 miles to the East Verdi exit. Past the off-ramp, stay straight to drive on 3rd Street. In 2.4 miles, turn right on Bridge Street. In 0.6 miles, turn right on Dog Valley Road, just past the

Dog Creek

Truckee River. In 0.3 miles, Dog Valley Road turns into Henness Pass Road at the California state line. In 2.1 miles, park at 39.5401, -120.0303 in a dirt shoulder in front of a forest service gate on the right side of the road. Henness Pass is a dirt road suitable for low-clearance two-wheel-drive vehicles under dry conditions. *30 mins.*

Looking across the rugged Dog Creek watershed

45 Oxbow Park

ESCAPE TO THE SHADY BANKS OF THE MAJESTIC TRUCKEE RIVER AT OXBOW PARK. HIKING through this hidden parcel of open space near downtown is enjoyable for all ages and abilities.

At a Glance

DIFFICULTY	Very easy	**DISTANCE/TIME**	1.0 miles/0.5 hours
ELEVATION GAIN	100 feet	**TRAIL TYPE**	Foot trail
SOLITUDE	Heavy use	**USERS**	Hikers
BEST SEASON	All	**LAND OWNERSHIP**	Nevada Department of Wildlife
ANIMALS	Birds, turtles, beavers	**FEATURES**	River, wildflowers

Nestled near downtown Reno, the Oxbow Nature Study Area is a little known pocket of open space along the Truckee River. In addition to providing easy access to the river, the park features lush vegetation, ponds, wetlands, and excellent birding opportunities.

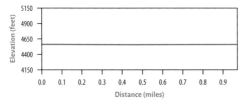

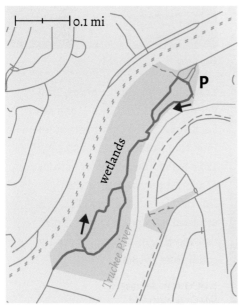

From the parking area, walk on the paved foot trail to the left away from the visitors center. In a few minutes, a boardwalk takes you to the bank of a large curved portion of the Truckee River, the oxbow. An oxbow is a U-shaped portion of a river named after the shape of the yoke of oxen. Erosion occurs faster on the outside of a river bend because the speed of water is greater than on the opposite side. At the same time, sediment deposits faster on the inside of a river bend as a result of the slower water movement. The result is that a river that runs through a meadow, like the Truckee River, will become increasingly curvy as it ages.

Turn right at the river to continue your flat riverside stroll and enter a grove of large Fremont cottonwoods. Park staff have placed wire around these handsome trees to protect them from resident beavers. Native cattails, wil-

Overlook at the Truckee River

lows, elderberries, and a wide variety of other water-loving plants line your path. Wildflowers are common in the spring in the meadow past the cottonwood grove.

In 0.4 miles, you will reach the southern end of the park marked by the onset of a subdivision. On your return, you can explore several trails that pass through wetland areas on the side of the park farther from the river.

From Reno. Take I-80 west for 0.5 miles to the Keystone Avenue exit. At the off-ramp, turn left onto Keystone Avenue. In an additional 0.5 miles, turn right onto 2nd Street. In 0.7 miles, 2nd Street becomes Dickerson Road. Follow Dickerson Road for 0.7 miles until you reach the Oxbow Nature Study Area located at 39.5186, -119.8463. *10 mins.*

A peaceful resting spot at the Truckee River

Green vegetation abounds at Oxbow Park

46 Steamboat Ditch

GO FROM THE BANKS OF THE TRUCKEE RIVER TO A DESERT PLATEAU IN THE FOOTHILLS OF Mount Rose Wilderness. This trail is great for a quick hiking or trail running trip close to downtown.

At a Glance

DIFFICULTY	Easy	DISTANCE/TIME	3.3 miles/2 hours
ELEVATION GAIN	500 feet	TRAIL TYPE	Foot trail
SOLITUDE	Heavy use	USERS	Hikers, bikers
BEST SEASON	All	LAND OWNERSHIP	County park, National Forest
ANIMALS	Deer, coyotes	FEATURES	River, streams

The Steamboat Ditch trail network is one of the many excellent hiking areas just outside of downtown Reno. The ditch is part of a large irrigation project in the Reno area constructed in the late 1800s to bring water from the Truckee River to farmland, and it is still in use today.

From the parking area, turn right on the paved trail that follows the Truckee River. As you walk on this flat path, the mighty river is framed by black cottonwoods, willows, and rabbitbrush. In 0.3 miles, turn left and cross the Truckee River via a bridge. Follow signs for the **Tom Cooke Trail**, which climbs 200 feet up the hillside before reaching a plateau in 0.4 miles. Continue straight for 0.2 miles

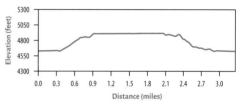

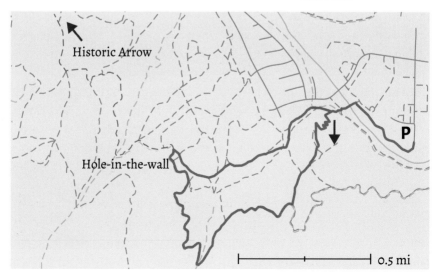

Enjoying the flat paved portion of the trail

on the main trail, and turn right at the junction when you arrive at Steamboat Ditch. For the next 1.1 miles, the trail follows the ditch on a flat contour. The terraced terrain here was sculpted by landslides over the last 100,000 years caused by periodic flooding of the Truckee River.

At the next trail junction, you have two options. To immediately complete the loop, turn right, and begin your approach back down to the Truckee River over the course of 0.8 miles. Near the river, there are several trail junctions, but as long as you walk toward the river, they all lead to the same place in a similar amount of time. Cross once again over the bridge, and follow the paved trail back to the trailhead.

Alternatively, if at the junction you are interested in extending your hike, continue straight and hike along the ditch for an additional 0.6 miles. At this point, dubbed "hole-in-the-wall" by locals, the water in the ditch enters a tunnel constructed by early engineers to limit landslides. Here, turn left onto a dirt road that climbs over the tunnel. When you reach the top of the road in 0.2 miles, turn right on another road heading north. Take this road for 0.2 miles until it terminates at a site with several large concrete slabs in the shape of an arrow. This artifact is one of many concrete arrows that once dotted the continental United States. The arrows were built in the 1920s to help pilots of the first air postal system navigate in an era before radar. To return to the trailhead from here, hike back to the junction at Steamboat Ditch, and then follow the directions in the preceding paragraph.

From Reno. Take I-80 west for 2.0 miles to the McCarran Boulevard exit. At the off-ramp, turn left onto McCarran Boulevard. In 0.9 miles, turn right onto 4th Street. In 2.0 miles, turn left onto Woodland Avenue. In 0.4 miles, park in the parking lot at 39.5035, -119.8968 at the end of the road. *15 mins.*

Steamboat Ditch

"Hole-in-the-wall"

47 Hunter Creek Falls

THIS BEAUTIFUL HIKE TRANSITIONS FROM DESERT TO FOREST AND CULMINATES IN MAJESTIC 30-foot waterfalls. An enjoyable trip all year round; summer visitors can cool off by swimming at the base of the cascades.

At a Glance

DIFFICULTY	Hard	DISTANCE/TIME	6.0 miles/4 hours
ELEVATION GAIN	1,500 feet	TRAIL TYPE	Foot trail
SOLITUDE	Heavy use	USERS	Hikers
BEST SEASON	All	LAND OWNERSHIP	National Forest
ANIMALS	Deer, bears	FEATURES	Waterfalls, streams

One of the enchanting aspects of hiking in the mountains at the outskirts of Reno is the experience of going from sunny, exposed desert to cool, shady forest. Nowhere is this transition as dramatic as on the trail to Hunter Creek Falls.

Past the forest service gate outside of the parking area, walk down the wide dirt road, and in 0.1 miles use the wooden bridge to cross Hunter Creek. Although its size fluctuates with the seasons, the creek contains water all year. Elderberry, gooseberry, wild roses, cattail, and willows make up the luscious vegetation along the creek bed.

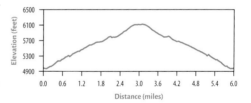

In 0.3 miles, a sign indicates you have reached the Mount Rose Wilderness area, and the views of the downtown Reno behind you recede into the distance as you hike deeper into the canyon. The trail is easy to follow, and there are no prominent junctions. For the next 1.9 miles, the path steadily climbs up the canyon through the sage steppe with only a handful of shady spots among isolated Jeffrey pines. The dense green band of vegetation lining the creek bed below is a constant reminder of the nourishing power of water. The trail crosses the remnants of several rock slides, which originated from the steep canyon walls to your right.

When you climb high enough, your

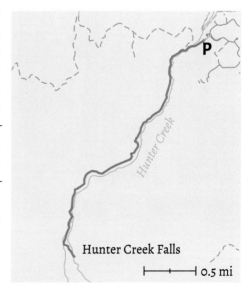

Hunter Creek Falls

⊢————⊣ 0.5 mi

Entering the canyon

world changes suddenly as you enter a dense forest of lodgepole pines, firs, and aspens. The shade and humidity are a welcome respite from the sun-exposed slopes. Hunter Creek splits into two tributaries here, and you will have to carefully use logs and rocks to cross them both. From the forest edge, it is only 0.6 miles farther to the 30-foot waterfalls. A small pool beneath the falls makes for enjoyable swimming in the summer. In the winter and early spring, snow blankets the forested area, and enormous icicles hang majestically from the waterfalls. There is a large flat area on the left side of the waterfalls that makes for an excellent break spot. Return to the trailhead the way you came.

From Reno. Take I-80 west for 2.0 miles to the McCarran Boulevard exit. At the off-ramp, turn left onto McCarran Boulevard. In 1.2 miles, turn right onto Mayberry Drive. In 1.3 miles, turn left onto Plateau Road, and in an additional 1.1 miles, turn right onto Woodchuck Circle. Follow Woodchuck Circle to reach the road's end in 0.8 miles and a parking lot located at 39.4929, -119.8946. *20 mins.*

A shaded break spot near the falls

Hunter Creek Falls

48 Rattlesnake

CLIMB TO THE TOP OF AN ANCIENT VOLCANO IN THE MIDDLE OF TRUCKEE MEADOWS AND
revel in outstanding views of the mountains that circumscribe Reno.

At a Glance

DIFFICULTY	Very easy	**DISTANCE/TIME**	1.6 miles/1 hour
ELEVATION GAIN	400 feet	**TRAIL TYPE**	Dirt road
SOLITUDE	Medium use	**USERS**	Hikers
BEST SEASON	All	**LAND OWNERSHIP**	Bureau of Land Management
ANIMALS	Coyotes, snakes	**FEATURES**	Expansive views

Near the Reno airport, a series of ancient volcanoes rises from the otherwise
flat valley of Truckee Meadows. The tallest of these conical domes is Rattlesnake
Mountain.

From the parking area, the towers on top of Rattlesnake Mountain are visible.
To begin your hike, walk across Alexander Lake Boulevard and onto the dirt road.
In 0.2 miles, turn left at the junction to continue on the main road that climbs
up the mountain. As the name implies, rattlesnakes are common here, so watch
your step. The Great Basin rattlesnake is the only species of rattlesnake in Greater
Reno, and it is venomous. Rattlesnakes are most active from April to October. You

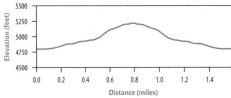

are most likely to see them from April to
June when they are warming themselves
up after hibernation.

After 0.6 additional miles, you reach
the top of Rattlesnake Mountain. All of
Truckee Meadows and the surrounding mountains are visible. Before Reno
existed, the Truckee Meadows consisted
of enormous wetlands surrounding the
Truckee River. The muddiest spot of
these meadows was probably right below
Rattlesnake Mountain at the airport, the
lowest point of the valley. After enjoying
the views, return to the trailhead the
way you came. This hike is often coupled
with Huffaker Hills (Hike 49) for a longer
outing.

From Reno. Take Highway 395/In-
terstate 580 south toward Carson City.

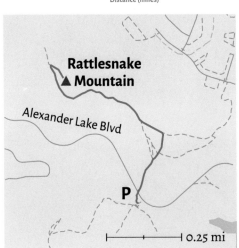

In 3.2 miles, take the exit for Moana Lane. At the off-ramp, turn left onto Moana Lane. In 0.2 miles, Moana Lane becomes Airway Drive. In 1.3 miles, turn left on McCarran Boulevard. In 0.6 miles, turn right onto Alexander Lake Boulevard. In 1.1 miles, turn right into the trailhead parking lot located at 39.4667, -119.7535. *15 mins.*

Rattlesnake Mountain

There are great views of the Virginia Range throughout this hike.

49 Huffaker Hills

ENJOY BRILLIANT SPRINGTIME WILDFLOWER DISPLAYS AND WONDERFUL VIEWS OF TRUCKEE Meadows with this relaxing and easy hike among the rolling desert terrain of Huffaker Hills.

At a Glance

DIFFICULTY	Very easy	**DISTANCE/TIME**	1.8 miles/1 hour
ELEVATION GAIN	300 feet	**TRAIL TYPE**	Foot trail
SOLITUDE	Medium use	**USERS**	Hikers
BEST SEASON	All	**LAND OWNERSHIP**	Bureau of Land Management
ANIMALS	Coyotes	**FEATURES**	Expansive views, wildflowers

The Huffaker Hills are a series of volcanic buttes that rise from the Truckee Meadows valley floor. A large network of trails offers many hiking opportunities for recreationists of all abilities. The area is particularly enjoyable to visit in the spring when colorful wildflowers carpet the hillsides against the snowy backdrop of the surrounding mountain ranges.

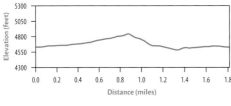

From the parking area, take the foot trail heading south through the sagebrush steppe. In 0.1 miles, turn left at the junction, and stay to the right at a second junction in an additional 0.2 miles. Over the next 0.6 miles, the trail gradually climbs to the cairn-adorned high point of the hills. Views of two reservoirs develop on the left along with increasing vast vantages of Truckee Meadows.

Once you have enjoyed the views at the top, continue down on the main trail to complete the back side of the loop. In 0.2 miles, turn right at the junction. In the spring, the hills are frequently covered in purple and yellow. The purple flowers are flaxes and Great Basin violets, and the yellows are from Hooker's balsamroot, buckwheats, and biscuitroot. In 0.2 additional miles, turn right at another junction to head north. Hiking 0.4 miles more brings you back to

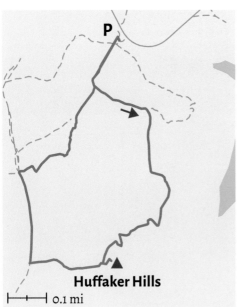

Huffaker Hills

0.1 mi

the first trail junction. Head straight through this last junction, and in 0.1 miles, you will be back to the parking area.

From Reno. Take Highway 395/Interstate 580 south toward Carson City. In 3.2 miles, take the exit for Moana Lane. At the off-ramp, turn left onto Moana Lane. In 0.2 miles, Moana Lane becomes Airway Drive. In 1.3 miles, turn left on McCarran Boulevard. In 0.6 miles, turn right onto Alexander Lake Boulevard. In 1.1 miles, turn right into the trailhead parking lot located at 39.4667, -119.7535. *15 mins.*

The Huffaker Hills trailhead

View towards Peavine and Rattlesnake Mountains

50 Steamboat Hills

CLIMB THROUGH SCENIC DESERT HILLS AT THE FOOTHILLS OF THE CARSON RANGE. ENJOY the snow-capped views of Mount Rose Wilderness without having to drive far up windy Mount Rose Highway.

At a Glance

DIFFICULTY	Easy	DISTANCE/TIME	3.4 miles/2 hours
ELEVATION GAIN	800 feet	TRAIL TYPE	Dirt road, off trail
SOLITUDE	Light use	USERS	Hikers, OHVs
BEST SEASON	All	LAND OWNERSHIP	National Forest
ANIMALS	Deer, coyotes	FEATURES	Expansive views

The Steamboat Hills rise at the foot of the Carson Range in south Reno. Because they rise largely in isolation from the surrounding landscapes, they afford excellent views of nearby Mount Rose Wilderness and the Virginia Range to the east. The hills are named for steam emitted by hydrothermal features on the east side of the mountains, which are harnessed by a geothermal power plant.

From the parking area, walk on the dirt road heading up into the hills. For the first 0.8 miles, follow the main road, which climbs 400 feet before reaching a sagebrush plateau. From here, the whole community of Galena is visible

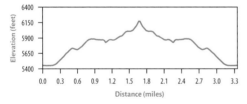

to the west with snow-capped Mount Rose (Hike 75) standing majestically in the background. To the south, Washoe Lake sitting beneath Slide Mountain is also visible.

Past the plateau, there are several crisscrossing dirt roads that all lead east. Regardless of which route you choose, turn right in 0.5 miles toward the Jeffrey pine trees and up to the saddle between the two high points of the peaks. Your destination is the western peak, which is the higher of the two and does not contain any towers. In 0.3 miles, turn off the dirt road, and follow a faint trail, which takes you most of the way up the

mountain. To get to the top, you have to hike the remaining 0.1 miles off trail. Few people hike this trail, so you will have the wonderful views at the top to yourself. Return to the trailhead the way you came.

Climbing above the community of Galena

From Reno. Take Highway 395/Interstate 580 south for 10.7 miles to the Mount Rose Highway exit. Take Mount Rose Highway (NV 431), and in 2.5 miles turn left on Fawn Lane. Drive to the end of the pavement in 0.9 miles, and park at the end of the street at 39.3752, -119.8057. *20 mins.*

Interesting rocky outcropping near the summit

Donner Pass

Granite Towers

Interstate 80 at Donner Pass provides easy access to the snowiest portion of the Greater Reno area. Although Donner Pass is best known for skiing during the winter and early spring, the large snowpack melts away to yield superb hiking adventures during the summer and fall. In this rugged landscape, more so than snow, granite is king. The beautiful rocks, sculpted by glaciers, are accentuated by crystal clear streams, powerful waterfalls, and a plethora of subalpine lakes.

For easy hikes along flowing water, explore Sagehen Creek (Hike 55), Alder Creek (Hike 58), or Coldstream Canyon (Hike 61). At Webber Falls (Hike 53), you can either take a short stroll to the top of the waterfalls or embark on an exhilarating off-trail adventure to their elusive base. Hikes with close access to gorgeous lakes include Summit Lake (Hike 57) and Webber Lake (Hike 52). Trek to more remote lakes with trips to Martis Creek Lake and Lake Ella (Hike 62) and Five Lakes (Hike 63).

As is typical throughout this book, the most difficult hikes are summiting adventures. Extraordinary views await those who complete the strenuous climbs to the tops of Mount Lola (Hike 54), Mount Judah, and Donner Peak (Hike 60). Jagged rock formations reveal the power of ancient volcanoes on the top of Sierra Buttes (Hike 51) and Castle Peak (Hike 56). If you are looking to warm up your legs with a shorter summiting experience, hike to the top of Boca Hill (Hike 59) for lovely views of Martis Valley and the surrounding mountains.

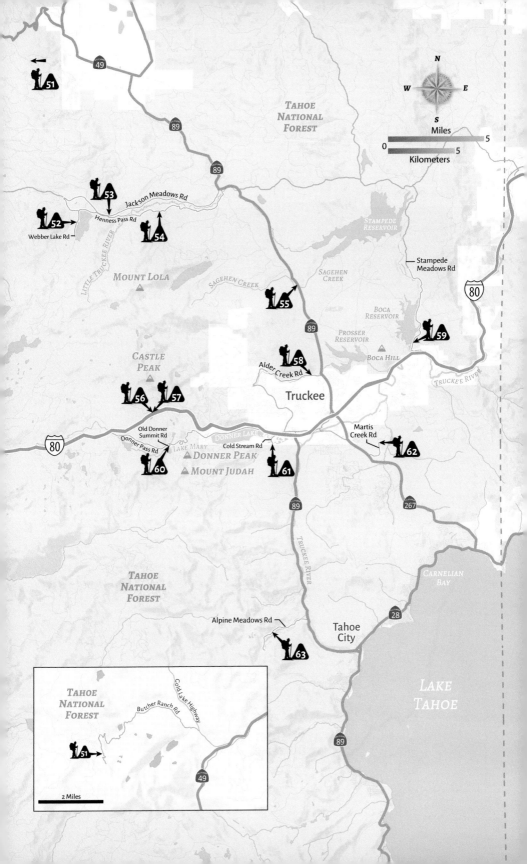

Map Labels

51

49

89

TAHOE
NATIONAL
FOREST

N
W · E
S

Miles
0 — 5

Kilometers
0 — 5

53 Jackson Meadows Rd

52 Henness Pass Rd

Webber Lake Rd

54

LITTLE TRUCKEE RIVER

MOUNT LOLA

Sagehen Creek

SAGEHEN CREEK

Stampede Meadows Rd

STAMPEDE
RESERVOIR

I-80

55

89

BOCA
RESERVOIR

PROSSER
RESERVOIR

Boca Hill

59

CASTLE
PEAK

58 Alder Creek Rd

Truckee

TRUCKEE RIVER

56 **57**

Old Donner
Summit Rd

I-80

Donner Pass Rd

DONNER LAKE

LAKE MARY

Cold Stream Rd

60

DONNER PEAK

MOUNT JUDAH

61

Martis
Creek Rd

62

267

89

TAHOE
NATIONAL
FOREST

TRUCKEE RIVER

CARNELIAN
BAY

28

Tahoe
City

Alpine Meadows Rd

63

LAKE
TAHOE

89

Inset Map

TAHOE
NATIONAL
FOREST

Cold Lake Highway

Butcher Ranch Rd

51

49

2 Miles

51 Sierra Buttes

STUNNING, JAW-DROPPING, AND DIZZYING ARE JUST SOME WORDS TO DESCRIBE SIERRA Buttes. Climb a nerve-racking set of stairs to the fire tower at the top to enjoy some of the best views imaginable.

At a Glance

DIFFICULTY	Hard	DISTANCE/TIME	4.7 miles/4 hours
ELEVATION GAIN	1,600 feet	TRAIL TYPE	Foot trail
SOLITUDE	Heavy use	USERS	Hikers, bikers
BEST SEASON	May–October	LAND OWNERSHIP	National Forest
ANIMALS	Deer, black bears	FEATURES	Expansive views, wildflowers

The pinnacles of Sierra Buttes in the northern Sierras pierce the sky like majestic towers amid a foreground of pristine lakes. While the hike features gorgeous wildflowers in the early summer and restful pine and fir forests, it is the one-of-a-kind view from the precariously perched fire tower at the top that makes this hike one of the most spectacular in California. Make sure to do this hike on a clear day so you fully experience the stunning summit panorama.

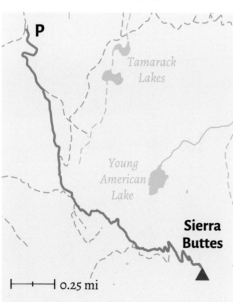

From the parking area, the trail immediately begins climbing through forest for the first 0.5 miles. The trail then flattens as it travels along an exposed ridge over the next 0.4 miles. In the early summer, this ridge bursts into a kaleidoscope of colors from blossoming mule's ears, buckwheat, paintbrushes, and mountain mint. Cragged Sierra Buttes and the fire tower are visible in the distance. Near the end of the ridge before you reenter the forest, peer beyond the cliffs for impressive views of Tamarack Lakes and at least two other glacially carved lakes in the distance.

Hike straight through the junction with the Pacific Crest Trail, and continue into the forest toward the fire tower. The trail climbs for 0.8 miles before it meets up with a jeep road.

Past the jeep road, the final ascent to the fire tower begins through a series of switchbacks. From here, it is 0.7 miles to the base of the tower. Although there are excellent views from the base of the pinnacles, the heart-pounding climb up 180 metal stairs to the fire tower makes this hike truly special. That being said, the stairs are certainly not something to be attempted by those with a fear of heights.

The panorama at the top is nothing short of breathtaking. Views of Upper and Lower Sardine Lakes impress below

Wildflowers are abundant in the first half of the hike.

180 steps to the top of Sierra Buttes

View from the top of Sierra Buttes

you to the north with Lassen Peak and countless other peaks making up a gorgeous backdrop. To the east, Mount Rose (Hike 75) and the Carson Range stand proudly in the sky with the desert ranges of the Great Basin visible farther in the distance. Scan the horizon in the southwest carefully for a peak rising above the haze of California's Central Valley. This blurry crest is Mount Hamilton of the San Francisco Bay Area and is more than 160 miles away. After you have savored the views, climb back down the stairs, and retrace your steps back to the trailhead.

From Reno. Take I-80 west for 29.9 miles to the Highway 89-North/267 exit. Turn right on Highway 89 toward Sierraville. Within the first mile, drive straight through two traffic circles. Drive a total of 27.9 miles on Highway 89 before merging onto Highway 49-North. In 12.9 miles, turn right onto Gold Lake Highway. In 1.3 miles, turn left onto Packer Lake Road. In 0.3 miles, turn right to stay on Packer Lake Road. In 2.6 miles, continue straight as Packer Lake Road becomes County Route 621. In 1.9 miles, turn left onto Butcher Ranch Road. In 0.2 miles, park at the signed trailhead at 39.6116, -120.6654. *1 hour, 40 mins.*

52 Webber Lake

ENJOY TRANQUIL WEBBER LAKE AND RESPLENDENT WILDFLOWERS IN LOWER AND UPPER Lacey Meadows. This flat adventure is excellent for all skill levels as long as you're willing to get wet when crossing Lacey Creek.

At a Glance

DIFFICULTY	Easy	**DISTANCE/TIME**	6.2 miles/3 hours
ELEVATION GAIN	300 feet	**TRAIL TYPE**	Foot trail, dirt road
SOLITUDE	Medium use	**USERS**	Hikers, bikers
BEST SEASON	May–November	**LAND OWNERSHIP**	Truckee Donner Land Trust
ANIMALS	Deer, bears	**FEATURES**	Lake, streams, wildflowers

North of Truckee, snow-capped mountains feed meandering streams that flow through a secluded 3,000-acre valley to form idyllic Webber Lake. In addition to hiking, the lake is a peaceful and easily accessible destination for camping, fishing, and non-motorized boating. Until recently, this beautiful portion of the Sierra Nevadas was owned by private ranchers and before then, a Gold Rush entrepreneur. A defunct hotel built in 1860 still stands at the edge of the lake.

This hike begins at Webber Lake, which by itself is a worthwhile destination. The most special aspect of the area, however, is the spectacular summer wildflowers that carpet Lower and Upper Lacey Meadows. Especially after a wet winter, the green grasses of these meadows are overtaken by blankets of blue camas lilies, purple larkspurs, pink checker-mallows, and white yarrows. Good conditions for wildflowers also mean that Lacey Creek will run high, and because there is no bridge, be prepared to get your feet and legs wet.

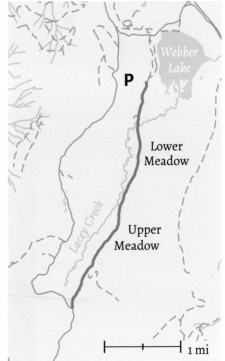

Out of the parking area, follow the dirt road past the trailhead kiosk and into the lodgepole pine forest. After 0.5 miles, the

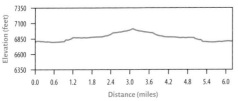

forest opens up as you enter Lower Lacey Meadows. Large Webber Lake stretches out behind you, and the even larger meadow invites you to walk farther. Gentle forested hills surround the valley in all directions. The water in this valley serves as an important stopover for a wide range of migratory birds. Particularly enchanting are the gigantic American

Crossing Lacey Creek in Lower Lacey Meadow

white pelicans and sandhill cranes.

As you walk through the meadow, make note of the colors of the wildflowers near Webber Lake so you can compare them to the different species that grow in drier regions farther from the lake. Soon, you will have to forge Lacey Creek if you wish to continue farther. The creek is wide and slow-moving, so even when the water is deep, the crossing is pleasant. In another 0.4 miles, the well-defined trail reenters lodgepole pine forest, which affords you welcome shade on a hot summer day.

The forest ends in 0.6 miles when you reach Upper Lacey Meadows. Although this meadow is much smaller than the first one, a benefit is that it is out of sight from the more popular lower portion of the trail. Lacey Creek continues its serpentine path here, and its tranquil banks with wildflowers all around make for an exquisite picnic spot. The relatively flat trail continues through Upper Lacey Meadows as the meadows narrow in its upper stretches. In 1.5 miles, you will reach Meadow Lake Road and the

Webber Lake

Camas and buttercup wildflowers

trail terminus. Retrace your steps back to the trailhead.

From Reno. Take I-80 west for 29.9 miles to the Highway 89-North/267 exit. Turn right on Highway 89 toward Sierraville. Within the first mile, drive straight around two traffic circles. Drive a total of 14.5 miles on Highway 89 before turning left on Jackson Meadows Road. Continue on Jackson Meadows Road for 8.1 miles, which is closed in the winter and early spring because of snow. Following the signs for Webber Lake, turn left. In several hundred feet, you will see Webber Lake. Veer to the right toward the campground. Turn left past the campground, and park in a dirt parking area at 39.4811, -120.4213. *1 hour, 20 mins.*

53 Webber Falls

COOL OFF BY HIDDEN YET EASILY ACCESSIBLE WATERFALLS IN THE NORTHERN SIERRA Nevadas. For an optional waterfall adventure of epic proportions, forge the Little Truckee River to access the magnificent base of the cascades.

At a Glance

DIFFICULTY	Very Easy or Hard	**DISTANCE/TIME**	0.2 miles/0.5 hours, or 0.9 miles/2.5 hours
ELEVATION GAIN	300 feet	**TRAIL TYPE**	Off trail, foot trail, dirt road
SOLITUDE	Medium use	**USERS**	Hikers
BEST SEASON	May–August	**LAND OWNERSHIP**	National Forest
ANIMALS	Deer	**FEATURES**	Waterfalls

The Little Truckee River is the largest tributary of the Truckee River. Just one mile downstream from its headwaters at Webber Lake (Hike 52), the Little Truckee River plunges 76 feet to form stunning Webber Falls. Despite their beauty, the falls are not well advertised, and the parking area to visit them is an unmarked road shoulder. Nevertheless, it is a short and very easy jaunt from the road to access the top of the falls. For an unforgettable and difficult adventure, forge the lower

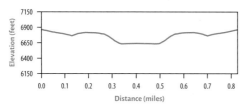

reaches of the creek and swim at the bottom of the falls.

Late spring, when the roads are clear of snow and the Little Truckee River is at its largest, is the best time to see the roaring

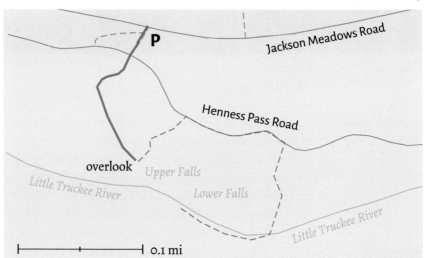

The base of the falls

Forging the Little Truckee River to access the lower falls

falls. The waterfalls are more crowded in the summer when the pools above the main waterfalls are popular swimming holes. Although during the summer, you are likely to encounter foolhardy individuals swimming in the middle pool, this activity is not safe, given the precipitous drop at the downstream end of the pool. Do not risk it! By late summer and fall, though, the waterfalls reduce to a trickle and are far less impressive from above. If you are up for a challenge, this time of year is when you can enter the steep canyon, wade through the river, and enjoy the falls from below.

After parking, carefully walk down the use-trail away from the road. In 150 feet, you will reach Henness Pass Road. Cross over this dirt road, and continue descending. Once on the other side of Henness Pass Road, you can faintly hear the falls during periods of high flow. Various small foot trails lead toward the falls over the remaining 0.1 miles.

Webber Falls consists of three cascades. The uppermost falls drop 25 feet into a large pool, and it is straightforward to view both its top and bottom. Shady areas near the upper fall's pool afford enjoyable sitting spots. The top of the more majestic middle falls are visible from this vantage point as well. However, because of the steepness of the terrain, it is not safe to get a full view of these cascades from this area. The middle falls drop 75 feet into a much larger pool followed by smaller cascades. The lowest falls cascade 15 feet and are completely hidden from the top vantage.

During periods of low flow, more adventurous hikers can experience the falls in all of their glory by taking a circuitous and wet route to access the spectacular pool at the base of the middle falls. For this approach, return to Henness Pass Road and turn right on this dirt road to head east. As you walk along this road, pay careful attention to the steep terrain in the canyon below you. The best place to enter the canyon is 0.15 miles along Henness Pass Road away from any sheer cliff faces. Navigate down the open ravine and a brief patch of very high brush near the water's edge. Once at the water, hike upstream for 0.1 miles to reach the falls.

Because you have to traverse slippery rocks and brush, sturdy shoes, good balance, and hiking poles are a must. Whenever crossing a stream, or in this case hiking in the middle of one, do not go barefoot. You are more likely to cut your feet and fall. Your boots and wool socks will dry out in no time. Only attempt this route during periods of low flow, which typically begin in late July. Although the bottom of Webber Falls is difficult to access, swimming in the lowermost pool is the experience of a lifetime.

From Reno. Take I-80 west for 29.9 miles to the Highway 89-North/267 exit. Turn right on Highway 89 toward Sierraville. Within the first mile, drive straight through two traffic circles. Drive a total of 14.5 miles on Highway 89 before turning left on Jackson Meadows Road. Continue on Jackson Meadows Road, which is closed in the winter and early spring because of snow, for 6.7 miles. Turn into a small unlabeled gravel parking area at 39.4857, -120.3912 on the left side of the road that is just past a sign for Lake of the Woods. *1 hour, 10 mins.*

View from the top of the falls

54 Mount Lola

PANORAMIC VIEWS OF THE NORTHERN SIERRA NEVADAS, VAST FIELDS OF WILDFLOWERS, large snowfields, refreshing streams, and hidden waterfalls await those who complete a strenuous, all-day trek to the top of Mount Lola.

At a Glance

DIFFICULTY	Epic	DISTANCE/TIME	10.4 miles/6 hours
ELEVATION GAIN	2,600 feet	TRAIL TYPE	Foot trail
SOLITUDE	Medium use	USERS	Hikers, bikers
BEST SEASON	May–October	LAND OWNERSHIP	National Forest
ANIMALS	Deer, bears	FEATURES	Expansive views, waterfalls, streams, wildflowers

Standing at 9,148 feet, Mount Lola is the largest peak in the Sierra Nevadas north of Interstate 80. Besides the outstanding summit views, there are many reasons to climb Mount Lola. Enjoy dozens of species of late-blooming wildflowers, hidden waterfalls, tranquil meadows, rushing streams, and a huge snowfield as you follow a well-maintained trail to the summit.

Out of the parking area, the trail begins unassumingly through open forest with manzanita understory. Within 0.3 miles, though, you pass through several groves of aspen growing alongside small streams. The climate and constant water supply provide ideal growing conditions for these trees, and the groves here contain some of the largest specimens of aspen in the Sierra Nevadas.

After the aspen groves, the trail

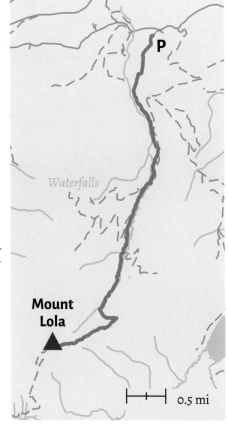

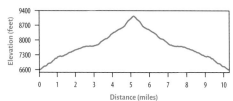

continues to climb, now through lodgepole pine–fir forest. In 0.4 miles, the forest opens up to reveal a small, rocky meadow filled with mule's ears flowers that bloom yellow in the summer. Soon thereafter, your path runs alongside perennial Cold Stream. This beautiful stream originates from the top of Mount Lola, and it is a convenient source of water to filter because the trail stays close to the stream for most of the hike.

After 1.0 miles of walking along Cold Stream, the trail briefly intersects a forest service road. Although both routes lead to same place, veer left to stay on the more enjoyable foot path. The trail here veers close to the stream and leads you through a dense field of exquisite purple-pink fireweed flowers, which typically bloom in August. Because this hike traverses a wide range of elevations in a wet portion of the Sierras, you can enjoy wildflowers from June to September, and the ever-changing mountain exhibits a unique floral display each week.

In 0.5 miles, your path crosses Cold Stream. There is no way to avoid getting wet in early summer, but in later months the stream is low enough to allow you to easily rock hop across. For the next 0.5 miles, the trail crosses several small tributaries before leaving the lodgepole pine–fir forest to give way to a large meadow. Dozens of species of wildflowers thrive here, and they bloom in every color of the

Fireweed flowers along the foot trail

Cold Stream and its peaceful banks

rainbow. Look for crimson columbines, red paintbrushes, pink shooting stars, orange lilies, yellow monkeyflowers, blue larkspurs, lavender asters, and purple lupines. The 0.3 mile walk through the meadow is the flattest portion of the hike, and there are nice sunny and shady spots to rest before you continue climbing.

Past the meadow, you reenter the forest and steadily climb for 1.0 miles. The trail then veers to the left as it diverges from Cold Stream. Before you leave Cold Stream, though, look for a faint trail heading to the right at this main bend. In a few hundred feet, this small trail leads you to a hidden set of lovely waterfalls flowing down a steep portion of Cold Stream canyon.

After enjoying the cascades, return the main trail that heads east away from Cold Stream. As you climb, expansive views of Sierra Valley to the north open up to your left. From the waterfalls, there are only 1.2 miles left to the summit, but the ascent during this portion is the steepest of the hike. After a switchback, the forest gradually gives way to sparse fields of windblown mountain hemlock. Mountain hemlock can be identified by their tight clusters of small bluish-green needles and small cones. They are well-adapted to the long-lasting snowpack and fierce winds on the upper slopes of Mount Lola. Despite its name, this tree is not related to the famous herb that killed Socrates. The trees are not poisonous, and, in fact, a tea can be brewed from their needles.

If you climb Mount Lola in early summer, you will find snow traction devices useful to traverse the large, steep snowfields during this final portion of the trail. Even in August, you will be able to cool down in snow that lingers on the north side of Mount Lola's large glacial-carved amphitheater. In welcome contrast to the steep slopes of the trail, the slopes of the treeless summit of Mount Lola are surprisingly gradual.

Unsurprisingly, though, the views from the top are outstanding. Circular White Rock Lake and oblong Independence Lake lie below to the west and east, respectively. The rugged spires of Castle Peak (Hike 56) are visible to the south. In the distance to the northwest, the towers of Sierra Buttes (Hike 51) pierce the sky. On a clear day, you will even be able to make out Lassen Peak about 100 miles to the north and a small sliver of Lake Tahoe to the south. If you wish, you can walk 0.5 miles north along Mount Lola's ridge to attain better foreground views to the north. From this vantage point, you can see all of Sierra Valley and Frenchman Lake (Hike 1). After you have savored the views, begin the long descent back to the trailhead.

From Reno. Take I-80 west for 29.9 miles to the Highway 89-North/267 exit. Turn right on Highway 89 toward Sierraville. Within the first mile, drive straight through two traffic circles. Drive a total of 14.5 miles on Highway 89 before turning left on Jackson Meadows Road. Continue on Jackson Meadows Road, which is closed in the winter and early spring because of snow, for 1.5 miles. Turn left onto a dirt road, following the sign pointing toward Independence Lake. Soon thereafter, a paved bridge takes you over the Little Truckee River. In 0.7 miles, turn right at the first intersection onto unlabeled Henness Pass Road. Drive 3.3 miles on this road until you reach a well-marked trailhead at 39.4884, -120.3399. Under dry conditions, all of the dirt roads are passable by low-clearance two-wheel-drive vehicles. *NOTE:* Digital mapping services give different driving directions that use rough roads that are inaccessible to most vehicles. *1 hour, 10 mins.*

At the summit

55 Sagehen Creek

A FLAT HIKE ALONG RELAXING SAGEHEN CREEK LEADS TO A BEAVER POND, A LARGE FIELD of wildflowers, and open views of Stampede Reservoir.

At a Glance

DIFFICULTY	Easy	**DISTANCE/TIME**	5.0 miles/2.5 hours
ELEVATION GAIN	300 feet	**TRAIL TYPE**	Foot trail
SOLITUDE	Heavy use	**USERS**	Hikers
BEST SEASON	April–December	**LAND OWNERSHIP**	National Forest
ANIMALS	Deer, beavers, bears	**FEATURES**	Lake, streams, wildflowers

Flowing through the northern Donner Pass area, perennial Sagehen Creek is one of many regional creeks that are sourced from heavy snowfall on nearby mountains. The hike follows an easy course for 2.5 miles from Highway 89 along the creek to Stampede Reservoir.

Out of the parking area, follow the trail through a mixture of Jeffrey pine and lodgepole pine. As the trail gets closer to the creek, the pine trees give way to dense groves of willows and aspen. The creek waters a wide range of wildflowers that bloom in early summer. Along the forest floor, look for yellow Rocky Mountain butterweed and mahala mat, a ground cover that blooms with clusters of tiny purple flowers.

After 1.0 miles of hiking, Sagehen Creek widens into a shallow pond formed by a beaver dam. Beavers are the largest rodents in North America and are

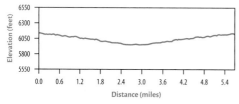

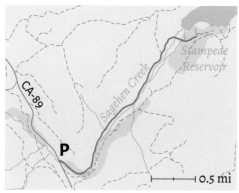

fascinating creatures. They use their large, strong incisors, which are bright orange due to their high iron content, to fell trees. They eat the inner bark and move the trees great distances over land and water to build their dams and lodges. Along the edge of the creek near the pond, you will notice many beaver-gnawed stumps.

After their dam successfully creates a pond, beavers build lodges as places to hide from predators, rear their young, and sleep during the day. A lodge consists of a conical mound of twigs and leaves, and is usually about 5 feet in diameter. If you look carefully, you will

At the banks of Sagehen Creek

spot a few beaver lodges from the trail. Because beavers are nocturnal, you are unlikely to see these animals during the day. However, Sagehen Creek is an excellent spot to watch beavers at work during a warm summer night in the light of a full moon.

As you hike past the beaver pond, notice the brownish-gray rocks on the open slopes above the trail to the left and farther in the background. These volcanic rocks are called andesite and were deposited from ancient lava flows. Andesite is the dominant rock in the Sagehen Creek area, in contrast to the granite that epitomizes the Sierra Nevada. In most of the Sierras, millennia of

Beaver-gnawed aspen stump

glacial action have eroded away the more recent lava flows. The Sagehen Creek basin, however, did not experience heavy glaciation, so these andesite lava flows are still present today. The porous rocks act like a sponge that holds more water than hard granite does. This geology allows Sagehen Creek to perennially flow even when the snow disappears in the summer.

Near the end of the trail, you reach a large meadow on the shores of Stampede Reservoir. Numerous wildflower species abound here in early summer. In wet years, the meadow is covered with purple camas lilies, a stunning sight that ap-

Walking through pines, mule's ears, and sage

pears as if it were taken straight out of a fairy tale. In these special years, the Sagehen Creek meadow is the best place in the northern Sierra Nevadas to view camas lilies in late May and early June. You may need to cross over Sagehen Creek, getting your feet wet or walking on a fallen log, to see them up close.

Various use-trails lead to the shores of Stampede Reservoir. Here at the interface between the meadow and the water, songbirds such as the mountain chickadee, dark-eyed junco, and Audubon's warbler intermix with water birds such as mergansers, the American white pelican, and bald eagles. Take a break at the water's edge to enjoy the views and wildlife before returning to the trailhead the way you came. If desired, you may return to Highway 89 via West Stampede Road on the opposite side of Sagehen Creek. This road is dirt, and the vegetation here is drier than on the main trailhead.

From Reno. Take I-80 west for 29.9 miles to the Highway 89-North/267 exit. Turn right on Highway 89 toward Sierraville. Within the first mile, drive straight around two traffic circles. Drive a total of 7.1 miles on Highway 89 before parking on the right side of the road at a well-marked trailhead at 39.4341, -120.2050. When snow is on the ground, there is no easy parking in this area, which effectively closes the trailhead during these times. *40 mins.*

The final meadow overlooking Stampede Reservoir

56 Castle Peak

ASCEND TO TURRETS IN THE SKY AT CASTLE PEAK FOR MAJESTIC VIEWS OF DONNER PASS and beyond. Enjoy scenic Castle Valley with streams and wildflowers along the way.

At a Glance

DIFFICULTY	Hard	**DISTANCE/TIME**	5.7 miles/3 hours
ELEVATION GAIN	2,000 feet	**TRAIL TYPE**	Foot trail, dirt road
SOLITUDE	Medium use	**USERS**	Hikers, bikers
BEST SEASON	April–November	**LAND OWNERSHIP**	National Forest
ANIMALS	Deer, bears	**FEATURES**	Expansive views, streams, wildflowers

Three spires of rock form a dominating landmark north of the high-point of Interstate 80 at Donner Pass. Although access to the trailhead is available year-round and is popular with cross-country skiers and snowshoers in the winter, the easiest times for hiking are during the spring, summer, and fall when snow levels are lower. With a summit at 9,103 feet, Castle Peak is only slightly lower than Mount Lola (Hike 54) and is one of the highest peaks in the Donner Pass region. The cragged volcanic outcroppings of Castle Peak, however, make the summit feel even higher. In this way, the summit of Castle Peak is reminiscent of much taller peaks in the southern Sierra Nevadas where such rugged peaks are common.

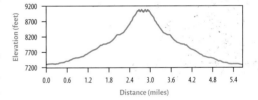

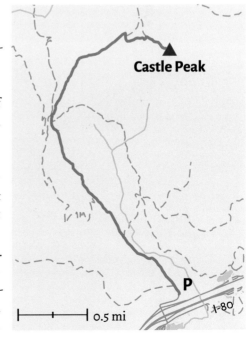

From the parking area, walk up the dirt forest service road through a forest of lodgepole pine and red fir. After 0.5 miles, the trail alternates several times between open meadows and forests. Take a moment to peer beyond the trees on the right to see Castle Valley with majestic Castle Peak in the background. In the meadows here, the many tributaries

Looking towards Castle Peak from Castle Valley

The narrow, well-defined trail up Castle Peak

of Castle Creek result in wonderful wild-flower displays in the summer. Large fields of lavender wandering daisies intermixed with tall corn lilies thrive here. Look also for patches of blue stickseed, purple lupines, and crimson columbines.

Continue straight on the main dirt road as it climbs more steeply through the shaded forest. After you hike 1.1 additional miles, the trail leaves the forest and begins to climb up the ridge toward Castle Peak. Lower down in the forest to the right, there is an additional parking area suitable for those with high-clearance four-wheel-drive vehicles who want to shave a round-trip total of 3.2 miles off the hike. Past the parking area, the road turns into a foot trail, and on a flat section of the ridge, you will soon reach a prominent trail junction. The path to the left leads to Round Valley, a popular cross-country skiing destination and wildflower viewing area. Instead of descending into Round Valley, veer right to continue to climb the ridge of Castle Peak. The elevation here is about 8,000 feet, and there is still more than 1,000 feet of climbing ahead.

On the exposed rocky ridge, a variety of wildflowers blooms from July to September. Look for yellow buckwheat, blue flax, pink narrow-tube skyrockets, and Leichtlin's mariposa lilies with brown spots on the yellow interior of their petals. Rocky outcroppings of cooled lava become more common the higher you climb. This section of the trail becomes increasingly steeper until you reach the summit. Hiking poles and shoes with good traction are highly recommended because loose pebbles make the trail slippery here. Additionally, large packs of snow can linger through the summer, depending on the wetness of the previous winter. As you climb, a few faint spur trails lead in various directions. Stay on the main trail, which is readily identified at all times by its relentless ascent.

A successful climb to the base of the towers of Castle Peak is rewarded with outstanding views in all directions. On a clear day, Lassen Peak is visible to the north about 100 miles away, and the many peaks of the northern Sierras surround you in the foreground. The trail loses definition at the base of the towers, and many faint trails weave around the three steep rock turrets. The true high point, which is atop the spire farthest to the east, is not climbed by many. Reaching the top requires a 25-foot nearly vertical climb. Although the volcanic rock provides numerous sturdy holds for hands and feet, this ascent is too dangerous for the average hiker. Fortunately, outstanding wraparound views are accessible from many locations at the base of the towers, and these panoramas are not too different from the one obtained at the true summit. After you have fully taken in the views, retrace your steps back down to your car.

From Reno. Take I-80 west for 40.8 miles to the Castle Peak/Boreal Ridge Road exit. After the off-ramp, turn right and follow the road for 0.2 miles. Park where the pavement ends near a forest service gate at 39.3409, -120.3476. *45 mins.*

Rock climbing skills are required to ascend the true high point.

57 Summit Lake

THIS EASY HIKE THROUGH FIRS AND WILDFLOWERS TO A SUBALPINE LAKE IS AN EXCELLENT outing for all ages. The cool climate at the high trailhead elevation makes it a welcome adventure during hot summer days.

At a Glance

DIFFICULTY	Easy	**DISTANCE/TIME**	6.3 miles/3 hours
ELEVATION GAIN	800 feet	**TRAIL TYPE**	Foot trail, dirt road
SOLITUDE	Medium use	**USERS**	Hikers, bikers
BEST SEASON	All	**LAND OWNERSHIP**	National Forest
ANIMALS	Deer, bears	**FEATURES**	Lakes, streams, wildflowers

As Interstate 80 traverses through Donner Pass, it passes by more than a dozen subalpine lakes. Summit Lake makes for an excellent hiking destination because it is readily accessible and yet there is no development around the lake. During hot summer days, Summit Lake is a popular swimming hole, so consider packing your swimsuit.

Out of the parking area, walk on the main dirt forest road that leads you through a forest of lodgepole pines and red fir trees intermixed with small meadows. A wide range of wildflower species abound in these meadows in the summer. After 0.6 miles of hiking, turn right at the prominent junction to take the lower route that crosses Castle Creek. After passing the creek drainage, the trail climbs gradually back into the trees.

The forest is dominated by large specimens of red fir. The bark on young red firs is gray, but the red-brown color of mature red firs like these gives them their

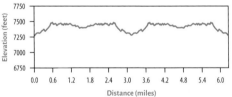

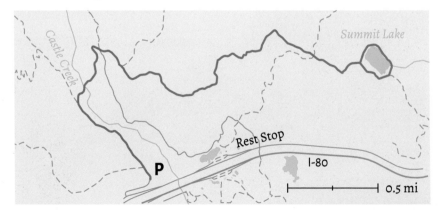

name. Notice the large quantity of wolf lichen growing on these red firs. Wolf lichen is readily identified by its bright chartreuse color and is frequently mistaken for a moss. While mosses are plants, lichens are composites of bacteria and fungi that grow together in a symbiotic relationship. Notice that the wolf lichen on these red firs does not occur at the base of the trees. The lichen cannot tolerate snow, so they are year-round markers of maximum snow depth.

At 0.4 miles past the creek, the trail bends to the right before reaching a trail junction. Walk straight through the junction and the second junction in another 0.2 miles. An obscured sign at the second junction points you in the direction of Summit Lake (mostly east) and not the **Pacific Crest Trail** (PCT) to the south. The trail now is relatively flat as it meanders around granite boulder fields and open terrain that fosters yet more fertile ground for wildflowers. Particularly enchanting are the prettyface flowers with six yellow petals and

Tall red firs with wolf lichen at their bases

Summit Lake is a popular swimming destination.

brown stripes. Large clusters of hot pink mountain pride flowers are sure to stop you in your tracks.

As you near Summit Lake, you will reenter the forest, cross over a forest road, and then pass several tributaries that nourish water-loving plants including ferns. The trail descends gradually to the lake and takes you directly to the shores. Lodgepole pines grow right up to the water's edge, giving the lake a definitive mountain feel. If you wish, you may continue on the trail, which circles the lake. Otherwise, enjoy a waterside break before returning to the trailhead the way you came.

From Reno. Take I-80 west for 40.8 miles to the Castle Peak/Boreal Ridge Road exit. After the off-ramp, turn right and follow the road for 0.2 miles. Park where the pavement ends at 39.3409, -120.3476. *45 mins.*

Mountain pride amid granite boulders

58 Alder Creek

AN EASY HIKE ALONG ALDER CREEK MEANDERS BETWEEN FOREST SHADE AND MEADOW sun. If you're looking for a longer hike or trail run, follow the well-maintained trail along the creek through a quiet Truckee neighborhood.

At a Glance

DIFFICULTY	Easy	DISTANCE/TIME	4.9 miles/2.5 hours
ELEVATION GAIN	400 feet	TRAIL TYPE	Foot trail
SOLITUDE	Heavy use	USERS	Hikers, bikers
BEST SEASON	All	LAND OWNERSHIP	National Forest
ANIMALS	Deer, bears	FEATURES	Streams, wildflowers

Like Sagehen Creek (Hike 55), Alder Creek is one of several perennial creeks in the Donner Pass area that cross Highway 89, making hiking access easy. Alder Creek is notable for being the campsite of 25 members of the Donner Party, who struggled to survive here during the winter of 1846–1847. The trail is a popular

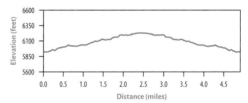

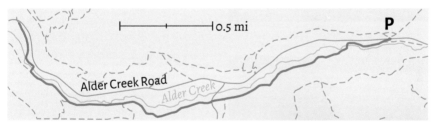

snowshoeing destination in the winter, but is equally popular in warmer months among hikers and mountain bikers.

Walk away from the highway along the well-defined trail. Within 0.3 miles, the trail crosses over Alder Creek via a sturdy wooden bridge. The trail passes through mixed coniferous and deciduous forest. Near the water's edge, aspens and several species of willows are plentiful though the trail is usually about 50 feet away from the water's edge. Conifers include lodge-

This trail is popular with both hikers and bikers.

Sturdy bridges allow you to more fully enjoy views of the creek.

pole pines, Jeffrey pines, and incense cedars. In addition, red firs, white firs, and Douglas firs, the three firs native to the Greater Reno area, are common here. The firs can be distinguished most readily by their needles. Branches of red firs contain tightly clustered bristly needles that stand upright. White firs and Douglas firs both have much flatter needles. Look carefully at the base of the needles where they meet the stem to distinguish between the two. While white fir needles grow straight off the stem at right angles, Douglas fir needles noticeably change directions at their base.

Carefully cross Schussing Way to continue on the trail 0.8 miles past the bridge. In another 1.1 miles, another well-constructed wooden bridge takes you to Alder Creek Road, the street on which you parked. If available, a second car can pick you up here. Otherwise, return the way you came back to the trailhead. Alternatively, you can explore farther upstream Alder Creek. The trail continues along the creek for an additional 2.1 miles, but this portion of the creek is surrounded by homes.

From Reno. Take I-80 west for 29.9 miles to the Highway 89-North/267 exit. Turn right on Highway 89 toward Sierraville. Within the first mile, drive straight around two traffic circles. Drive a total of 2.2 miles on Highway 89, and then turn left on Alder Creek Road. In 0.4 miles, park on the left side of the road at a well-marked trailhead at 39.3672, -120.1902. *40 mins.*

Alder Creek

59 Boca Hill

A GENTLE CLIMB TO BOCA HILL, A PEAK IN THE MIDDLE OF TRUCKEE'S LARGEST VALLEY, LEADS to excellent views of the surrounding reservoirs and mountains.

At a Glance

DIFFICULTY	Hard	DISTANCE/TIME	6.3 miles/4 hours
ELEVATION GAIN	1,200 feet	TRAIL TYPE	Dirt road
SOLITUDE	Light use	USERS	Hikers, OHVs
BEST SEASON	All year	LAND OWNERSHIP	National Forest
ANIMALS	Deer, bears	FEATURES	Expansive views

Driving east on Interstate 80 from Reno, you dramatically serpentine out of the steep Truckee River Canyon about 10 miles past the Nevada-California border and emerge in large and flat Martis Valley. Just right of the highway, Boca Hill, a peak of mounded forest, rises in isolation above the valley. At 6,700 feet above sea level, Boca Hill is not high compared to other peaks in the Donner Pass area such as Mount Lola (Hike 54), Castle Peak (Hike 56), and Mount Judah (Hike 60), all of which are well above 8,000 feet. What it lacks in elevation, though, Boca Hill makes up for in prominence.

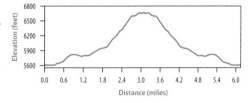

In topography, prominence is a measure of how high a mountain is above the surrounding landscape. From a summit, you always have to hike down to a lower point before you start climbing a higher second summit. How far down you go defines the prominence of the first mountain. For example, Boca Hill has 920 feet of prominence, which means from the top of Boca Hill, you must descend at least 920 feet to reach a higher point. Because high prominence peaks tower above the surrounding terrain, the views are usually excellent on top of these summits. In the case of Boca Hill,

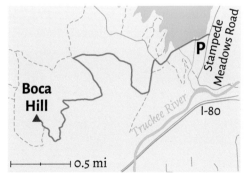

there are outstanding views of the Martis Valley and the surrounding mountains.

Boca Hill is a straightforward mountain to climb. If you park before Boca Reservoir, first walk over the dam. Boca Dam was constructed in 1939 to control the flow of the Truckee River and prevent flooding of downtown Reno during years with wet winters. Once on the other side of the reservoir, walk 0.2 miles on

Mount Rose Wilderness from Boca Hill

the paved road, and turn left on the second dirt road on the left. This dirt road climbs up Boca Hill. In 0.3 miles, turn right at the first junction you encounter. This fainter dirt road heads west, and in 0.9 miles terminates at another junction. Turn left here, and stay on this road as it climbs 1.5 miles to the top of Boca Hill.

The summit of Boca Hill is mostly open, affording you excellent views in all directions. Because the ascent up Boca Hill is relatively gradual, it can be hiked year-round, although snowshoes are needed in the winter and early spring. After you are finished taking in the views, return the way you came.

From Reno. Take I-80 west for 24.2 miles to the Hirschdale Road exit. After the off-ramp, turn left. Drive over the Truckee River and the railroad tracks. In 0.8 miles, park at 39.3910, -120.0922 in a large dirt shoulder on the left side of the road near the Boca Reservoir dam. If snow levels are low, you may cross the dam and park on the opposite side of the reservoir. *30 mins.*

Boca Reservoir and beyond

60 Mount Judah and Donner Peak

SUMMIT THE TOPS OF MOUNT JUDAH AND DONNER PEAK AS PART OF A BEAUTIFUL LOOP that features incredible wildflower displays throughout the summer and vast Donner Pass views.

At a Glance

DIFFICULTY	Hard	DISTANCE/TIME	5.5 miles/4.5 hours
ELEVATION GAIN	1,500 feet	TRAIL TYPE	Foot trail
SOLITUDE	Medium use	USERS	Hikers
BEST SEASON	May–October	LAND OWNERSHIP	National Forest
ANIMALS	Deer	FEATURES	Expansive views, wildflowers

The Donner Pass exit on Interstate 80 is a portal to high-elevation recreation for thousands of visitors. Given the ski resorts and housing developments in the area, a series of peaks south of Donner Pass that are protected by the forest service provide welcome respite for the wilderness seeker. Here, the Pacific Crest Trail runs part of its 2,653-mile-long course connecting Mexico to Canada via some of the continent's most mountainous landscapes.

From the parking area, head east and begin your hike on the well-marked **Pacific Crest Trail**. In a few hundred feet, you will walk through a beautiful shady subalpine garden filled with aspen trees, ferns, and multiple species of wildflowers. Beyond this garden, the trail begins to switchback up the mountainside via steps carved into the granite. As you climb, look for mountain maple trees, which are nourished by water that slowly percolates out of the hillside. During July and August, many of the green leaves are covered by a film of bright red bumps. These bumps, or galls, are caused by mites, which feed on the leaves.

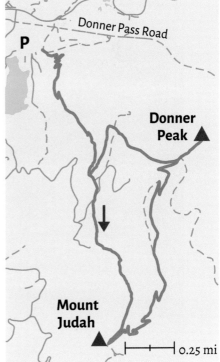

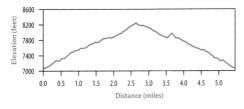

Past the granite steps, the trail continues to climb along the western slopes of the Pacific Crest. Views of Lake Mary below and Lake Van Norden farther west open up. A few rugged Jeffrey pines, tattered by harsh winds, grow on these slopes against the odds. After 0.9 miles total of hiking, you will reach a trail junction. The path to the left climbs up to Donner Peak. If you want a shorter outing, turn left here and hike out to Donner Peak and back for a round-trip distance of 3.9 miles.

For the complete loop to both Mount Judah and Donner Peak, continue straight through this junction instead. The trail here alternates between forest and exposed slopes. On hot summer days, any of the shaded forests make for good breaking spots because the upper portions of the trail are very sunny. After 1.0 miles of additional hiking, a trail sign marks a junction and points to Mount Judah to the left. As you climb this new trail and leave the **Pacific Crest Trail**

View from Donner Peak

behind, look down below at Roller Pass, the saddle point between Mount Judah and Mount Lincoln to the south. Roller Pass was one route that pioneers in the 1840s used to traverse the Sierra Nevadas. Although still quite a climb, Roller Pass is not as steep as Donner Pass. As a result, wagons did not have to be disassembled to cross Roller Pass like they were when crossing Donner Pass.

From the trail junction, it takes 0.7 more miles and 400 feet of climbing to reach the summit of Mount Judah. The views from the top are outstanding, and countless snowy peaks are visible in all directions. Enjoy a bird's-eye perspective of the big blue waters of Donner Lake below.

The most difficult climbing of the trail is behind you at this point, and continuing on to Donner Peak is not strenuous. Navigate the talus-strewn ridgeline between the two peaks as you gently descend to a saddle point in another 1.0 miles. At the junction, veer to the right to climb Donner Peak, which is only 0.2 miles away and 100 feet above you. Views of Donner Lake are even more impressive from Donner Peak.

After you have soaked in the panorama, retrace your steps for 0.2 miles back down to the trail junction. Head right to take a new trail at this point. This spur trail takes you through lovely fields of rainbow-colored wildflowers that bloom in late summer. In 0.6 miles, you once again reach the **Pacific Crest Trail**. Turn right at the junction, and follow your footsteps back to your car.

Mule's ears, desert paintbrushes, and lupines

From Reno. Take I-80 west for 33.2 miles to the Donner Pass Road exit. Drive on Donner Pass Road for 6.9 miles. Turn left on Old Donner Summit Road, and in 0.2 miles, park on the side of the road at 39.3147, -120.3272 near Lake Mary. *50 mins.*

61 Coldstream Canyon

EXPLORE THE RUGGED ALPINE TERRAIN OF DONNER PASS WITH THIS EASY HIKE THROUGH scenic Coldstream Canyon. Look for abundant wildlife near Cold Creek and the adjoining ponds.

At a Glance

DIFFICULTY	Very Easy	DISTANCE/TIME	3.3 miles/1.5 hours
ELEVATION GAIN	300 feet	TRAIL TYPE	Dirt road, foot trail
SOLITUDE	Heavy use	USERS	Hikers, bikers
BEST SEASON	All	LAND OWNERSHIP	Truckee Donner Land Trust
ANIMALS	Deer, beavers, bears	FEATURES	Lakes, stream, wildflowers

In the heart of Donner Pass, a massive glacier plowed eastward and carved dramatic Coldstream Canyon. Corralled by mountains on three sides that rise more than 1,000 feet from the canyon floor, this hike provides visitors with a distinct alpine feel with minimal climbing. With easy trail access, the trail can be enjoyed year-round. Snowshoeing through the heavy snowfall in winter and early spring is a magical experience. However, the beauty of the surrounding landscape and the majesty of nearby Cold Creek make this hike enjoyable no matter the season.

Past the parking area, Cold Stream Road heads south and climbs into Coldstream Canyon. Although many hikers choose to walk up this road, it is more enjoyable to walk up the smaller dirt trail to the left of the road, closer to Cold Creek. For the first 0.4 miles, the trail is fairly steep, but the rest of the hike is almost entirely flat.

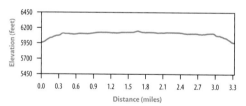

After the climb and 0.6 miles of more hiking, you will reach the smaller of two large ponds. There are many parallel trails and roads throughout this hike. The exact path you take is unimportant because all of the trails head in the same direction and never deviate from one another for long. The ponds and this complicated assembly of trails is a relic of the mining history of Coldstream Canyon. High-quality gravel, formed from millennia of glacial action, was mined here throughout the twentieth

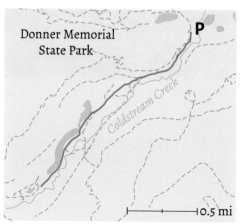

century. More recently, various agencies came together to restore the canyon's wetlands and open the land to the public.

Shortly past the first pond, you will reach the larger second pond, which although narrow, is nearly 0.5 miles long. Birding opportunities abound here. Osprey, bald eagles, and various songbirds are common. Look for tree stumps that have been gnawed by beavers. When you reach the end of the second pond, you can return to the trailhead by any of the parallel trails that take you back to the parking area.

From Reno. Take I-80 west for 33.2 miles to the Donner Pass Road exit. In 0.2 miles, turn left on Cold Stream Road. In 0.6 miles, park in a dirt parking area on the side of the road at 39.3170, -120.2299. *40 mins.*

This hike is shaded and relatively flat.

Beaver tracks preserved in dried mud

The second pond

62 Martis Creek Lake and Lake Ella

ADVENTURE TO TWO EASILY ACCESSIBLE LAKES IN THE MIDDLE OF GRAND MARTIS VALLEY.
The lakes offer excellent birding opportunities and great places to enjoy a picnic.

At a Glance

DIFFICULTY	Easy	DISTANCE/TIME	6.2 miles/3 hours
ELEVATION GAIN	600 feet	TRAIL TYPE	Paved road, foot trail
SOLITUDE	Medium use	USERS	Hikers, bikers
BEST SEASON	May–November	LAND OWNERSHIP	U.S. Army Corps of Engineers, Truckee Donner Land Trust
ANIMALS	Deer, bears	FEATURES	Lakes, streams, wildflowers

The mountains that form the northern rim of Lake Tahoe receive plenty of snow. In spring, snowmelt on the northern slopes of these mountains flows into large Martis Valley. The water in this area provides a haven for wildflowers and wildlife, and this hike takes you to the two lakes in the valley.

Martis Valley is named for the ancient Martis people, the first Native Americans to inhabit the Greater Reno area. Archaeological evidence indicates that people have resided in Martis Valley for at least 2,000 years. The Washoe people camped in Martis Valley, where they hunted game and foraged for blue camas

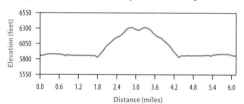

bulbs and other wild edibles, up until the 1910s.

To begin your adventure, walk past the gate at the trailhead and onto Martis Dam Road. This

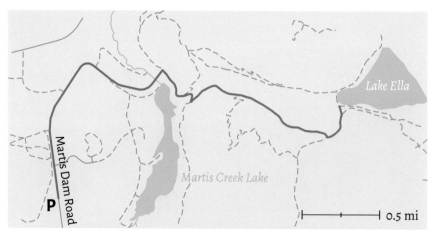

portion of the road is only accessible to maintenance vehicles associated with the Martis Dam. Because the road is paved to the dam, the first section of this hike is perfect for young families with strollers. Bikers often ride the first 1.5 miles of the trail to the other side of the dam before stashing their bikes away to begin hiking when the pavement ends.

The trail begins through mixed vegetation dominated by sagebrush, bitterbrush, and ponderosa pines. In 1.2 miles, cross the top of Martis Dam. Martis Creek Lake, formed by the dam, is a favorite fishing spot for anglers and birds of prey such as osprey and bald eagles. Morning fog is common in Martis Valley as a result of the large bodies of water and relatively low elevation. As you cross the dam, excellent views of the Sierra Nevadas that border Lake Tahoe appear to your right. Snow lingers late in the season on the ski runs of Mount Pluto, and Martis Peak (Hike 64) stands tall in the background to Mount Pluto's left.

Tall trees provide shade throughout much of this hike.

After you cross the dam, follow the sign to Waddle Ranch, which leads you to a foot trail to the right. In early summer, wildflowers are common here as the trail

Martis Creek Lake with Mount Pluto in the background

follows the lakeside for 0.3 miles. Soon, you will pass a small creek that nourishes cattails and other water-loving plants. This creek originates from Lake Ella, your next destination. You will take a tight switchback and walk eastwardly with the creek parallel on your left.

To reach Lake Ella, continue on this trail and begin climbing to enter the Waddle Ranch Preserve. You're now on **Matt's Trail**, and it gently climbs 500 feet over the next 1.0 miles. As you climb, you enter a hidden world consisting of a vast forest of stately ponderosa pines mixed with red firs and white firs. Continue on the trail to descend to Lake Ella over the next 0.3 miles.

Lake Ella is a picturesque 70-acre lake that is home to a number of bird species including song sparrows, western tanagers, mountain bluebirds, yellow warblers, and various ducks. A lakeside picnic table provides excellent views from a shady vista. Although Lake Ella is called Dry Lake on some maps, it holds water throughout the summer most years. Several use-trails allow you to explore along the lake's southern and western shores.

After your visit to Lake Ella is complete, return via Matt's Trail. At the high point of Matt's Trail 0.3 miles from the lake, there is a well-marked junction. If you want to tack on additional mileage, you can turn left on **Erika's Trail**. This trail adds 0.9 miles as it winds through forest before it loops back to Matt's Trail. Parts of Erika's Trail boast some nice views of Martis Valley, and there is a small grove of sugar pine trees about halfway through the trail. Once common throughout the Lake Tahoe Basin, these trees are becoming increasingly rare, perhaps due to a particular sensitivity toward climate change. Regardless of whether you take Erika's Trail, walk back across the dam and return to the trailhead.

From Reno. Take I-80 west for 29.9 miles to the Highway 89-North/267 exit. Turn left onto Highway 267. In 2.9 miles, turn left onto Martis Dam Road. Drive 1.2 miles until the road ends at a closed gate. Park at the well-marked trailhead on the left side of the road at 39.3170, -120.1264. The trailhead is open from May until the first snowfall, typically in November. *40 mins*

A bench at the shores of Lake Ella

63 Five Lakes

HIKE TO FIVE SUBLIME SUBALPINE LAKES SURROUNDED BY GRANITE-PUNCTUATED wilderness. Choose the lake with your favorite scenery, and take a plunge. Or better yet, swim in them all!

At a Glance

DIFFICULTY	Easy	**DISTANCE/TIME**	4.9 miles/3 hours
ELEVATION GAIN	1,300 feet	**TRAIL TYPE**	Foot trail
SOLITUDE	Heavy use	**USERS**	Hikers
BEST SEASON	May–October	**LAND OWNERSHIP**	National Forest
ANIMALS	Deer, bears	**FEATURES**	Lakes

Among the forests on the west side of Lake Tahoe, ancient glaciers carved a series of majestic granite bowls and cirques. This scenic landscape is preserved in aptly named Granite Chief Wilderness. The gorgeous **Five Lakes Trail** takes you to a series of granite bowls that are filled year-round with snowmelt. These subalpine lakes sit among a stunning alpine backdrop and provide idyllic swimming holes for aquatic enthusiasts.

From the parking area, cross the street, and begin hiking on the signed trailhead. The trail immediately starts to climb through a lodgepole pine forest mixed with red and white firs. Look and listen for iconic birds of these coniferous forests such as the mountain chickadee and red-breasted nuthatch. In 0.6 miles, the trail continues to climb, but it leaves the forest to give away to exposed rocky terrain, taking you under ski lifts and over granite boulders. Lovely views of Alpine Meadows Ski Resort and its mountain backdrop open up to the south.

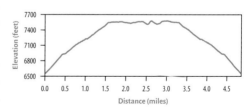

After you climb an additional 0.9 miles, a sign welcomes you to the Granite Chief Wilderness.

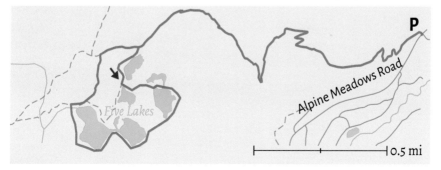

Even more welcoming is the flat terrain and shade provided by gigantic red firs. In 0.2 miles, you will be able to spot the first unnamed lake through the trees to the left of the trail. Take a narrow unofficial trail to the left that leads to the lake.

Each of the lakes has its own character and feel. The route described here will lead you to increasingly larger lakes. The smaller volume of the first lakes allows the sun to warm them up more in the summer, while the larger later lakes contain colder, clearer water.

Continue past the first lake, and when you reach the shores of the second lake, turn left. Follow an ill-defined trail to reach the north shore of the third lake, which is far less grassy and muddy than the first two. You will also pass by a smaller body of water to the left, which is apparently deemed a pond, not a lake, lest the area be called Six Lakes. A small trail circumvents the third lake, and the eastern end of the trail climbs a granite

Steps during the initial ascent

Swimming in the second lake

ridge that provides beautiful views of the canyon below to the left.

Follow the trail to the fourth lake, which contains the clearest water yet. In late summer, wildflowers abound in the meadow between the third and fourth lakes. A small creek connects the fourth and fifth lakes. The fifth lake is arguably the most beautiful of them all as its eastern boundary is defined by a dramatic granite cliff that is the foreground of a spectacular rugged alpine background.

Find your way around the eastern edge of the fifth lake before regaining the official Five Lakes Trail on the northern shore. From here, it is only 0.4 miles to the original trail junction that led you to the first lake. Stay straight through this junction, and retrace your steps for 1.7 miles to descend back to your car.

From Reno. Take I-80 west for 32.2 miles to the Highway 89-South exit. Turn left onto Highway 89, and in 9.8 miles, turn right onto Alpine Meadows Road. In 2.1 miles, park on a dirt shoulder on the left side of the road at 39.1791, -120.2298 across the street from the trailhead. *50 mins.*

The fifth and largest lake

Heading down back to the trailhead

North Lake
Tahoe

Grandiose Lake Views

Lake Tahoe is paradise for those who love the outdoors. Crystal clear waters, peaceful streams, dense forests, abundant wildlife, and spectacular views await those who make the easy drive to the north side of the lake from Reno.

For flat shoreline views of Lake Tahoe, hike to Sand Harbor (Hike 68) and Chimney Beach (Hike 69). Alternatively, for exquisite higher vantages of the lake, climb to Martis Peak (Hike 64), to Stateline Point (Hike 67), and to a rocky pinnacle perched above a spectacular portion of the Tahoe Rim Trail (Hike 65). The Incline Flume Trail (Hike 66) is an excellent flat hike with bird's-eye views that is a good option for those wishing to escape the summer crowds.

Lastly, explore the backcountry high above Lake Tahoe's east shore with a challenging trip to Marlette Lake (Hike 70). This hike also features an easy side trip to scenic Spooner Lake, a nice alternative for those wanting an easier adventure.

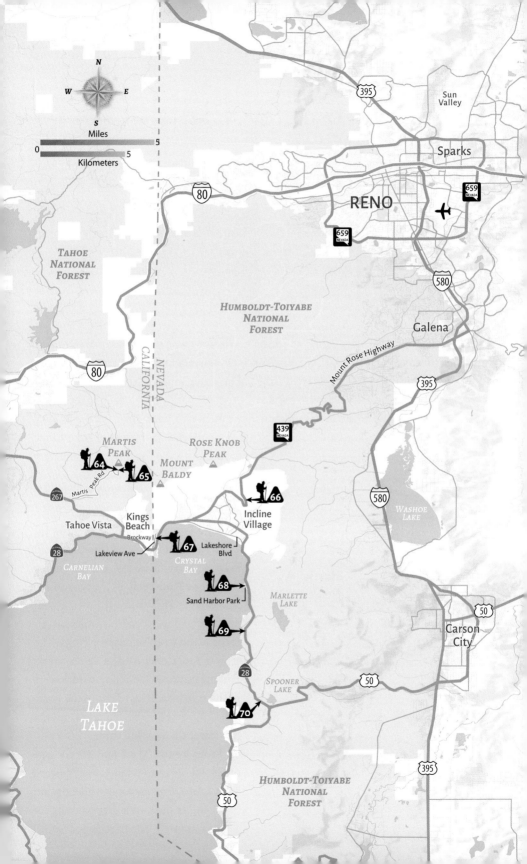

64 Martis Peak

HIKE THROUGH A LUSH FOREST TO THE MARTIS PEAK FIRE LOOKOUT WITH TOWERING VIEWS of Lake Tahoe. With short and long options, there is a variation of this hike for everyone.

At a Glance

DIFFICULTY	Very easy or Hard	DISTANCE/TIME	1.1 miles/0.5 hours or 7.3 miles/4 hours
ELEVATION GAIN	300 feet or 1,500 feet	TRAIL TYPE	Paved trail
SOLITUDE	Medium use	USERS	Hikers, bikers
BEST SEASON	May–November	LAND OWNERSHIP	National Forest
ANIMALS	Deer, bears	FEATURES	Expansive views, wildflowers

Just north of Lake Tahoe, the deep red fir forests on the slopes of Martis Peak encompass a large swath of open space with myriad hiking opportunities. For a short adventure with elevated Lake Tahoe views, climb to the Martis Peak fire tower from the end of Martis Peak Road. From the parking area, walk past the gate and up the paved road for 0.5 miles to the century-old tower. There is a picnic table at the top where you can eat lunch while enjoying excellent views of Lake Tahoe to the south. To the north, the entirety of Martis Valley is visible at the foot of Truckee as well as Castle Peak (Hike 56) and more distant Lassen Peak.

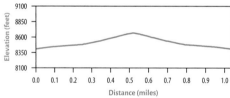

For a longer hike and an option for when Martis Peak Road is snowbound, start from Highway 267, and hike along the **Tahoe Rim Trail** all the way to the fire tower. This route follows a well-marked trail and steadily climbs past fir forests and granite outcroppings. The trail is replete with Lake Tahoe views and meadows of blooming wildflowers in the summer. Regardless of the route you choose, return to your car from the fire tower the way you came.

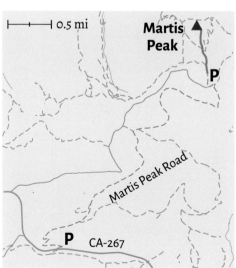

From Reno. Take I-80 west for 29.6 miles. Merge onto Highway 267 toward Lake Tahoe. For the longer hike option, in 9.1 miles park in a dirt parking lot

on the right side of the road at 39.2585, -120.0645. For the shorter hike option, in 8.1 miles, turn left onto unlabeled Martis Peak Road, which is closed in the winter and early spring. Drive 3.4 miles on Martis Peak Road, and park at 39.2867, -120.0332 by the closed forest service gate. *NOTE:* Digital mapping services sometimes give incorrect driving directions to this location. *1 hour.*

Picnic table next to a huge western juniper tree near the top

View of Lake Tahoe from the fire tower
View north from the summit

65 Kings Beach Tahoe Rim Trail

EXPLORE A BEAUTIFUL STRETCH OF THE TAHOE RIM TRAIL THOUSANDS OF FEET ABOVE LAKE Tahoe. Travel through dense forests and fields of wildflowers, and enjoy mind-bending views of the lake and surrounding mountains.

At a Glance

DIFFICULTY	Hard	DISTANCE/TIME	9.1 miles/6 hours
ELEVATION GAIN	1,400 feet	TRAIL TYPE	Foot trail
SOLITUDE	Medium use	USERS	Hikers
BEST SEASON	May–November	LAND OWNERSHIP	National Forest
ANIMALS	Deer, bears	FEATURES	Expansive views, wildflowers

High above the community of Kings Beach on the north side of Lake Tahoe lies one of the most beautiful stretches of the **Tahoe Rim Trail,** a 165-mile loop that circumnavigates the lake along the surrounding ridges of the Sierra Nevadas. The hike affords increasingly spectacular views of Lake Tahoe before it culminates in a jaw-dropping panorama from atop a rocky alpine perch.

From the parking area junction, walk east on a dirt spur road. The small wildflower-filled meadow you immediately encounter with its auspicious vantage of Lake Tahoe foreshadows much grander views to come. In 0.1 miles, turn left at the signed junction to begin your hike on the **Tahoe Rim Trail.**

Over the next 1.5 miles, the trail gently climbs through the shade of red fir forest. Then the trail bends south-ward as it levels out at the top of a ridge. To your left, dramatic cliffs define a rugged canyon that forms the headwaters of Juniper Creek, a tributary of the Truckee

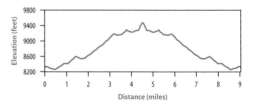

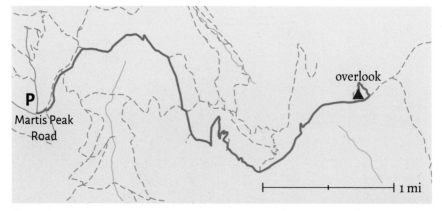

River. Far beyond this drainage, Stampede and Boca Reservoirs are visible on the opposite side of the Truckee River in the distance.

In another 0.3 miles, cross straight through the junction to stay on the main trail, which now resumes ascending. In 1.0 miles, a sign welcomes you to Nevada as you leave California. How different the subalpine landscape is here from the stereotype of Nevada as barren desert! In fact, the astounding views of Lake Tahoe begin past the state line.

Hikers and backpackers both revel in the beauty of this trail.

For the next 1.0 miles, the trail alternates between sunny meadows and cool forests of red fir, interspersed with the occasional western juniper tree that clings to crumbling slopes of weathered granite. In the last 0.5 miles on the **Tahoe Rim Trail** described here, you traverse the largest meadow yet. In the sum-

Enjoying the stellar views

mer, this meadow is carpeted in acres of mule's ears, blooming in cheery yellow. Despite the steep terrain above and below you, the trail here is completely flat, which allows you to fully appreciate the spectacular views of Lake Tahoe below.

The high elevation and open landscape make this portion of the Tahoe Rim Trail among the most magnificent. You can continue hiking along the **Tahoe Rim Trail** for as far as you like; Relay Peak (Hike 76), the highest point on the trail, is 5.6 miles farther from here at 10,338 feet above sea level. The route mapped here, though, takes you to a large sheer rocky outcropping on the hillside to your left, which possesses even grander views.

Turn left onto a narrow spur trail, which climbs to the top of the turret-shaped rocks in 0.2 miles. The summit is flat, and on a calm, windless day, you can take time to soak in your surroundings. Without a doubt, Lake Tahoe will grab most of your attention, but there are also outstanding views of the rest of Mount Rose Wilderness to the east. After you have savored the panorama, return to the trailhead the way you came.

From Reno. Take I-80 west for 29.6 miles. Merge onto Highway 267 toward Lake Tahoe. In 8.1 miles, turn left onto unlabeled Martis Peak Road, which is closed in the winter and early spring. Drive 3.2 miles on Martis Peak Road, and park at 39.2853, -120.0329 in a turnout on the right side of the road. *NOTE:* Digital mapping services sometimes give incorrect driving directions to this location. *1 hour.*

At the hike's high point with stunning views

66 Incline Flume Trail

RAMBLE ALONG A MOUNTAINSIDE ABOVE LAKE TAHOE ON THIS FLAT TRAIL. THIS HIKE IS A great option for those seeking an easy adventure away from summer crowds.

At a Glance

DIFFICULTY	Easy	DISTANCE/TIME	5.1 miles/3 hours
ELEVATION GAIN	300 feet	TRAIL TYPE	Foot trail
SOLITUDE	Medium use	USERS	Hikers, bikers
BEST SEASON	All	LAND OWNERSHIP	National Forest
ANIMALS	Deer, bears	FEATURES	Streams, expansive views

On the **Incline Flume Trail,** enjoy a flat hike 1,500 feet above Lake Tahoe with lovely lake views and stately forests. On busy summer days, this hike is a quieter alternative for those who find the parking area at Tahoe Meadows (Hike 80) too hectic.

After parking, carefully cross Mount Rose Highway, and embark on the foot trail that begins at the signed trailhead at the road's bend. For the first 1.0 miles, your path is shaded by fir trees and Jeffrey pines. Below you to the right, gaps between the tall trees tease you as they yield intermittent views of the grand lake.

Pass straight through the signed trail junction to stay your course on the main trail.

Over the next 0.8 miles, the trail bends past the canyons of the

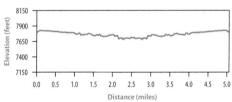

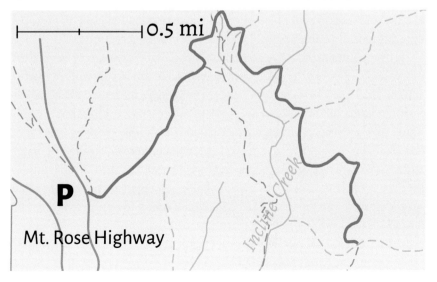

This trail is enjoyable no matter the time of year.

Incline Creek drainage. On your way, you will pass over two perennial branches of the creek and several more tributaries during wet months. During the winter and spring, the rush of the creek is loud, but its path is obscured by snow and ice bridges that span the ravines' large granite boulders. When the snow has melted, the true course of the water is revealed, and it bounces energetically off the rocks, flittering quickly in alternating directions with sparkling splashes.

As the mountainside above and below you becomes increasingly steep, trees can no longer grow on the precipitous gravelly soils. As a result, you are greeted with majestic open views of Lake Tahoe. Lake Tahoe is the largest alpine lake in North America and the second deepest lake in the United States, trailing only Crater Lake in Oregon. Unlike Crater Lake, which is volcanic in origin, Lake Tahoe was created gradually through the faulting action of tectonic plates. The same faults gave rise to the Sierra crest west of Lake Tahoe and the Carson Range to the east. Because of Lake Tahoe's large volume and depth, it contains the cleanest and clearest water in the nation. Agricultural runoff from nearby homes and businesses has led to a steady decrease in water clarity, which a generation ago exceeded 100 feet. Fortunately, strict laws regulating pollution have been successful in slowing the deterioration in water quality.

Although the Incline Flume Trail continues for 3.5 more miles past the start of the grand views, a good place to turn around is when the trail re-enters forest in 0.7 miles at another tributary of Incline Creek. From here, follow the trail back to your car.

From Reno. Take Highway 395/Interstate 580 south for 10.7 miles to the Mount Rose Highway exit. Drive on Mount Rose Highway (NV 431) for 19.6 miles, and park in a large paved turnout at the right side of the road at 39.2676, -119.9300. *40 mins.*

Mountains, pines, and manzanita

View of Lake Tahoe from the trail

67 Stateline Point

SOAR HIGH ABOVE LAKE TAHOE WITHOUT MUCH EXERTION. THE FIRST HALF OF THE HIKE is on a paved trail and features superb views, making it an excellent wheelchair-friendly adventure.

At a Glance

DIFFICULTY	Easy	DISTANCE/TIME	2.9 miles/2 hours
ELEVATION GAIN	900 feet	TRAIL TYPE	Paved road, foot trail
SOLITUDE	Heavy use	USERS	Hikers, bikers
BEST SEASON	April–December	LAND OWNERSHIP	National Forest
ANIMALS	Deer, bears	FEATURES	Expansive views

Hang gliding above Lake Tahoe is an exhilarating experience, and the steep cliffs at the Nevada-California state line make for a popular launching point for aerial enthusiasts. For those of us who are more grounded, take a quick climb to Stateline Point, and enjoy the extraordinary Lake Tahoe views.

To the left of the parking area, walk on the paved road past the forest service gate. After climbing 300 feet in 0.7 miles, you reach the stone foundation of where a fire tower once stood. Turn left and onto a foot trail that makes a 0.3-mile loop. The loop affords exquisite views of Lake Tahoe and is outfitted with signs that explain the history of the fire tower and surrounding area.

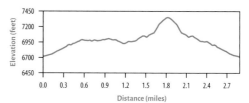

Stateline Point panorama

After completing the loop, hike back down on the main paved road for 0.2 miles. At the junction, turn left onto the dirt trail going up the hillside, a side trip that should be skipped if traveling via wheelchair. For the next 0.3 miles, the path climbs gradually through a dense forest of Jeffrey pines and white firs complemented by an understory of manzanita and bitterbrush. Shortly after the trail levels out, turn right on a faint foot trail that leads farther up the mountain. In 0.2 miles, the forest transitions into open rocky slopes with sagebrush and scattered wildflowers. Climb an additional 0.1 miles to the plateau at Stateline Point for mesmerizing views of Lake Tahoe. When you have finished taking in the views, hike back down the mountain for 0.6 miles until you reach the paved road. Turn left, and return via the road to the trailhead.

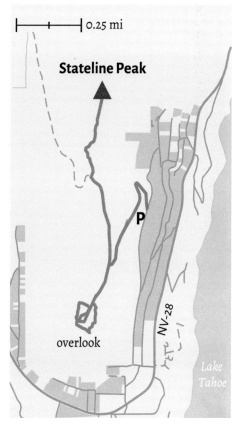

From Reno. Take Highway 395/ Interstate 580 south for 10.7 miles to the Mount Rose Highway exit. Drive

on Mount Rose Highway (NV 431) for 24.1 miles. Turn right at the roundabout onto Highway 28, and in 1.6 miles, turn right onto Beowawie Road. In 0.2 miles, turn left onto Tuscarora Road. In 0.1 miles, turn right onto Lakeview Avenue. In 0.3 miles, park on a shoulder on the right side of the road at 39.2372, -120.0041. *50 mins.*

Hiking up the main trail

Looking west across Lake Tahoe

68 Sand Harbor

THERE IS NEVER A BAD TIME TO REVEL IN THE MAGNIFICENCE OF LAKE TAHOE'S EAST SHORE. Replete with sandy beaches, granite coves, mountain vistas, and teal waters, this popular hike is unforgettable.

At a Glance

DIFFICULTY	Easy	**DISTANCE/TIME**	6.1 miles/3 hours
ELEVATION GAIN	900 feet	**TRAIL TYPE**	Paved trail, dirt trail, beach
SOLITUDE	Heavy use	**USERS**	Hikers, bikers
BEST SEASON	All	**LAND OWNERSHIP**	State Park
ANIMALS	Birds	**FEATURES**	Lake

On Lake Tahoe's eastern shore in Nevada, experience the crown jewel of shoreline Tahoe hiking at Sand Harbor. The highways that circle Lake Tahoe are famous for being some of the most scenic roads in the nation. With a newly constructed trail outfitted with several bridges that span ravines, hikers can enjoy this majestic landscape safely away from the highway. The main pathway is paved and flat, which makes for fast hiking, but the glorious views will have you stopping in your tracks. Numerous signed dirt spur trails lead to secluded coves, picnic areas, and lakeside bouldering opportunities.

From the parking area, first explore Sand Harbor's beautiful white sandy beach. The shoreline here is dotted with granite boulder islands and turquoise waters. Turn right past the beach, and head to the **Tahoe East Shore Trail**, which begins at Sand Harbor's northern limit. In 0.6 miles, two spur trails lead you to Sunset Cove and Emerald Cove. These two coves are on opposite sides of a small peninsula. Sunset Cove's southwest vantage makes it the better choice for

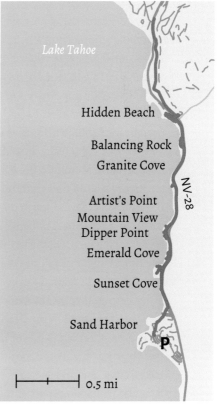

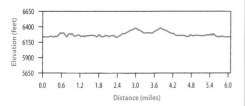

Hidden Beach

viewing sunsets in the winter, while Emerald Cove's northwest vantage is ideal for watching summer sunsets.

Enjoy more lakeside views 0.1 miles past Emerald Cove via a short trail to Dipper Point. In addition to the Jeffrey pines and white firs, this area has one of the few satellite populations of canyon live oaks in Nevada. Unlike most oaks, canyon live oaks can tolerate cold temperatures, and their large acorns were an important food source for Native Americans.

Past Dipper Point, walk an additional 0.2 miles on the main trail to reach two more spur trails, **Mountain View** and **Artist's Point**. From these viewpoints, most of the mountains on the western rim of Lake Tahoe can be seen. Two tall sets of peaks are visible. To the north on the far right side of the horizon, Incline Peak (Hike 79) and other nearby peaks along the Tahoe Rim Trail above Kings Beach (Hike 65) can be seen. On the left side of the horizon on the opposite side of Lake Tahoe lies a cluster of tall peaks in the Desolation Wilderness, which include Mount Tallac and Pyramid Peak.

After getting inspired at Artist's Point, head back to the main trail, and hike 0.3 miles to the junction for Granite Cove. Because it is relatively far from any parking area, this cove is one of the least visited on the **Tahoe East Shore Trail**, despite being arguably the most scenic. In addition to fantastic views of most of Lake Tahoe, the cove features numerous flat granite boulders that make for spectacular picnicking spots at the water's edge.

Back on the main trail, walk an additional 0.3 miles to the south entrance of Balancing Rock. At the shoreline, look for a large boulder that appears to be balancing on top of a smaller rock. There are a number of such balancing rocks around Lake Tahoe, and they each are comprised of one boulder that has been selectively eroded to form a narrow pedestal. In 0.1 miles, the Balancing Rock spur trail takes you back to the main path through a second northern entrance.

In 0.1 additional miles, turn left at the signed entrance for Hidden Beach. Like Sand Harbor, this beach is sandy and perfect for swimming and birding. Common birds of Lake Tahoe include water species such as gulls and mergansers, songbirds such as western tanagers and dark-eyed juncos, and birds of prey such as bald eagles, golden eagles, and red-tailed hawks.

Those who want a flat hike can turn around at Hidden Beach. Otherwise, cross underneath the tunnel that leads to the other side of Highway 28. The paved trail then climbs 150 feet over the next 0.4 miles, resulting in lovely views of Lake Tahoe from a higher vantage point. In another 0.4 miles, the trail terminates after descending to the Tunnel Creek parking area. Turn around here, and return via the main trail to the Sand Harbor parking area in 2.7 miles.

From Reno. Take Highway 395/Interstate 580 south for 10.7 miles to the Mount Rose Highway exit. Drive on Mount Rose Highway (NV 431) for 21.9 miles, and turn left onto Country Club Drive. In 2.3 miles, turn left onto Highway 28. In 3.7 miles, turn right and enter Sand Harbor, part of Lake Tahoe Nevada State Park. Park in the main parking lot at 39.1982, -119.9310. There is a $10 parking fee, and the park is open from 8 a.m. until sunset. *55 mins.*

Numerous exquisite and secluded coves await you on this hike.

69 Chimney Beach

ENJOY A SCENIC STROLL TO LAKE TAHOE'S GORGEOUS CHIMNEY BEACH AND AN accompanying perusal alongside peaceful Marlette Creek. This easy hike is suitable for toddlers, grandparents, and everyone in between.

At a Glance

DIFFICULTY	Very easy	DISTANCE/TIME	1.9 miles/1.5 hours
ELEVATION GAIN	600 feet	TRAIL TYPE	Foot trail
SOLITUDE	Medium use	USERS	Hikers
BEST SEASON	All	LAND OWNERSHIP	National Forest
ANIMALS	Birds	FEATURES	Lake

Eastern Lake Tahoe's rocky shorelines and sandy beaches have a reputation for being incredibly picturesque. Unfortunately, though, popular destinations like Sand Harbor (Hike 68) get so crowded, particularly in the summer, that it can be difficult to find a place to park, let alone find some solitude for a hike. For those busy days, consider a hike to Chimney Beach, which is off the beaten path but equally beautiful as Sand Harbor.

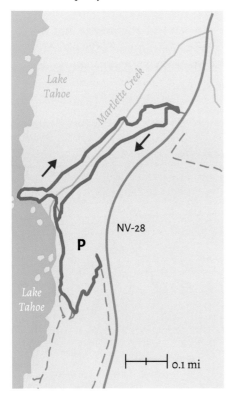

From the southern portion of the parking area, walk on the forest service road that heads down. Almost immediately after beginning on the road, follow the sign to the right that demarcates a foot trail to the beach. The trail goes through a mixed forest of Jeffrey pines and firs with manzanita understory, vegetation typical of Lake Tahoe's shores.

In 0.2 miles, the path turns right and travels along the lake. Numerous spur trails lead to the shoreline, but after a bridged crossing of Marlette Creek, you reach Chimney Beach in 0.4 miles. The location is named after a stone chimney that stands on the sandy shores, which is all that remains

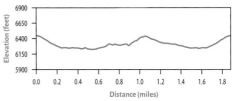

Chimney Beach

from a lakeside cabin. Large granite boulders are jumbled on the beach's peninsula and extend out into the water, entertaining visitors in the mood for some challenging rock hopping. A lone sugar pine tree, easily identified by its enormous pine cones, grows out of a small patch of soil among the rocks.

After you have enjoyed Chimney Beach, continue your hike by walking up along Marlette Creek on a foot trail along the beach side of the creek. Here, deciduous alders and willows join the evergreen trees. In 0.3 miles, cross to the other side of the creek via a small footbridge. Use the stairs to climb out of the creek drainage, and in 0.2 miles you will still be in the forest, but close to Highway 28. At this point, turn around and take a path that leads to the left and back down to the shoreline on the opposite side of the creek. From here, retrace your steps for 0.4 miles to return to the trailhead.

From Reno. Take Highway 395/Interstate 580 south toward Carson City for 36.1 miles. Merge onto Highway 50 west toward Lake Tahoe. In 9.7 miles, turn right onto Highway 28. In 5.1 miles, turn left into a paved parking lot at 39.1635, -119.9307. *55 mins.*

70 Marlette Lake

HIGH IN THE MOUNTAINS ABOVE LAKE TAHOE EXISTS A LESSER-KNOWN ALPINE LAKE OF great beauty. Travel through fields of wildflowers and aspen-lined creeks to reach the cold waters of remote Marlette Lake.

At a Glance

DIFFICULTY	Hard	DISTANCE/TIME	10.6 miles/6 hours
ELEVATION GAIN	1,400 feet	TRAIL TYPE	Foot trail, dirt road
SOLITUDE	Heavy use	USERS	Hikers, bikers, equestrians
BEST SEASON	May–November	LAND OWNERSHIP	State Park
ANIMALS	Deer, bears	FEATURES	Lakes, streams, expansive views, wildflowers

It is hard to dream up something more sublime than gazing down 1,500 feet at Lake Tahoe, the largest alpine lake in North America, while standing near the banks of a second alpine lake. Such magnificent views are what you will find at Marlette Lake.

At 350 acres, Marlette Lake is the second largest, after Fallen Leaf Lake, of the subsidiary lakes within the Lake Tahoe rim. Unlike Fallen Leaf Lake, though, there are no private lands or private vehicles around Marlette Lake, giving the area a distinct backcountry feel. The dam at Marlette Lake was built in the 1870s to provide water for mining operations in Virginia City and the surrounding desert. Today, the lake is a popular fishing area and serves as a spawning site for several trout species, including the threatened Lahontan cutthroat trout.

Marlette Lake

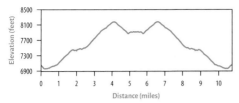

Near the parking area, take any of the several short foot trails that quickly convene. Walk past the sign for **North Canyon Road** and **Marlette Lake Trail**. The dirt road first passes through an open area of sagebrush and bitterbrush with some scattered pines. In the summer, daises and lupines line the trail.

Past the meadow, the trail gradually climbs along perennial North Canyon Creek. A number of species of water-loving plants inhabit this area, including the pink Sierra Nevada pea, yellow sticky cinquefoil, and the highly toxic white death camas. Soon, you pass Spencer's Cabin, an old sheltering place for a cowboy who once worked this country and lived among the colorful aspen. In 0.8 miles, veer left onto Marlette Lake Trail as opposed to continuing on North Canyon Road. Both routes lead to Marlette Lake, but the Marlette Lake Trail is closed to mountain bikers.

The trail climbs steadily through a mixed forest of Jeffrey pines and white fir. On the shallow volcanic soils here, yellow mule's ears, orange paintbrushes, and mountain mint are common. In 1.0 miles, the trail crosses over Secret Harbor Creek via a small bridge. In the summer, look for yellow monkey flowers and crimson columbines, and in the fall, enjoy the dense thickets of golden-leaved aspens in this riparian area.

For the next 2.1 miles, the trail continues

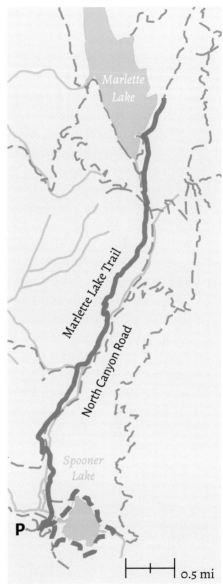

Spencer's Cabin

to climb. Here, the forest transitions to lodgepole pines and red firs, two trees that tolerate the colder temperatures at these higher elevations. At the high point of the hike, there is a prominent trail junction. Stay straight to descend to Marlette Lake over the next 0.8 miles.

Instead of immediately descending to Marlette Lake, if desired, you can first turn left at the junction for a quick detour to outstanding views. Hike up this spur trail for 0.3 miles to its high point and another junction. At the junction, turn left off trail to climb the forested unnamed peak in 0.2 miles. The peak is adorned with a granite outcropping, and from its top, you are treated to a gorgeous view of Marlette Lake sitting in its basin, overhanging Lake Tahoe.

At Marlette Lake, you reach the shores of the lake near an outhouse. Turn left at the restrooms, and cross a short levee to reach a small island. The island is an excellent spot to break for lunch and take in the views. Past the island, you can continue hiking north to explore the east side of the lake. This trail is downhill or flat for the next 0.5 miles. Past this point, the trail crosses a creek and begins to ascend the hillside with additional outstanding views, but to avoid more climbing, here is a good place to turn around.

Return to the trailhead the way you came. Back near the parking area, you can also explore Spooner Lake if you have the energy for more adventure. The flat 2.2-mile loop around the lake is a pleasing trip that can also serve as an alternative hike for those not up for the longer trek to Marlette Lake.

From Reno. Take Highway 395/Interstate 580 south toward Carson City for 36.1 miles. Merge onto Highway 50 west toward Lake Tahoe. In 9.7 miles, turn right onto Highway 28. In 0.7 miles, turn right into Lake Tahoe Nevada State Park at 39.1062, -119.9164. There is a $10 parking fee, and the park is open from 8 a.m. until sunset. *50 mins.*

View of Marlette Lake and Lake Tahoe from atop the nearby high point

The Carson Range

The Sierra Nevada Experience

The Carson Range is the Sierra Nevada playground for the Reno metropolitan area. In the summer, hikers can meander through meadows of colorful wildflowers and cool off in subalpine lakes, streams, and waterfalls. In the winter, plowed Mount Rose Highway provides access to a wonderland of snow and ice.

Most of the hikes begin either near the high point of Mount Rose Highway or at the base of Mount Rose Wilderness outside the community of Galena. At lower elevations, enjoy hikes of varying difficultly alongside creeks such as Thomas and Whites (Hike 72), Brown's (Hike 74), Ophir (Hike 82), and Jones on the way to Church's Pond (Hike 73). Hiking opportunities are also numerous at higher elevations and range from easy strolls, such as those to scenic Tamarack Lake (Hike 77), rugged Upper Thomas Creek (Hike 71), and verdant Tahoe Meadows (Hike 80), to epic summiting experiences on Mount Rose (Hike 75) and Mount Houghton and Relay Peak (Hike 76).

An easy hike with excellent bird's-eye views takes you to Chickadee Ridge (Hike 81). More challenging ascents to Tamarack Peak (Hike 78) and Incline Peak (Hike 79) are hidden gems that offer spectacular views of Lake Tahoe. These two hikes, along with Tamarack Lake (Hike 77), are good choices for those seeking more solitude in what is otherwise a popular wilderness area. An adventure through the Genoa Loop (Hike 83) is a chance to explore the more rugged southern portion of the Carson Range.

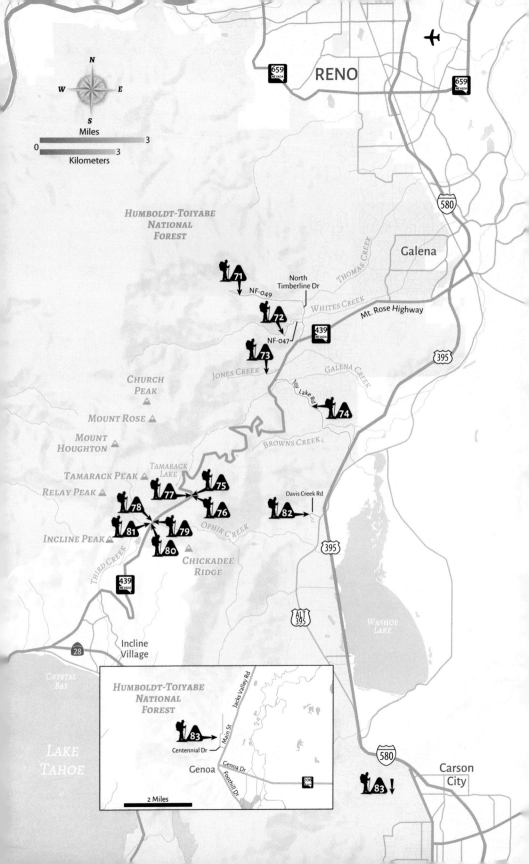

71 Upper Thomas Creek

EXPLORE THE PRISTINE HEADWATERS OF THOMAS CREEK IN THE HEART OF MOUNT ROSE Wilderness. Cool down in the shade of the forest in the summer, or relish the vibrancy of the aspens in the fall.

At a Glance

DIFFICULTY	Hard	**DISTANCE/TIME**	7.4 miles/5 hours
ELEVATION GAIN	1,700 feet	**TRAIL TYPE**	Foot trail
SOLITUDE	Heavy use	**USERS**	Hikers, bikers
BEST SEASON	May–November	**LAND OWNERSHIP**	National Forest
ANIMALS	Deer, black bears	**FEATURES**	Streams, wildflowers

In the Sierra Nevadas, the birthplace of an alpine stream is revered and enigmatic. Perhaps the waters begin from drips off of high-elevation snow that incessantly accumulate in crevasses or muddy puddles before they join forces in myriad rivulets. Perhaps instead the waters originate from springs seeping from below towers of exposed rock. This water might then percolate furtively underground before revealing itself as fragile and swampy meadows that later yield to crystal clear rills.

The birthplace of Thomas Creek is of both snow and springs. For half of the year, these headwaters are buried in deep snow. In summer, the land bursts alive in bright green frog-filled grasses. In autumn, the meadows are set ablaze in golden shimmers of countless quaking aspens.

To explore this special place, walk 100 feet up the road from the parking area. Look for a foot trail heading down to the creek on the left side of the road. Although the trail parallels the road for the next 0.5 miles, the scenery is spectacular. Aspens line the creek, and a mixed forest of Jeffrey pine, firs, and mountain mahoganies grows farther from the water. It is the sheer rock outcroppings on the opposite side of the creek, though, that will grab most of your attention.

After the first 0.5 miles, the trail intersects with the dirt road. Follow the road for 0.1 miles as it crosses Thomas Creek. Past the

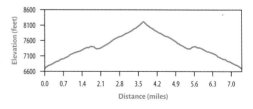

Thomas Creek

P

1 mi

The start of the trail features colorful aspen and conifers.

The trail weaves in and out of shade and sun.

creek, a sign points you toward a foot trail, which allows you to deviate from the road. From here, the trail steadily climbs away from the creek for the next 1.1 miles. The trail then levels out, but the surrounding terrain steepens to become a precipitous hillside. From this vantage point, there are stunning views looking toward Reno down the Thomas Creek watershed.

In 0.6 miles, the trail takes you back to the creek. This higher portion of Thomas Creek contains even denser stands of aspen, which peak in color in late October. The trail continues mostly along the creek for the next 1.4 miles. As you approach the headwaters of the creek, notice the increasing number of grasses that make up the wetlands of the springs.

At the headwaters, the trail abruptly turns north and begins a long series of switchbacks up the mountainside. Although the trail system continues for dozens of miles, here is a good place to turn around. Return to your car the way you came.

From Reno. Take Highway 395/Interstate 580 south for 10.7 miles to the Mount Rose Highway exit. Take Mount Rose Highway (NV 431) for 4.5 miles, and turn right on North Timberline Drive. In 1.2 miles, turn left on an unlabeled forest service road. The road is dirt, but it is suitable for low-clearance two-wheel-drive vehicles under dry conditions. Drive for 1.8 miles, and park in a parking area for 4–5 cars on the left side of the road at 39.3943, -119.8714 near a bridge over Thomas Creek. *35 mins.*

Colorful alder along the creek

72 Thomas and Whites Creeks Loop

EXPLORE THE WATERSHEDS OF TWO PERENNIAL CREEKS WITH AN INTERMITTENT POND IN between. In the summer, this shaded hike is an excellent outing to get away from summer heat.

At a Glance

DIFFICULTY	Hard	DISTANCE/TIME	6.2 miles/3 hours
ELEVATION GAIN	1,100 feet	TRAIL TYPE	Foot trail
SOLITUDE	Heavy use	USERS	Hikers, bikers
BEST SEASON	April–November	LAND OWNERSHIP	National Forest
ANIMALS	Deer	FEATURES	Streams

Heavy snowfall and a series of subalpine springs create two perennial streams on the eastern side of Mount Rose Wilderness. Because these two creeks, Thomas and Whites Creeks, are only 0.5 miles apart, the watersheds of both can be enjoyed on a relatively short hike. The hike is mostly shaded, making it a great candidate for those looking to get away from the heat without driving up the pass of Mount Rose Highway.

Out of the parking area, pass the trailhead kiosk and walk on the wide dirt trail. There are several parallel paths here, and the exact path you take is not important. The initial vegetation is typical of the lower elevations of the Carson Range and consists of Jeffrey pine forest mixed with red fir, white fir, mountain mahogany, and sagebrush.

Soon, you will hear the babbling of Whites Creek to the right. Notice the stark change in vegetation as you walk along the peaceful creek. Mountain alder with its toothed leaves, various willows with their lance-like leaves, and black cottonwood with its heart-shaped leaves flourish on the stream's banks. These young deciduous trees grow where there is sufficient water, and their local range moves to accommodate the ever-changing streams. Look for older conifers near the creek as well. These trees are sometimes heavily affected by the changing path of the creek, and erosion can eliminate much of their soil,

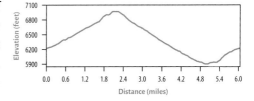

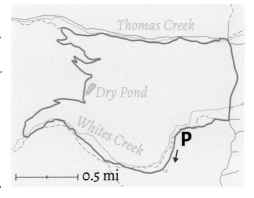

Whites Creek flowing in mid-summer

exposing parts of their massive root systems that cling to the remaining stream banks.

After 1.3 miles of gradually climbing alongside Whites Creek, you will reach a trail sign and a junction. At this stage, turn right onto the **Dry Pond Trail**, and cross over Whites Creek via a sturdy bridge. As you head away from the creek, you will quickly exit the Jeffrey pine forest and enter exposed grassland dotted with mountain mahogany trees. This south-facing slope receives too much sun to support a coniferous forest.

While the trail switchbacks up the hillside, enjoy outstanding views of Washoe Valley in front of you and Mount Rose behind you. In 2017, a 29-acre fire burned in this area, and you will surely notice the scorched mountain mahoganies. This portion of the route is the steepest and sunniest. If you hike this trail early in the morning or on a cool day, complete the loop in the direction described here. However, if you are hiking on a hot afternoon, it is best to park at Thomas Creek Trailhead and complete the loop in the opposite direction so you can walk downhill through this section of the trail.

After 0.8 miles of climbing 500 feet, the trail levels off at Dry Pond. During the spring or after a series of summer thunderstorms, this pond is by no means dry. After you pass by Dry Pond, you will begin your descent into the Thomas Creek

Dry Pond

watershed. In 1.1 miles, you will reach the banks of Thomas Creek.

There is more flow in Thomas Creek as compared to Whites Creek, and as a result, the two creeks support slightly different vegetation profiles. Dense stands of aspen line Thomas Creek that are not present along Whites Creek, but the aspen are also accompanied by alders, willows, and black cottonwoods. During your 1.4-mile walk along the creek, you will pass through several scenic groves of aspen. Enjoy how the sunlight bounces off their flickering leaves, which rustle soothingly in the wind. This trail is a delightful hike in autumn when the aspen leaves change to yellow.

After the 1.4 miles, you will reach Thomas Creek Trailhead. It is ideal to leave a second car here or have somebody pick you up if possible. Otherwise, you will have to walk back to the Whites Creek Trailhead. Do this by walking down paved North Timberline Drive for 0.6 miles. Turn right onto the forest road on which you previously drove. From

Aspens line the trail in several spots.

here, it is another 0.7 miles to your car. Although you can walk on the road, there is a trail that runs along the road and Whites Creek that is more enjoyable.

From Reno. Take Highway 395/Interstate 580 south for 10.7 miles to the Mount Rose Highway exit. Drive on Mount Rose Highway (NV 431) for 4.5 miles, and turn right on North Timberline Drive. In 0.5 miles, turn left on an unlabeled forest service road. The road is dirt, but it is suitable for low-clearance two-wheel-drive vehicles. The parking area is located at the end of the road in 0.8 miles at 39.3781, -119.8481 and is listed on some maps as the Whites Creek Dry Pond Trailhead. On hot summer afternoons, start instead at the Thomas Creek Trailhead. To get there, drive 1.3 miles on North Timberline Drive, and go to the large dirt parking area at 39.3935, -119.8388. *25 mins.*

73 Church's Pond

THIS HIKE IS A CALF-BURNING CLIMB UP TO SCENIC CHURCH'S POND. COOL YOUR MUSCLES off in the pond before enjoying excellent views of Washoe Valley on the way back down.

At a Glance

DIFFICULTY	Hard	DISTANCE/TIME	6.5 miles/4 hours
ELEVATION GAIN	2,100 feet	TRAIL TYPE	Foot trail
SOLITUDE	Heavy use	USERS	Hikers
BEST SEASON	May–November	LAND OWNERSHIP	National Forest, county park
ANIMALS	Deer, bears	FEATURES	Expansive view, streams, pond, wildflowers

James Church, a professor at the University of Nevada, Reno, developed the first device to measure snow depth in the early 1900s. His measurements of snow depth at Mount Rose were instrumental in developing early water supply–forecasting systems. Church Peak, which lies 0.6 miles north of its parent peak, Mount Rose, is named in his honor. Below Church Peak lies scenic Church's Pond, which is fed each year by heavy snowmelt off the Mount Rose-Church ridgeline.

Hike to the top of the Jones Creek watershed, relax at Church's Pond, and enjoy excellent views while meandering in and out of forests during your ascent. Start your adventure on a dirt trail originating on the northwest side of the parking

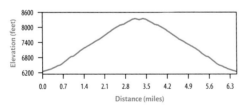

area. The trail heads west and climbs up the expansive slopes of Mount Rose. The vegetation during the first 0.5 miles of the trail is fairly open as you mostly traverse past sage and bitterbrush

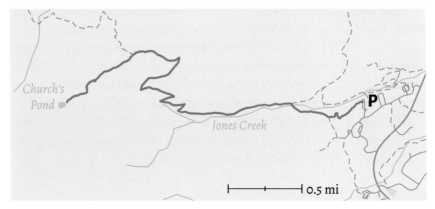

mixed periodically with Jeffrey pine. During the next 0.1 miles, though, you head
towards perennial Jones Creek, and the
trail becomes shaded in a Jeffrey pine forest. Follow the trail sign, and turn left at the
junction after the creek to continue your
westward and upward approach. The trail is
never overbearingly steep, but it maintains
a consistent and heart-pumping slope the
whole way. As you climb, the canyon below
you carved by Jones Creek becomes dramatically steep.

In another 0.5 miles, you will pass a sign
informing you that you have entered Mount
Rose Wilderness. In this roadless land,
mechanized vehicles of any sort, including
bicycles, are strictly forbidden. Soon, the
Jones Creek Canyon bifurcates as you reach
its headwaters. As a result, impressive views
open up, and to your left, the entire south
basin of rugged Chocolate Peak is laid out
before you.

The trail then begins to switchback up
and over the northern fork of Jones Creek.

Desert paintbrush with Washoe Lake in the background

Small spur trails that lead to cool aspen groves at a few of the creekside bends
make for good resting spots. Soon, though, the trail diverges from the creek, and
the path becomes rocky and open. Clumps of mountain mahogany replace Jeffrey
pines in the exposed soil.

At the bend of the final switchback, you are afforded outstanding views of
Washoe Lake to the east and Mount Scott (Hike 92) behind it. Slide Mountain
dominates the view south. Finally, on this exposed ridgeline, the trail begins
to flatten out. Wildflowers abound here in the summer. Look for orange desert
paintbrush, vibrant yellow sulfur flowers, and soft mule's ears. Mount Rose (Hike
75) becomes visible in the distance ahead of you.

Now, 1.6 miles past the Mount Rose Wilderness sign, cross straight through
a well-marked trail junction. The trail here brings you through a moist area that
supports aspen, lodgepole pines, and western white pines. In early summer, also
notice the Anderson's lupine blooming near the trail. Unlike most lupines, whose
petals are purple, this lupine blooms with white flowers. With Church Peak in

the background, Church's Pond serves as a peaceful lunch area and summer swimming hole.

After enjoying this idyllic spot, for the most direct return, head back down the slopes the way you came. Optionally, for a much longer hike, you can take a left at the junction 0.6 miles away from Church's Pond. This trail goes to Whites Creek and adds 3.3 miles and 500 feet of elevation gain. Part of this approach is also accessed in the Thomas and Whites Creek Loop (Hike 72).

From Reno. Take Highway 395/Interstate 580 south for 10.7 miles to the Mount Rose Highway exit. Drive on Mount Rose Highway (NV 431) for 5.6 miles, and then turn right into Galena Creek County Park. Drive on the main park road for 0.5 miles before turning right into a large parking lot, located at 39.3622, -119.8575, past the main visitors center. *20 mins.*

Relaxing at the shores of Church's Pond

74 Brown's Creek

PERUSE THE LOWER FOOTHILLS OF THE CARSON RANGE ALONG TWO SCENIC TRIBUTARIES.
This hike is snow free most months and features wildflowers in the summer,
making it a great outing all year-round.

At a Glance

DIFFICULTY	Easy	**DISTANCE/TIME**	4.3 miles/2 hours
ELEVATION GAIN	1,000 feet	**TRAIL TYPE**	Foot trail
SOLITUDE	Heavy use	**USERS**	Hikers, bikers
BEST SEASON	All	**LAND OWNERSHIP**	County park
ANIMALS	Deer	**FEATURES**	Streams, wildflowers

Snowmelt and springs combine to form perennial Brown's Creek on the
northeastern slopes of Slide Mountain. Explore the lower stretches of the Jeffrey
pine forests in the Carson Range on land protected by the Washoe County park
system outside the community of Galena.

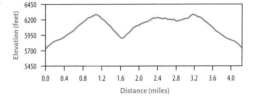

The trailhead originates across the
street from the parking area. During
the first 1.1 miles, you will steadily climb
400 feet up a north-sloping ridge. The
vegetation here consists of Jeffrey pines
with sage, bitterbrush, and manzanita
understory. Mountain mahoganies grow
in some of the rockier, more exposed
soils. Jeffrey pines, along with ponderosa
pines, are nicknamed "yellowbellies" for
their yellow inner wood, which is apparent on several of the trees in this
area. Scratch and smell the trees' inner
bark and twigs. The wood of the Jeffrey
pine gives off a delightful citrusy-vanilla
odor. As you climb, views of Reno and
the Truckee Meadows open up between
the trees.

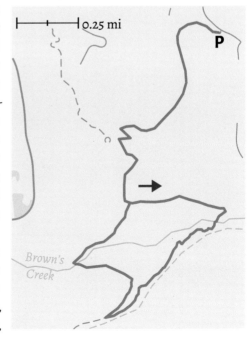

At the top of the ridge, a small spur
trail to the left leads to a sunny bench
with open views of Washoe Valley. Below
you and obscured by forest lies Joy Lake,
which, as the interpretive sign explains,

The initial climb up to the Brown's Creek watershed affords excellent views of Reno.

Manzanita and Jeffrey pines

was the site of a western-themed amusement park in the 1950s.

Back on the main trail, the path begins to descend into the Brown's Creek basin. In 0.1 miles, you will reach a fork, which marks the beginning of the loop route around the creek. Turn left at the junction for the most enjoyable route.

As you approach the creek, blooming wildflowers such as delicious-smelling mountain mint, yellow buckwheat, and deep purple royal penstemon become increasingly common in the early summer. In 0.5 miles, cross the footbridge over the creek. This portion of the trail sits in between two tributaries of the creek just before their confluence and is particularly lush. Enjoy the shade of dense pockets of deciduous trees, including black cottonwood, mountain alder, and Pacific willow.

Continue following the trail, which now rises alongside the second smaller tributary for 0.7 miles. The trail then returns via a switchback to the main branch of the creek in 0.4 miles. Cross over Brown's Creek once again using a well-constructed footbridge. Gently ascend for another 0.3 miles to complete the loop, and then descend back to the trailhead over the course of 1.2 miles.

From Reno. Take Highway 395/Interstate 580 south for 10.7 miles to the Mount Rose Highway exit. Drive on Mount Rose Highway (NV 431) for 5.9 miles before turning left on Joy Lake Road. Drive 1.5 miles on Joy Lake Road. The parking area is a large C-shaped gravel turnout on the left side of the road located at 39.3491, -119.8328. *25 mins.*

Buckwheat flowers on sandy slopes

75 Mount Rose

SUMMIT THE HIGHEST PEAK IN WASHOE COUNTY FOR MIND-BLOWING VIEWS IN ALL directions. If you're not up for the long climb, turn around at the beautiful Galena Creek waterfalls instead.

At a Glance

DIFFICULTY	Epic	DISTANCE/TIME	10.4 miles/6 hours
ELEVATION GAIN	2,200 feet	TRAIL TYPE	Foot trail
SOLITUDE	Heavy use	USERS	Hikers
BEST SEASON	May–October	LAND OWNERSHIP	National Forest
ANIMALS	Deer, pikas, bears, Clark's nutcrackers	FEATURES	Expansive views, waterfalls, streams, wildflowers

At 10,776 feet above sea level, Mount Rose is the highest peak in Washoe County, the tallest peak in this book, and the second highest peak in the Lake Tahoe basin. Unsurprisingly, then, the views from the top are about as grand as they come. On a clear day, you can see well over 100 miles in almost every direction. From downtown Reno, Mount Rose is a prominent landmark, and in the summer months, it is last locale in view with snow.

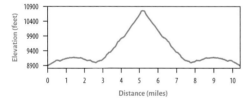

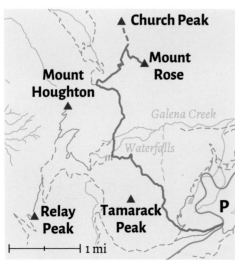

Despite its immense stature, it is straightforward though challenging to summit Mount Rose. In fact, the **Mount Rose Trail** is probably the most popular trail in all of northern Nevada, so expect companions on this hike no matter the time of year. Most people on the trail, however, do not climb Mount Rose and instead turn around after reaching the Galena Creek waterfalls in 2.5 miles. The flat, 5-mile out-and-back trip to the waterfalls takes about 2.5 hours to complete.

From the parking area, walk past the restrooms toward the trailhead kiosk. Climb up the well-carved rock steps to the right to start your adventure on Mount Rose Trail. Over the next 0.5 miles, the trail gradually climbs through open subalpine terrain covered by sagebrush and pinemat manzanita.

In the late summer, colorful wildflowers bloom including yellow sulfur flowers, fuzzy mule's ears, purple lupines, and sunset-colored paintbrushes.

The scattered pine trees here are mostly of the lodgepole and ponderosa variety. However, in addition to these two species, a few specimens of a third, very rare species of pine tree called the Washoe pine can be found. Mount Rose Wilderness is one of the few places in the world where this mysterious tree grows. Because it has

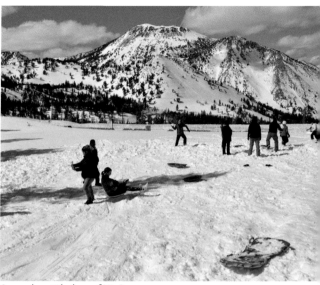

Snow play at the base of Mt. Rose

characteristics similar to both the ponderosa and Jeffrey pines, the Washoe pine is difficult to identify. The best way to distinguish the Washoe pine from others is by its new pine cones on mature trees. Unlike green Jeffrey pine cones, the new pine cones are reddish-purple, and unlike ponderosa pine cones, the barbs on the cones do not prickle your hands when squeezed.

Beautiful views of Tahoe Meadows (Hike 80) with Lake Tahoe in the background lie in front of you as you continue to climb. The trail then gradually turns north as you enter a lodgepole pine forest. The next 2.0 miles of the path are flat and mostly shaded. Early on in the forest, Tamarack Lake (Hike 77) is visible between the trees to the right. On your left, the slopes of Tamarack Peak (Hike 78) rise steeply above you.

Toward the end of this portion of the hike, a sloped meadow containing Galena Creek opens up to the right. If you listen carefully, you will hear the waterfalls before spotting them in the distance. The 60-foot waterfalls are quite lovely and contain water all year long. Because the trip out to the waterfalls is mostly flat, it is a popular snowshoeing destination in the winter. The main trail leads you to the best views at the base of the waterfalls. However, a spur trail wraps up and around the falls to the left if you feel like attaining a different vantage point. Regardless of how you view the waterfalls, break here, and restore some energy for the steep climb to the summit ahead.

Past the waterfalls, follow the trail signs that direct you to Mount Rose summit. The route here continues through the meadow of Galena Creek and past several small streams that will get your feet wet in the spring months. Beyond

Lake Tahoe from the top of Mount Rose

the meadow, the trail steadily climbs and switchbacks in and out of forests. The higher you ascend, the grander the views east across Washoe Valley become.

The lodgepole pine forests also become increasingly dominated by whitebark pine trees. Listen for the loud metallic screech of the Clark's nutcracker, which is the most common sound in these forests. The gray-and-black Clark's nutcracker and the whitebark pine have a symbiotic relationship. The birds are one of the few animals that can crack open its pine nuts, and a forgotten cache of nuts stored away by the Clark's nutcracker is the main way the whitebark pine proliferates.

After 1.2 miles of climbing, you will reach a saddle point and a trail junction. Follow the sign, and turn right to continue your ascent of Mount Rose. Now as you approach 10,000 feet in elevation, the forest consists of pure stands of whitebark pines. As you climb, take breaks to appreciate the lovely view of Mount Houghton (Hike 76) with Lake Tahoe in the background developing behind you. You still have about 1,000 feet of climbing ahead, but the climbing is made easier by the spectacular views.

Eventually, you will pass the tree line as you enter a rocky and exposed world. This area is one of the few truly alpine environments in the Lake Tahoe basin. In early fall, wildflowers will be in bloom, but in summer, there may still be large packs of snow to traverse. With only 300 feet left of elevation gain, you will reach the saddle between Church Peak and Mount Rose. The trail turns right, and after 0.3 miles of rocky climbing, you will finally reach the summit at 39.3439, -119.918.

The panorama is truly spectacular. If the atmospheric conditions are favorable, you will be able to see as far south as northern Yosemite, as far north as Lassen Peak, and as far east as the Shoshone Mountains in central Nevada. Each of these landmarks is more than 125 miles away. All of Lake Tahoe is visible below you to the southwest. If you look carefully, you will also be able to see Fallen Leaf Lake, a gorgeous lake in its own right that will appear as if it is floating above the southern edge of Lake Tahoe.

After you have soaked in the views to your heart's content, head back down to the saddle between Mount Rose and Church Peak. Although most hikers will be too tired, if you are looking for additional adventure, you can take a short off-trail side trip to Church Peak. From the saddle, it is 0.4 miles and about 200 feet of climbing to the summit of Church Peak, located at 39.3521, -119.9233.

The views from Church Peak offer a slightly different perspective of the Greater Reno area, but they are no better than those on Mount Rose. The reason to explore Church Peak is to witness the pikas near the summit. As a result of the effects of climate change and habitat loss, these adorably squeaky rabbits are becoming increasingly rare in the Lake Tahoe basin.

Whether you originate from Church Peak or Mount Rose, follow your footsteps down more than 2,000 feet back to the trailhead.

From Reno. Take Highway 395/Interstate 580 south for 10.7 miles to the Mount Rose Highway exit. Drive on Mount Rose Highway (NV 431) for 16.0 miles, and at the top of the pass, turn right into the large paved Mount Rose parking area located at 39.3136, -119.8974. *35 mins.*

Spectacular Lake Tahoe views are common on the upper portions of this hike.

76 Mount Houghton and Relay Peak

ASCEND TWO MASSIVE PEAKS AS PART OF THE CROWN JEWEL CLIMBING EXPERIENCE OF the northern Sierra Nevadas.

At a Glance

DIFFICULTY	Epic	**DISTANCE/TIME**	11.3 miles/7 hours
ELEVATION GAIN	2,200 feet	**TRAIL TYPE**	Foot trail, dirt road
SOLITUDE	Medium use	**USERS**	Hikers
BEST SEASON	May–October	**LAND OWNERSHIP**	National Forest
ANIMALS	Deer, bears, Clark's nutcrackers	**FEATURES**	Expansive views, waterfalls, streams, wildflowers

Mount Houghton and Relay Peak are two of the most spectacular peaks in the Carson Range of the Sierra Nevadas. They offer extraordinary and unique foreground and background views that dazzle the eye. Multiple species of conifers, purple and white phlox, yellow sunflowers, and purple lupines are just a few of the wildflowers in the area. Babbling creeks, backcountry lakes and ponds, and waterfalls are all present on this truly magnificent hike. What's even better is that while a hundred people might scurry to the top of Mount Rose on days when the weather is good and the snowpack is low, far fewer people hike to these two peaks.

The sights and sounds you experience on this hike as well as the number of calories you burn will vary widely depending on the season. In spring and early

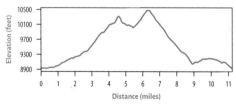

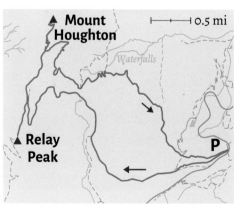

summer, you will need snowshoes and will forge deep streams. In late summer and early fall, you will encounter relatively little snow and enjoy good weather. Other times of the year, the weather may be too cold and unpredictable to make for an enjoyable trip.

Out of the parking area, head past the restrooms to find the main trailheads. Take the **Tamarack Lake Trail**, which runs to the left and is lower than the more popular Mount Rose Trail. After about 0.7 miles, take a junction to the left, which will quickly connect you to the forest service road just below you. If you miss this junction, you will notice that the trail takes a sharp turn to the right and begins climbing, where it quickly crosses over the upper Mount Rose Trail you did not take.

Once on the forest service road, your path gradually climbs through an open area westward over the next 1.0 miles with beautiful views of Lake Tahoe. Hike a mile farther as the trail slowly meanders northward through pine forest and you see scenic Third Creek below you to the left. The trail does not cross Third Creek proper, but most times of the year, small tributaries flow down the mountainside of Tamarack Peak (Hike 78) to your right that you will cross. At the 3-mile mark, you will hike alongside perennial Frog Pond, a small body of water that is part of Third Creek. Both make for good water to filter.

At Frog Pond, there is a well-marked trail junction. Hike straight through the junction and farther up. The trail becomes moderately steeper as you make

Galena Creek Waterfalls

your way up to Relay Ridge. You will pass a large dilapidated ski structure 0.3 miles past Frog Pond. The trail switchbacks up for an additional 2.7 miles, and exquisite views open up. At the top of Relay Ridge, turn left and hike for 0.6 miles to Relay Peak, located at 39.315400, -119.9471.

Views of Lake Tahoe, the desert ranges of Nevada, and most of Mount Rose Wilderness are breathtaking. Depending on the time of year, the top of the peak could be buried in dozens of feet of snow or be dry and filled with thousands of butterflies and ladybugs. In early October one year, the authors delighted in viewing millions of California tortoiseshell butterflies blown into the summit by mountain air currents. They were enamored with the hundreds of butterflies resting on their bodies as they rested and enjoyed lunch. Clear days in August, September, and October make for the easiest snow-free hiking.

View of Lake Tahoe from Relay Peak

When you are ready to relinquish the awe-inspiring panorama atop Relay Peak, hike back down the way you came 0.6 miles to the middle of Relay Ridge. At the junction, continue straight toward Mount Houghton to the north. In 0.8 miles, you will reach another junction. Stay left on the trail, which climbs up Mount Houghton. Fortunately, your route across the saddle between the two peaks means you have to climb less than 500 feet to reach Mount Houghton from Relay Peak. From the junction, the path to the summit is another mile and consists of many tight switchbacks across talus.

The views on top of Mount Houghton, located at 39.3341, -119.9395, are arguably even more exhilarating than those on Relay Peak. Although Mount Rose (Hike 75) blocks your views to the north, you otherwise have a phenomenal 270° view, the majesty of which is impossible to describe in words. Particularly enchanting foreground views will have your eyes locked on the back side of Relay Ridge. The steep terrain of this glacier-carved amphitheater is both harrowing and inspiring.

Tear yourself away from Mount Houghton's special views and hike down 1.0 miles to the trail junction you previously crossed. This time, though, turn left at the junction to descend off of Relay Ridge. The trail descends consistently down Relay Ridge with the switchbacks saving you undue compression on your knees. After 1.3 miles of descent from the junction, you will reach another junction. You are only 0.1 miles away from the Frog Pond junction you encountered on your ascent, but the two junctions are distinct. Head straight through the junction on your way to Galena Creek waterfalls.

The beautiful waterfalls are only 0.5 miles away at this point and are right along the trail you need to take to get to your car. There are limited views from the top, but the trail also takes you to the bottom so you can more fully appreciate the 60-foot waterfalls.

Past the falls, take the fork to the right and follow the trail back to the Mount Rose parking area. This section of the trail makes for your easiest hiking of the entire trip and is relatively flat. Be on the lookout for picturesque Tamarack Lake (Hike 77) between the pine trees to the left when you are about 0.5 miles away from your car.

From Reno. Take Highway 395/Interstate 580 south for 10.7 miles to the Mount Rose Highway exit. Drive on Mount Rose Highway (NV 431) for 16.0 miles, and at the top of the pass, turn right into the large paved Mount Rose parking area located at 39.3136, -119.8974. *35 mins.*

The terrain is rugged on the slopes of Mount Houghton.

77 Tamarack Lake

RELAX AT PICTURESQUE TAMARACK LAKE IN A GORGEOUS SUBALPINE SETTING. ROMP through forests and a meadow smattered with streams and wildflowers along the way.

At a Glance

DIFFICULTY	Easy	**DISTANCE/TIME**	3.6 miles/1.5 hours
ELEVATION GAIN	300 feet	**TRAIL TYPE**	Foot trail
SOLITUDE	Medium use	**USERS**	Hikers, bikers
BEST SEASON	April–November	**LAND OWNERSHIP**	National Forest
ANIMALS	Deer, bears	**FEATURES**	Streams, lake, wildflowers

From the Mount Rose trailhead, instead of following in the footsteps of most people who hike to Galena Creek waterfalls or summit Mount Rose, enjoy a casual outing to tranquil Tamarack Lake. At an elevation of 8,800 feet, this subalpine lake forms from snowmelt off the western slopes of nearby Tamarack Peak. The lake is also the source of one of the main upper tributaries of Galena Creek and provides excellent habitat for wildflowers and wildlife. A careful observer will likely see bear scat on the trail because the lake is a favorite stopover for black bears. Many different birds also visit the lake, including the multicolored western tanager, the yellow-rumped warbler, and the mountain chickadee.

From the parking area, head past the restrooms to the trailhead signage. Do not climb up the steps carved into the rock, and instead take the lower path, the **Tamarack Lake Trail**, to the left. The first 0.8 miles of this trail are flat and parallel to Mount Rose highway. The path then sharply turns to the right, crosses over **Mount Rose Trail**, and climbs 100 feet in 0.2 miles up to a ridge. From the ridge, witness wonderful views of Lake Tahoe behind you. Because this portion of the trail passes through exposed vegetation, it is a great place to see colorful displays of wildflowers such as mule's ears, paintbrushes, sulfur flowers, and lupines. From the ridge, hike down

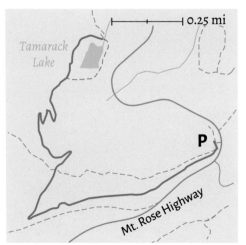

the gently switchbacking trail, which leads you to Tamarack Lake in 0.6 miles.

During your descent, you first meander through a lodgepole pine forest that is interspersed with red fir and mountain hemlock. As you exit the forest and enter the meadow surrounding the lake, blooming wildflowers abound in the summer. Species include columbines, lupines, penstemons, and water-loving corn lilies. You will also cross many small streams; the exact number will vary depending on the time of year.

View from the trail as it heads down towards Tamarack Lake

At the shores of Tamarack Lake

The trail continues to the north side of the lake, where there is a dirt shore that makes for a good resting spot. If desired, you may take a faint trail that wraps around the east side of the lake. By the time you reach the southern end of the lake, though, the trail disappears entirely, and you will have to hike through some brush off trail to reconnect with your main route. Regardless of whether you loop around the lake, once on the main trail, retrace your steps back to your car.

From Reno. Take Highway 395/Interstate 580 south for 10.7

miles to the Mount Rose Highway exit. Drive on Mount Rose Highway (NV 431) for 16.0 miles, and at the top of the pass, turn right into the large paved Mount Rose parking area located at 39.3136, -119.8974. *35 mins.*

78 Tamarack Peak

GET AWAY FROM IT ALL IN THE CENTER OF MOUNT ROSE WILDERNESS. THE VIEWS FROM this off-trail pursuit to the top of Tamarack Peak are sure to impress, and you'll have the views to yourself!

At a Glance

DIFFICULTY	Hard	DISTANCE/TIME	3.8 miles/2.5 hours
ELEVATION GAIN	1,400 feet	TRAIL TYPE	Foot trail, off trail
SOLITUDE	Medium use	USERS	Hikers
BEST SEASON	May–October	LAND OWNERSHIP	National Forest
ANIMALS	Deer, bears	FEATURES	Expansive views, streams

Mount Rose Wilderness is one of the most popular recreation areas in Nevada. Despite the busyness of the area, few residents ascend Tamarack Peak because there are no official trails to the top, which causes far more visitors to climb other nearby peaks like Mount Rose (Hike 75) and Mount Houghton and Relay Peak (Hike 76). This situation allows you to enjoy Tamarack Peak, a gem of a mountain with outstanding views, in near solitude.

Hike to the west out of the parking area into the forest. Within a few hundred feet, you will cross over a small tributary of Third Creek on your right. Continue heading north on this trail, which climbs upward and, after about 0.7 miles, travels alongside the main branch of perennial Third Creek. Hike an additional 0.7 miles. At the end of this stretch, the main trail will take you away from the creek and terminate at a larger trail, Relay Peak Road. You could alternatively take the beginning approach for Relay Peak (Hike 76) until you reach this point.

At this junction, turn neither left nor right onto the trail. Instead, cross straight over the trail and off trail up the slopes of

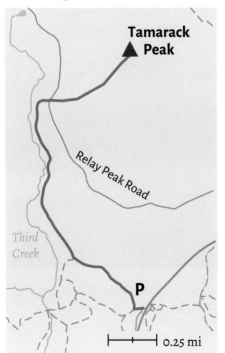

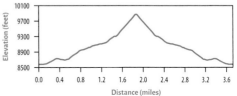

Hiking along Third Creek

Tamarack Peak. You will be able to spot the large amphitheater to the west formed by Relay Ridge as the densely forested slopes of Tamarack Peak rise above you to the east. The slopes of Tamarack Peak are moderately steep, but manageable under most conditions. Avoid this hike during periods of high avalanche danger because avalanches have occurred on Tamarack Peak.

View from the top

The dense forest soon gives rise to rocky meadows as you near the rounded top of Tamarack Peak. In summer months, this area is blanketed with wildflowers. The vista on the summit, located at 39.3184, -119.9217, is spectacular. Enjoy beautiful views of Lake Tahoe, Relay Peak, Mount Rose, Mount Houghton, and Slide Mountain. Return the way you came.

From Reno. Take Highway 395/Interstate 580 south for 10.7 miles to the Mount Rose Highway exit. Drive on Mount Rose Highway (NV 431) for 17.5 miles. Turn right into a dirt parking area located at 39.3007, -119.9205. *35 mins.*

79 Incline Peak

CLIMB THROUGH A BEAUTIFUL FOREST, AND HIKE ALONG CLEAR STREAMS BEFORE SOAKING in mesmerizing overhanging views of Lake Tahoe on this hidden gem of an adventure.

At a Glance

DIFFICULTY	Hard	DISTANCE/TIME	3.9 miles/2.5 hours
ELEVATION GAIN	1,200 feet	TRAIL TYPE	Foot trail
SOLITUDE	Medium use	USERS	Hikers, bikers
BEST SEASON	May–October	LAND OWNERSHIP	National Forest
ANIMALS	Deer, bears	FEATURES	Expansive views, streams, wildflowers

There are many phenomenal views of Lake Tahoe throughout the northern Sierra Nevadas. Although the large summer crowds might make you think otherwise, the best views are not from the shore. The truly spectacular views are those from the surrounding mountains. Some of these mountain vistas are close to Lake Tahoe, while still being high enough to see the entire lake. The impressive result is that Lake Tahoe fills a large segment of your field of view.

Ascend Incline Peak for one of the best views in the entire Lake Tahoe basin. At the summit, you will feel as if you are on top of the entire lake! What's even

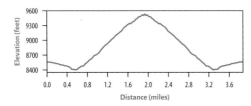

better is that because there is only an unofficial foot trail to the top, you are likely to have the views to yourself.

From the parking area, pass by the green forest service gate,

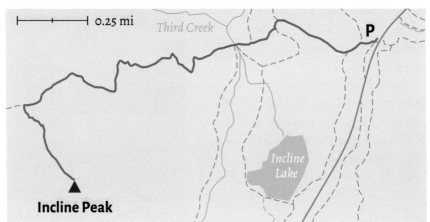

and hike on the wide dirt trail for 0.4 miles as it descends into a lush aspen grove filled with myriad species of wildflowers in the summer. After 0.4 miles, the wide trail begins a hairpin turn. At this turn, look carefully for a small foot trail to the right and follow it. Whereas the original wide trail heads down toward Incline Lake to the south, the correct narrower path is flat initially and continues west.

After 0.1 miles of hiking on this path, you will cross scenic Third Creek using a sturdy wooden bridge. After the creek crossing, the trail steadily climbs up through shaded forest. The trees here consist primarily of lodgepole pines and red firs, but there are also a few specimens of enormous western white pines right along the trail.

Depending on the time of year, you will also pass several small streams during your ascent. Eventually, you leave the lodgepole-fir forest and enter more open terrain along a developing ridge. Look for a small foot trail to the left that appears 1.0 miles after the Third Creek crossing. This spur trail runs south along the ridge and reaches Incline Peak in 0.3 miles. In the winter, this ridge receives heavy snowfall and strong winds. As a result, the forest here is sparse and contains hearty mountain hemlock and whitebark pine trees.

The beginning of this hike takes you through lush forests and groundcover.

Bridged crossing of Third Creek

From your perch atop Incline Peak, the views of Lake Tahoe are truly stunning. Have lunch on any of the large boulders at the top that make for good picnic tables. Once you are done savoring the views, return to your car the way you came.

From Reno. Take Highway 395/ Interstate 580 south for 10.7 miles to the Mount Rose Highway exit. Drive on Mount Rose Highway (NV 431) for 17.5 miles. Turn right into a dirt parking area located at 39.3007, -119.9205. *35 mins*

A tributary of Third Creek along the trail
Lake Tahoe views from the top

80 Tahoe Meadows

WHETHER YOU COME TO SNOWSHOE OR TO BASK IN THE MAJESTIC WILDFLOWER DISPLAYS, there is always something special to discover at Tahoe Meadows.

At a Glance

DIFFICULTY	Very Easy	DISTANCE/TIME	2.5 miles/1.5 hours
ELEVATION GAIN	300 feet	TRAIL TYPE	Foot trail, boardwalk
SOLITUDE	Heavy use	USERS	Hikers, bikers
BEST SEASON	All	LAND OWNERSHIP	National Forest
ANIMALS	Deer	FEATURES	Wildflowers, streams

Straddled between Slide Mountain and Chickadee Ridge, Tahoe Meadows affords excellent year-round recreation that is readily accessible and appropriate for all skill levels and ages. In the winter, dozens of feet of snow often blanket the area. As home to the highest year-round snow-plowed pass in the Sierra Nevadas, Mount Rose Highway allows you to easily enjoy this winter wonderland.

The flat terrain of Tahoe Meadows is popular for snowshoeing, and sledding with kids. As the snow melts in the spring, a grassy field emerges, and a plethora of tiny streams flows through the meadows to form the headwaters of Ophir Creek (Hike 82). With further warming, only the largest rivulets remain in the meadows as they provide the moisture that powers a spectacular wildflower show in the summer.

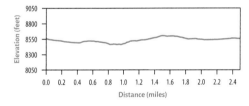

Each week of summer in Tahoe Meadows is a unique experience. Any particular species of subalpine wildflower does not bloom for very long. Fortunately, there are so many different types

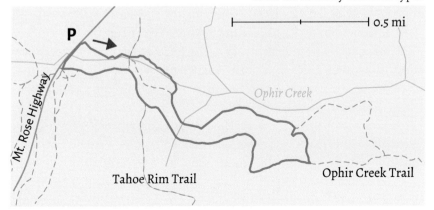

A sturdy, wide boardwalk takes you along Ophir Creek and wildflowers.

of wildflowers here that no matter when you visit in the summer, Tahoe Meadows will be beautiful, even if it has been a dry winter. In the middle of June, thousands of yellow plantain-leaved buttercups populate the area. A few weeks later purple meadow penstemons and white marsh marigolds abound. Lavender-colored tundra asters are also common. In July, look for the odd-shaped elephant head flowers, which are generally pink and indeed resemble the head of a pachyderm. Alpine shooting star will also bloom in purple in wetter areas during this time. Once August comes, the colors in Tahoe Meadows will change further yet. Lupines of various species and the vibrant crimson columbines burst into bloom.

All summer, look for bushes of stinging nettle along the stream banks. These plants are equipped with hundreds of tiny sharp hairs, which cause an unpleasant stinging sensation if they touch bare skin. Despite this unpleasant feature, the plants are quite valuable culinarily and medicinally. When cooked, the nutritious leaves taste like a mixture of spinach and cucumber. Teas from the leaves are purported to treat a number of ailments. Archaeological evidence up to 4,000 years old indicates that Native Americans had a long history of processing various foodstuffs such as stinging nettle and pine nuts in the fertile Tahoe Meadows area.

Off of Mount Rose Highway, head east toward flat and open Tahoe Meadows. Walk on the well-constructed boardwalks and bridges that take you across the meadows and over various streams. The many boardwalks and trails in this area can be stitched together to form loops of almost any desired length, and the entire area is very well signed. Please stay on established boardwalks, which were installed to preserve the fragile ecosystem of Tahoe Meadows. The route mapped here takes you 1.0 miles east before you turn right and return to your car through lodgepole pine forest. This hike can also be combined with nearby Chickadee Ridge (Hike 81).

From Reno. Take Highway 395/Interstate 580 south for 10.7 miles to the Mount Rose Highway exit. Drive on Mount Rose Highway (NV 431) for 16.9 miles. Once past the high point of the highway, you will descend into Tahoe Meadows. After the road levels out, pull off to the side of the road into the large shoulders on either side of the highway at 39.3022, -119.9185. *35 mins.*

Ophir Creek flows year round.

Tundra aster in Tahoe Meadows

81 Chickadee Ridge

WALK THROUGH A FOREST FILLED WITH MOUNTAIN CHICKADEES, AND THEN ENJOY A
bird's-eye view of Lake Tahoe from the ridgeline or the summit.

At a Glance

DIFFICULTY	Easy	DISTANCE/TIME	3.7 miles/2 hours
ELEVATION GAIN	300 feet	TRAIL TYPE	Foot trail
SOLITUDE	Heavy use	USERS	Hikers, bikers
BEST SEASON	March–November	LAND OWNERSHIP	National Forest
ANIMALS	Deer, bears	FEATURES	Expansive views

From the parking area, walk on a dirt trail on the east side of Mount Rose
Highway. The path begins by going through a level forest of lodgepole pine trees.
Follow signs at well-marked junctions to stay on the **Tahoe Rim Trail**. Bikers are
only allowed on this trail on even-numbered days, so it is best to hike this trail
on an odd-numbered day if you are visiting during a busy summer weekend. As
the trail turns and climbs to the south, you meander in and out of the forest. In
more open areas, look for asters, lupines, and other wildflowers.

After 1.1 miles of travel, the trail flattens out as you reach Chickadee Ridge with
excellent views of Lake Tahoe. Locals refer to this area as Chickadee Ridge because
of the large number of these small white, gray, and black birds in the area. Listen
for the "fee-bee-bee" of their song. If you stand still, the mountain chickadees
here may flitter about closer to you than other wild birds. Unfortunately, this
friendly behavior is a result of human feeding. Never feed wild animals of any kind! Feeding animals ingrains in them unnatural behaviors that are usually dangerous to their own species and others in their ecosystem.

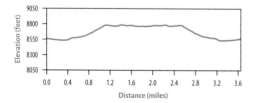

You can continue hiking on this relatively flat portion of the Tahoe Rim Trail for as long as you like. The entire loop is 165 miles and is a popular two-week backpacking trip. After 0.7 miles of hiking on Chickadee Ridge, the trail will pass a steep ravine. Until late spring, water flows through the ravine. If you are up for more adventure, you can ascend to the high point of Chickadee Ridge by

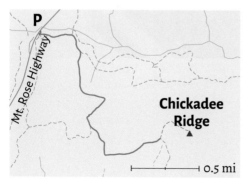

Lake Tahoe from the top of Chickadee Ridge

walking off trail alongside this ravine. The high point is 450 feet above the trail and has excellent views of Tahoe Meadows and Lake Tahoe.

After 0.2 miles of hiking up the ravine, turn right at the sandy saddle point. The last terrain to the summit is steep, so route-finding and bouldering skills are required. The lodgepole pine trees on this peak are of the krummholz variety. They are stunted and extremely windblown from fierce winds that originate over Lake Tahoe during storms. Enormous granite boulders scatter the top of the beautiful summit.

Regardless of whether you make it to the top of Chickadee Ridge, return to the trailhead by retracing your steps. This hike can also be combined with nearby Tahoe Meadows (Hike 80).

From Reno. Take Highway 395/Interstate 580 south for 10.7 miles to the Mount Rose Highway exit. Drive on Mount Rose Highway (NV 431) for 16.9 miles. Once past the high point of the highway, you will descend into Tahoe Meadows. After the road levels out, pull off to the side of the road into the large shoulders on either side of the highway at 39.3013, -119.9195. *35 mins.*

82 Ophir Creek

WITNESS THE POWER OF NATURE ON THIS STEEP CLIMB ALONGSIDE THE CANYON OF Ophir Creek, which was carved by massive flash flooding and landslides.

At a Glance

DIFFICULTY	Hard	DISTANCE/TIME	4.1 miles/2.5 hours
ELEVATION GAIN	1,100 feet	TRAIL TYPE	Foot trail
SOLITUDE	Medium use	USERS	Hikers
BEST SEASON	March–December	LAND OWNERSHIP	County park, National Forest
ANIMALS	Deer, bears	FEATURES	Streams

The steep slopes of Slide Mountain make for spectacular scenery. While the more popular and less strenuous way to enjoy the top of this terrain is to drive up to Tahoe Meadows (Hike 80), a lower starting point near Ophir and Davis Creeks will give you a greater appreciation for the Carson Range's ruggedness.

The **Ophir Creek Trail** starts at Davis Creek Regional Park near Interstate 580 in the Washoe Valley and ascends nearly 4,000 feet over 7 miles before terminating at Tahoe Meadows. The entire trail is very difficult to complete as an out-and-back in one day, especially because the trail is hard to follow past Rock Lake. Nonetheless, just making it to the banks of Ophir Creek is a pleasant adventure, and if you are looking to add more miles, you can continue on to Rock Lake with an additional 2.8 miles of hiking round-trip and 800 feet of elevation gain.

Out of the parking area, follow signs for the Ophir Creek Trailhead, which

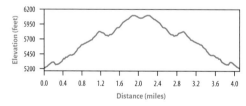

begins in sage, manzanita, and Jeffrey pine forest. The first 0.3 miles of gentle climbing belies the steep climbing that later becomes the norm. During this initial section of the trail, you will cross over two intermittent tributaries of Davis Creek. The tributaries typically have fairly steady flow and do not dry up until fall.

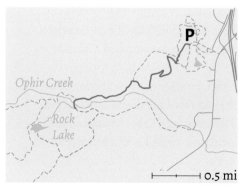

Pass through the junction turnoffs for the **Discovery Trail**, which is a short route to Davis Creek Pond. Instead of going to the pond, climb up along the Davis Creek ravine on the main trail. The wide trail climbs 100 feet over 0.1 miles before switchbacking to the left. At the

Aspens make this hike beautiful in the fall.

bend, prepare to get your feet wet if crossing Davis Creek in early spring.

The climb continues up another 300 feet over the next 0.4 miles through picturesque ponderosa pine forest. Take note of the occasional large granite boulders in the area. At this low elevation, many of the boulders are partially shrouded by pine needles and manzanita vegetation. These boulders are debris from Slide Mountain's famously large landslides. Throughout your ascent, notice how the boulders become increasingly prevalent and exposed. The more recent and relatively less powerful landslides did not have enough power to hurl the boulders farther down the mountain.

Soon the dramatic canyon that corrals Ophir Creek becomes visible to your left. This canyon is unlike any other in the Carson Range. The canyon is more than 200 feet deep here, and the loose granitic sands easily give way. The steep canyon banks strewn with fallen trees dwarf Ophir Creek, which during wet months is considerably mighty in its own right. The depth of the canyon is not the result of the typical slow erosional action of a stream. Rather, massive flash flooding triggered by the periodic landslides off Slide Mountain has torn open the canyon.

After 0.4 miles of additional climbing, the forest opens up to give way to an exposed ridge. Quickly, though, you will gently descend back into the Jeffrey pines before the climb resumes after another 0.2 miles. The trail now leads you even closer to the Ophir Creek canyon. From here, you can not only appreciate the canyon but also see all the way down to Washoe Valley and its Virginia Range backdrop. This vantage point makes for a good breaking spot before embarking on the final climb to the waters of Ophir Creek.

Ascend another 350 feet over the next 0.4 miles along the gradually narrowing canyon. When the trail starts descending, you are close to the creek. Here, the forest opens up to a beautiful unnamed meadow. Like many meadows at around 6,000 feet in the Carson Range, this land is carpeted with colorful wildflowers in early summer. Spectacular views of the impressive slopes of Slide Mountain open up above you. The ends of the meadow are straddled by two tributaries of Ophir Creek, each of which babbles with crystal clear water. It is the massive cluttering of the meadow with hundreds of enormous granite boulders, however, that makes this spot truly unique. These boulders fell from Slide Mountain in 1983 after a large portion of the peak's southeastern cliff face collapsed after wet May weather. The resulting landslide decimated Lower Price Lake, created the boulder field in this meadow, and transported debris all the way down to Interstate 580.

If you are in the mood for more climbing, you can cross a log bridge over the second tributary of Ophir Creek, continue back into the forest, and take a circuitous route to Rock Lake. The landslide of 1983 also strewed boulders into this aptly named lake. Home to larger animals like deer and black bears, Rock Lake also provides habitat for the endangered mountain yellow-legged frog. In the spring, the trail to Rock Lake can be difficult to follow because of the large quantities of snowmelt in the area. Regardless of whether you head to Rock Lake or stop at Ophir Creek, turn around, and enjoy the steady downhill return to the trailhead.

The rock field at the base of Slide Mountain

From Reno. Take Highway 395/Interstate 580 south for 18.8 miles to the Bowers Mansion Road/Old US 395 exit. Follow the signs to enter Davis Creek Regional Park. Once in the park, pass the campground on the right, and turn left on Davis Creek Picnic Road. Park in the dirt parking lot at 39.3050, -119.8338, which has space for 4–5 cars and is in front of the trailhead. *20 mins.*

83 Genoa Loop

THIS LOVELY HIKE IN A RUGGED PORTION OF THE SOUTHERN CARSON RANGE HAS A LITTLE bit of everything. Enjoy spectacular views of the Carson Valley, steep canyons, waterfalls, and the oldest town in Nevada.

At a Glance

DIFFICULTY	Hard	DISTANCE/TIME	8.3 miles/5 hours
ELEVATION GAIN	1,900 feet	TRAIL TYPE	Foot trail, road
SOLITUDE	Medium use	USERS	Hikers, bikers
BEST SEASON	May–December	LAND OWNERSHIP	National Forest
ANIMALS	Deer, bears	FEATURES	Expansive views, waterfalls, wildflowers

Although Mount Rose Wilderness forms the most popular hiking area of the Carson Range, some of the range's most dramatic scenery is found much farther south. The historic town of Genoa sits at the eastern escarpment of the southern portion of the range, where the mountains rise over 4,000 feet to the west in only 2 miles. Travel to Genoa to hike this exciting loop that takes you into the steep canyons above the Carson Valley. In addition to being treated to gorgeous valley views, the hike passes by waterfalls and through the charming town of Genoa, the oldest settlement in Nevada.

From the parking area, walk down to the end of Snowshoe Lane, and take the well-signed **Sierra Canyon Trail**. The trail climbs through a forest mixed with firs, Jeffrey pines, and ponderosa pines together with sage and manzanita understory. In 0.5 miles, a footbridge crosses the creek that runs through Sierra Canyon. Deciduous trees such as alders and black cottonwoods thrive near the moist creek drainage.

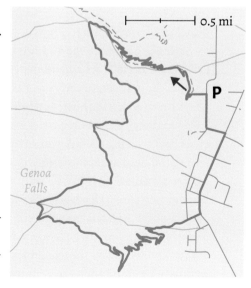

Past the creek, the trail switchbacks up the canyon, and increasingly expansive views of the Carson Valley develop behind you. Simultaneously, the steepness of the opposite side of the canyon

The Carson Valley in the distance

becomes apparent. Fortunately, the well-maintained trail allows you to navigate this precipitous terrain without issue. In 1.1 miles, turn left at the signed junction toward the **Genoa Canyon Trailhead**.

In 0.1 miles, the trail crosses the creek a second time. There are two creek crossings signed "Main Creek Crossing" and "Alternate Crossing." During most times of the year, both unbridged routes are easily manageable. However, during periods of high creek flow, the main route is advisable because a small handrail has been installed to aid in rock hopping.

Back on the original side of the creek, spectacular views of the valley develop ahead of you. The trail is narrow here, and because of the steepness of the terrain, the remainder of this hike is not recommended for those with a fear of heights. The trail itself, however, is relatively flat for the next 2.3 miles. During this stretch, the trail meanders in and out of several canyons. Notice how the sunny, south-facing canyon walls contain much drier vegetation such as mountain mahogany and sagebrush as compared to the shady north-facing walls, which are blanketed in conifers. This directional flora motif is common throughout the Carson Range, but it is especially pronounced on this hike because of the sharp angles of the canyon walls. A second ramification of the steep terrain is that the flat carved trail causes water to accumulate and freeze on the trail during the wetter months. For this reason, traction devices are highly recommended if you hike this trail in the winter or early spring.

At Genoa Canyon, a short spur trail at a signed junction takes you to Genoa Falls. The waterfalls are approximately 10 feet tall and usually contain water all times of the year except early fall. Past the waterfalls, the trail briefly climbs out of a secondary drainage before descending through dozens of switchbacks to a lower section of Genoa Creek over 2.3 miles. Carefully hop on rocks to cross the creek before hiking 0.2 miles down the trail to the **Genoa Canyon Trailhead**.

The trailhead lies at the terminus of Carson Street. Walk down Carson Street, and in 0.2 miles, turn left on Main Street. Just like that, you will be walking through downtown Genoa. Genoa was founded in 1851, and many of the houses and shops are originals from this era. The locals are accustomed to seeing hikers and will likely try to persuade you to buy some local antiques or farm fresh eggs. Past downtown, follow the fence lines of farmhouses along Main Street. After 0.6 miles of walking on Main Street, turn left on Centennial Drive. Centennial Drive veers to the right in 0.1 miles, and your car is just 0.2 miles farther.

From Reno. Take Highway 395/Interstate 580 south for 34.4 miles. At this point, the interstate ends; continue on Highway 395 (Carson Street) by turning left. Drive an additional 1.3 miles before turning right onto Jacks Valley Road. In 8.1 miles, turn right onto Centennial Drive just before downtown Genoa. Centennial Drive bends to the right, and in 0.4 miles, park on the right side of the street where it meets with Snowshoe Lane at 39.0139, -119.8454. *55 mins.*

Forested canyon views

Genoa Falls

The Virginia Range

The Peaceful Desert

The vast mountains of the Virginia Range stretch across the eastern edge of Reno. Most of this area is devoid of human development, giving you countless opportunities to experience a variety of desert landscapes away from crowds.

A very easy hike along Washoe Lake (Hike 91) is refreshing and scenic. Climb to the top of Chalk Bluff (Hike 84) for excellent views of the lower Truckee River meandering through the desert. Trips to Hidden Valley Peak (Hike 85), Hidden Valley Canyon (Hike 86), and Geiger Grade (Hike 89) take you past vibrantly colored canyons and hillsides. Explore Nevada's gold country at Basalt Hill (Hike 93).

For hikes with challenging elevation gains, trek to Louse Benchmark (Hike 88), Mount Davidson (Hike 90), and Mount Scott (Hike 92). Mount Davidson is the highest point in the Virginia Range, and the exposed summits of all three mountains afford towering panoramas of the Greater Reno area.

The most challenging hike and arguably the most rewarding in this chapter is an off-trail adventure through gorgeous Lagomarsino Canyon, which teems with wildlife and lush vegetation (Hike 87). However, what makes this hike truly special is discovering the prehistoric rock art that makes up the largest collection of Native American petroglyphs in all of Nevada.

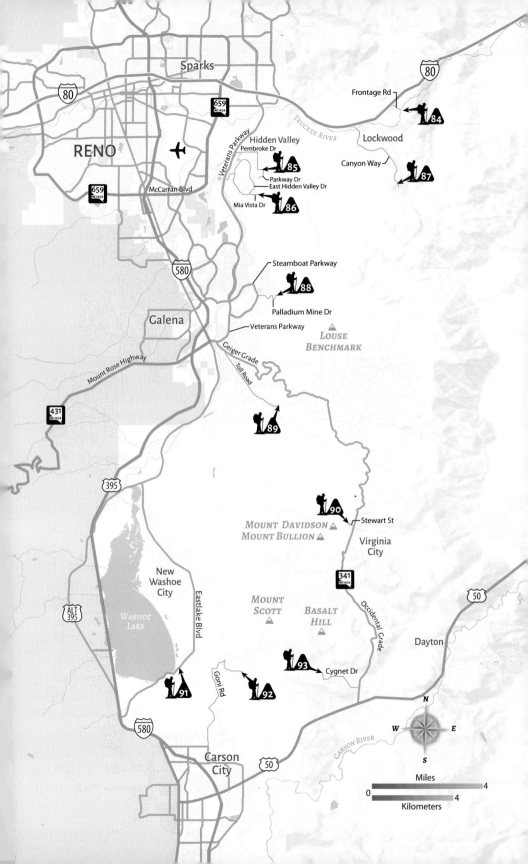

84 Chalk Bluff

HIKE IN THE WETLANDS OF THE MIGHTY TRUCKEE RIVER BEFORE EMBARKING ON A SHORT climb to a desert peak with excellent views of the Virginia Range.

At a Glance

DIFFICULTY	Hard	**DISTANCE/TIME**	5.3 miles/3.5 hours
ELEVATION GAIN	900 feet	**TRAIL TYPE**	Foot trail, dirt road, off trail
SOLITUDE	Light use	**USERS**	Hikers, anglers
BEST SEASON	All	**LAND OWNERSHIP**	Bureau of Land Management
ANIMALS	Bighorn sheep, water fowl, wild horses, jackrabbits	**FEATURES**	River, expansive views, colorful rock formations

The ecosystem around the lower Truckee River as it flows past the Virginia Range is very different from the upper montane headwaters near Lake Tahoe. Here, cottonwood and willow trees replace pines, and the large river deltas provide excellent habitat for water birds. Hike along the Truckee River and then up to Chalk Bluff, an open desert plateau that affords outstanding views of the river basin and surrounding mountains.

Out of the parking area, enter the banks of the Truckee River by passing through a gate in the adjacent fence to a popular fishing area. Follow the dirt paths as you make your way downstream along the river, heading east. If you

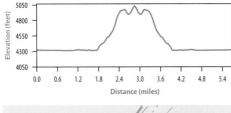

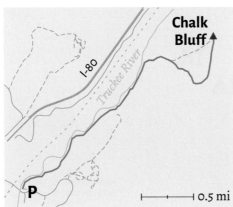

wish, you can use several small footpaths that weave around tall bushes right along the river bank. For a more straightforward route, take the larger, more open path slightly away from the river that leads you past high grasses, horsetails, and cattails. Regardless of the trail you choose, enjoy the sound of the raging river, and be on the lookout for impressive aquatic birds such as American white pelicans, double-crested cormorants, and American avocets, all of which are quite common here.

After 1.0 miles of walking on the trail, you will reach aptly named Mustang Road, a dirt road that takes you past an industrial building on the right. Follow the road past a set of popular fishing areas. After 0.5 miles of additional walking, you will pass the last fishing area, a powerful cascade in the Truckee, and the dirt road will turn back into a dirt trail. Continue downstream for an additional 0.3 miles through increasingly rocky terrain that is a favorite spot for wild horses. At this point, you should see a canyon to your right, adorned with brown and white rocks. Head east up the sandy ravine until you reach the top of the gentle sloping canyon in 0.7 miles. If you are feeling more adventurous, you can head up a steeper ravine to the left. This route features a short section that requires some hands and knees rock scrambling

Bighorn sheep on rocky outcropping

amid the chalk-colored rocks. Either way, after exiting the canyon, head north through the grass toward the top of Chalk Bluff, located at 39.5388, -119.5836.

As you ascend, scan the hills around you for bighorn sheep. These magnificent animals love the open, rocky terrain here, especially because they can easily stop by the Truckee for a drink. Before Europeans nearly hunted them to extinction, tens of thousands of bighorn sheep roamed all over Nevada, often in groups of several dozen. In the Virginia Range, the last sheep was observed in the early 1900s, but in 2010, the Nevada Department of Wildlife released about 40 sheep in these mountains. Since then, the local herd has grown to nearly 100. Other sheep restoration efforts across the state have also been successful, and now the population of the state animal is several thousand in the Great Basin Desert.

At the top of Chalk Bluff, enjoy tranquil views of the Pah Rah Range to the north and the rest of the Virginia Range to the south. To the west, marvel at the snow-capped Carson Range, and to the east, let your eyes follow the Truckee River's meandering course. Return down through the gentle main canyon ravine and along the Truckee River to your car.

From Reno. Take I-80 east 10.1 miles to the Mustang exit. After the off-ramp, turn right on Frontage Road, and in 0.7 miles, cross over the Truckee River. Immediately after the river, park in a dirt parking area at 39.5191, -119.6181 on the left side of the road. *15 mins.*

Wild horses grazing near Chalk Bluff

85 Hidden Valley Peak

CLIMB UP A SECLUDED WASH, AND TOP IT OFF WITH EXCELLENT VIEWS OF GREATER RENO.
You'll never believe this hidden adventure is so close to the city.

At a Glance

DIFFICULTY	Hard	DISTANCE/TIME	4.6 miles/3 hours
ELEVATION GAIN	1,600 feet	TRAIL TYPE	Foot trail, dirt road, off trail
SOLITUDE	Light use	USERS	Hikers
BEST SEASON	September–June	LAND OWNERSHIP	County park, county
ANIMALS	Wild horses, rabbits	FEATURES	Colorful rock formations, caves, expansive views

At 480 acres, Hidden Valley Park is large for a county park. Located in the foothills of the Virginia Range, numerous trails through the park lead to even more open space farther east outside the park. Although this adventurous hike begins on trails within the park, your journey will take you on a climb up a canyon deep in the Virginia Range before you reach the top of Hidden Valley Peak, where you will be treated to expansive views of the Greater Reno area.

Out of the parking area, pass through the gate and walk to the left on the large dirt trail for only 100 feet. At this point, take a smaller dirt trail to the right. Walk on this trail for 250 feet before turning right onto another dirt trail. Note that there are several dirt trails in the area, some better defined than others. Your exact approach at this stage is not important, as long as you are generally heading east, away from the park lowlands. Cross the fence through the green gate 300 feet away.

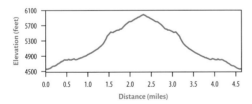

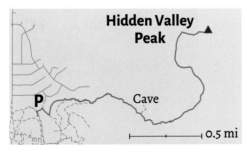

Fences throughout Hidden Valley Park were installed in an attempt to keep out wild horses, which are plentiful here. The horses always find ways around the fences, and it is quite likely you will see horses within the park, perhaps even close to the tennis courts. These animals are a majestic symbol of the American West. The horses' unregulated breeding has led to beautiful color patterns that are not typical in domesticated lines. It is breathtaking to watch mustangs gallop in unison across open sage country with a cloud of dust being kicked up behind them. Unfortunately, wild horses are nonnative animals that destroy native plants and compete with native animals for resources. Because horses were expatriated from North America more than 10,000 years ago and were reintroduced by the Spanish in the 1500s, they are properly called feral horses, not wild. The wild horse problem is exacerbated in Hidden Valley Park by inconsiderate individuals who illegally feed the horses.

After passing through the green gate, head north toward some homes at the edge of the park. Giant blazing stars bloom with their large yellow petals along the trail here in the summer. The path will veer to the right, and in 0.3 miles a sign and a large pile of rocks will mark the easternmost point of the park's Highland Loop trail. Instead of looping back toward the park entrance, continue heading east onto another dirt road that drops you down in 0.2 miles to the base of a large canyon with several large pink, white, and tan boulders. From here, the sandy ravine is your trail for the next 0.8 miles as you trek up the gorgeous canyon. The canyon walls are steep with crumbly boulders and outcroppings of sedimentary rocks, which have been highly modified by flash floods both ancient and present.

For a short and steep side trip, climb up to a small cave on the canyon's northern slope. The cave is only 0.1 miles away, but you must plan your route carefully due to steep and loose terrain.

Farther up the canyon, piñon trees with pine nuts line the steep slopes. Your route on the sandy ravine bottom, however, is fairly gradual and only becomes steep in a short final push out of the canyon. Your successful ascent is rewarded with easy travel on a dirt road. Turn left on the dirt road toward the large power lines.

There are great views of downtown Reno throughout this hike.

Cave entrance on slopes of the canyon

Now, out of the canyon, a vast secret world is revealed to you. Miles and miles of rolling desert terrain stretch out before you as you look east across the Virginia Range. Hike up the gentle dirt road for 0.6 miles toward rocky Hidden Valley Peak in front of you. At this point you will reach a junction, where you should take the faint trail to the right to reach the summit at 39.4975, -119.6889 in an additional 0.2 miles. Views of the Virginia Range, the Pah Rah Range, and Reno are outstanding. After you have taken in the panorama, head back down the way you came.

From Reno. Drive east on I-80 for 5.1 miles to the Sparks Boulevard exit. Turn right onto Sparks Boulevard, which in 0.5 miles becomes Veterans Parkway. In 2.0 miles, turn left on Pembroke Drive. In 0.6 miles, turn right on Parkway Drive to enter Hidden Valley Park. Once in the park, turn on the first dirt road to the left, and in 0.2 miles park in a small dirt parking area on the left side of the road at 39.4895, -119.7112. The dirt road is well maintained and suitable for low-clearance two-wheel-drive vehicles. Hidden Valley Park is open daily from 8 a.m. to sunset. *15 mins.*

View of Carson Range from the summit of Hidden Valley Peak

86 Hidden Valley Canyon

SCRAMBLE UP A HIDDEN CANYON AMONG RED, YELLOW, AND PINK ROCK OUTCROPPINGS.
Bask in the shade of a secret rock wall grotto. Great outing for teenagers!

At a Glance

DIFFICULTY	Hard	DISTANCE/TIME	1.2 miles/1 hour
ELEVATION GAIN	500 feet	TRAIL TYPE	Foot trail, off trail
SOLITUDE	Light use	USERS	Hikers
BEST SEASON	All	LAND OWNERSHIP	County park
ANIMALS	Wild horses, rabbits	FEATURES	Colorful rock formations

Numerous fault lines have slowly cut steep canyons across the western edge of the Virginia Range. For several million years, hot, pressurized water seeped through these fault lines and decomposed sulfur-containing minerals in the rocks, creating sulfuric acid. The sulfuric acid then reacted with and altered iron-containing minerals, which over the years rusted to varying extents to give colorful shades of yellow, pink, and red. Large portions of these hydrothermally altered rocks are exposed for your enjoyment in Hidden Valley Canyon.

To get to this beautiful canyon from the parking area, walk east toward the mountains across the small playground lawn. When you are in open sage steppe, head southeast on a dirt trail that is part of the park's **Perimeter Loop** route. After 0.1 miles, walk through one of the park's green gates to get to the other side of a fence meant to keep wild horses at bay. At this point, hike 0.1 miles off trail farther southeast to reach the sandy ravine at the bottom of the canyon. Flash floods occasionally occur in canyons like this one throughout the Virginia Range, spreading gravel and boulders out from the canyon mouths to form what is called an alluvial fan. Millions of years of periodic flash flooding have resulted in consolidated alluvial sediment that forms the bulk of Hidden Valley Park.

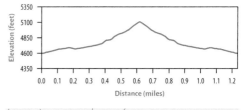

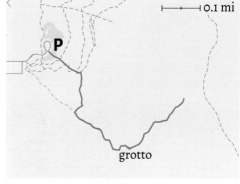

Hike up the sandy ravine for 0.2 miles until you reach a 50-foot rock wall. Marvel at the sheerness of this wall, which is evidence of massive uplifting along the faults in this area. In addition to its geological significance, this grotto also serves as a shady break spot. It is not safe for the average hiker to rock climb up the cliff face. Instead, go around the rock wall by hiking up the steep gravelly hillside to the left. Afterward, dip back down into the upper portion of the canyon, and continue your ascent, now to the north. As you climb farther, yellow, pink, and purple hydrothermally altered rocks become increasingly common. The wash has loose footing and some occasional steep steps that require the use of hands or knees for additional support. As such, this hike is great for teenagers and nimble adults, but it is not suitable for the less agile among us.

Hidden Valley Canyon ends about 0.2 miles beyond the grotto. At the upper reaches of the canyon, you will encounter large patches of halite, the mineral form of table salt, which resembles cauliflower in this ravine. There are also large platelets of a clear mineral called gypsum, which is used in the manufacture of drywall. Gypsum is so soft that you can confirm its identity by scratching it with your fingernail. At the top of the canyon, there are excellent views of downtown Reno and the Carson Range behind it. Return the way you came, back down the canyon to your car.

From Reno. Drive east on I-80 for 5.1 miles to the Sparks Boulevard exit. Turn right onto Sparks Boulevard, which in 0.5 miles becomes Veterans Parkway. In 2.0 miles, turn left on Pembroke Drive. Turn right at the first cross street in 0.4 miles onto Piping Rock Drive. In 0.3 miles, turn left onto East Hidden Valley Drive. In 1.3 miles turn left onto Mia Vista Drive, and drive to the end of the park to enter a playground area at 39.4774, -119.7139 that is part of Hidden Valley Park. This park is open daily from 8 a.m. to sunset. *20 mins.*

Colorful outcropping of hydrothermally altered rocks

Grotto rock wall

87 Lagomarsino Petroglyphs

FOR THOSE LOOKING FOR A TRULY MAGICAL DESERT HIKING EXPERIENCE, THIS IS IT. Bushwhack through a basalt canyon lined with lush vegetation, and enjoy the largest collection of petroglyphs in Nevada.

At a Glance

DIFFICULTY	Epic	DISTANCE/TIME	10.2 miles/10 hours
ELEVATION GAIN	800 feet	TRAIL TYPE	Off trail, foot trail, dirt road
SOLITUDE	Light use	USERS	Hikers
BEST SEASON	April–November	LAND OWNERSHIP	County
ANIMALS	Fish, frogs, water fowl, wild cattle, wild horses	FEATURES	Petroglyphs, colorful rock formations, springs, caves, wildflowers

Venture through wild, rugged, and isolated Lagomarsino Canyon. Witness its steep rock walls, straddle its long perennial creek teeming with wildlife, and experience solitude in this remote corner of the Virginia Range. Even better is that a successful journey through the canyon ends with an enormous one-of-a-kind petroglyph site, the largest in all of Nevada. Most of the hike does not follow any trail and involves extensive amounts of navigation through moderately dense vegetation and countless stream crossings. No matter the time of year, prepare for your feet to get wet. Although the elevation gain through the canyon is small, the constant adventuring around ponds, stream channels, boulders, and bushes will make you feel like Indiana Jones.

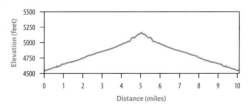

Out of the dirt parking area, walk east through the canyon. For the first mile, there is a faint dirt foot trail on the left side of Long Valley Creek. Although the size of this creek varies with the seasons, water flows year-round thanks to a multitude of springs scattered throughout the Virginia Range. After 0.8 miles of hiking, notice the small cave to your left, which you can explore if you wish. The canyon then begins to open up considerably, and rugged cliffs with rocks tinted light yellow and red

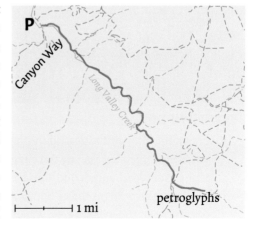

Wild horse near the parking area

Sheer basalt canyon walls

appear on both sides. The slow action of hot, pressurized water underground has altered the rocks to give them their exotic colors and craggy exterior. Groves of piñons and ponderosa pines grow in the altered acidic soil here, the latter of which are the only conifers of this kind you will encounter on this hike.

In an additional 0.3 miles, the dirt trail will meet a dirt road that comes in from terraced Washington Hill to your right. Washington Hill is owned by a company that is excavating the hillside to make cement. You will cross a pipe that is tapped into the ground to pump spring water up the hill to a reservoir for the company's operations. In dry months, look carefully for a small puddle on the dirt road here. Gas bubbles rhythmically rise from the ground through the perennial puddle, evidence that the ancient hydrothermal activity that altered the cliffsides is still active today.

Follow the dirt road for another 0.1 miles into the canyon before the road fades into a footpath. Soon, though, this footpath also fades away, and you are left to navigate the canyon off trail until you are fairly close to the petroglyphs, which are still 4.0 miles away.

For the next 2.7 miles, continue your sinuous southeast trek up the canyon. The vegetation, wildlife, and geology are remarkably varied during this portion of the hike, and with all of the moisture provided by Long Valley Creek, you will likely forget that you are traveling to the interior of an arid desert mountain range. At several points, 100-foot basalt walls above you are completely sheer and leave you with no choice but to wade in Long Valley Creek. Large stands of cottonwoods and willows keep you in the shade. Wildflowers are abundant and include wild roses, prickly poppies, and various species of penstemons. Several thousand fish and frogs inhabit the creek. The fish are particularly surprising, given that in the summer months, Long Valley Creek dries up before it reaches the Truckee River. The fish thus become trapped in the numerous small ponds that form in the summer, and they must wait until the winter snowmelt restores the creek level before they can return to the Truckee. Taking advantage of this situation, ducks and related birds feast here.

After you travel these 2.7 miles, the canyon will split at a large open fork. A 50-foot rock tower standing like a candlestick in the middle of the canyon fork is a noteworthy landmark. Lousetown Creek flows through the canyon trending to the southwest, but in summer months it will be dry. Take the canyon that contains perennial Long Valley Creek that continues to head left in the southeast direction. Watch out for feral cattle that enjoy grazing here. Like their more common wild horse counterparts, the unchecked breeding of these feral cows has given them interesting colorations, with some of the animals having red and white spots. Feral bulls must be treated with respect and are probably more dangerous than black bears. They can weigh more than 2,000 pounds and are angered easily. Make your presence known early by talking loudly, and give them as much space as you can.

In another 0.6 miles of hiking through the canyon, you will begin to see signs of dirt trails and pass a dilapidated pink car. The dirt road from which this car was dispatched is not much farther away, and you will find yourself at a T-junction of two dirt roads. Exit the main canyon, and hike your final 0.5 miles east on the dirt road. As you reach the headwaters of one of the springs, the ravine becomes relatively open, and the lush vegetation is abruptly replaced with sage, Mormon tea, and sporadic piñon trees. You are here, though, for the massive petroglyphs, which are signed and gated at 39.4427, -119.5670.

More than 2,200 petroglyphs were carved in the surrounding field of basalt boulders.

A petroglyph is a type of rock art in which designs are created by scratching or scraping away a rock's outer surface. Petroglyphs are different than pictographs, or rock paintings. The Lagomarsino petroglyphs were carved in basalt rock, which possesses an outer brown weathered surface and a white interior that is exposed by the artist. Although petroglyphs are difficult to date, experts believe some of the oldest panels here are as much as 10,000 years old. Human stick figures and myriad abstract designs abound. Bighorn sheep, lizards, birds, and insects are depicted. Many theories exist, but the precise meaning of these magnificent works of art will never be known.

The purpose of the large rock wall on southern slope of the canyon, opposite the petroglyphs, is also unknown. It may have been built to make hunting easier by corralling big game to the perennial spring below. Although a few milling sites and spear points have been found in the area, not enough artifacts have been found to suggest Lagomarsino was the permanent dwelling site of native peoples. Instead, the canyon probably was an important stopover point for people traveling elsewhere. In total, there are 2,229 panels of petroglyphs, most of them concentrated in a few acres!

While sitting among these boulders, imagine the ancient people sitting in the same spot several thousand years ago. Please tread lightly here, and respect this magical spot. Although it would be easy to spend a whole day enjoying this ancient art, you must make the long return journey to your car.

From Reno. Drive 8.7 miles east on I-80 to the Lockwood exit. The highway exit takes you to Canyon Way, which crosses over the Truckee River. In 3.3 miles, park at 39.4823, -119.6206 in a large dirt parking area on the left side of Canyon Way. *20 mins.*

Long Valley Creek

88 Louse Benchmark

TAKE A LONG WALK THROUGH THE SCENIC INTERIOR OF THE VIRGINIA RANGE. ASCEND through dense piñon forests to the summit of Louse Benchmark, which offers exquisite views.

At a Glance

DIFFICULTY	Epic	DISTANCE/TIME	10.7 miles/7 hours
ELEVATION GAIN	2,600 feet	TRAIL TYPE	Dirt road, off trail
SOLITUDE	Light use	USERS	Hikers, OHVs
BEST SEASON	September–June	LAND OWNERSHIP	County
ANIMALS	Wild horses, jackrabbits	FEATURES	Expansive views

On the border of Washoe and Storey Counties, the summit of Louse Benchmark offers exquisite views of the Truckee Meadows, Mount Rose, the Virginia City area, and the vast highlands east of Reno. The peak is named after the ghost town of Lousetown, which was situated about 1.5 miles east of the peak and existed from 1860 to 1880. Apparently the miners here did not have the best reputation, for "Louis" was changed to "Louse" early on. Lousetown was a toll road town that profited from controlling road access across the highlands from Virginia City to Reno alongside Lousetown Creek.

Out of the parking area, leave the subdivision behind, and head into the hills. The plotted route first heads north along a dirt road and rises steeply above Truckee Meadows into the Virginia Range. An adventurous alternative is to head directly east from the starting point into Eagle Canyon, which is visible from the trailhead. The 0.8-mile-long beautiful canyon has no trail, is steep, and requires ample rock scrambling, including some daring maneuvers not for the faint of heart. For those wanting to stay standing, the dirt roads highlighted on this map avoid the canyon entirely.

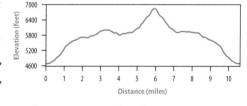

At the 2-mile point of the plotted route, there is a junction to the right. The shorter route is to turn right and cut in front of Camel Back Peak. Instead of heading straight, a loop hike can be had as shown, which only

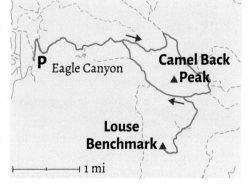

The three humps of Camel Back Peak

adds 1.2 miles to the overall trip. This route traverses the east side of Camel Back. With this route, it is about 4.5 miles until a junction appears heading south. This rocky jeep road is not maintained and gains about 700 feet in 1.0 miles. The peak is clearly visible as a forested high point for the majority of the trek up this road. After approximately 1.0 miles, the road stops climbing and loses altitude as it continues on toward ranches in the Virginia City Highlands.

The high point in the road is the best time to cut over and make your bushwhack up to Louse Benchmark, which is 0.2 miles nearly due west. This entry point will allow you to reach the top with some light rock scrambling among singleleaf piñon. Heading off trail sooner yields a steeper, more challenging ascent.

This area receives a healthy amount of snowfall in the winter, and with an elevation near 7,000 feet, the dense piñon forests are optimal for pine nut harvesting in the fall and early winter. There are plenty of delicious pine nuts for both you and the birds.

The actual peak of Louse Benchmark, located at 39.4096, -119.6645, consists of a pile of rocks rising only slightly above a piñon-covered plateau. A large wooden cross, which is visible from downtown Reno to those with keen eyesight, adorns the top.

Enjoy the views and come back down the steep rocky road that took you to the top. To shorten the descent, return via the west side of Camel Back. You will get an enchanting glimpse of Reno-Sparks through the backside portal of Eagle

Canyon as you look westward.

From Reno. Take Highway 395/Interstate 580 south for 8.7 miles to the Damonte Ranch Parkway exit. Turn left onto Damonte Ranch Parkway, and in 0.7 miles turn left onto Steamboat Parkway. In 1.6 miles, turn right onto Rio Wrangler Parkway, and after an additional 0.3 miles, turn left onto McCauley Ranch Boulevard. Continue straight through the traffic circle, and in 0.3 miles turn right on Palladium Mine Drive. In 0.2 miles, turn left on Claim Jumper Way. In an additional 0.2 miles, turn left on Tellurium Mine Drive, and park near 39.4273, -119.7008. *20 mins.*

Looking east from the summit

89 Geiger Grade

WALK IN THE FOOTSTEPS OF NINETEENTH-CENTURY PROSPECTORS AND PIONEERS through a vibrant canyon that leads to Virginia City. The route is a straightforward out-and-back climb, but a second vehicle can make it a very easy downhill stroll.

At a Glance

DIFFICULTY	Easy	**DISTANCE/TIME**	4.2 miles/2 hours
ELEVATION GAIN	1,100 feet	**TRAIL TYPE**	Dirt road
SOLITUDE	Medium use	**USERS**	Hikers, bikers, OHVs
BEST SEASON	All	**LAND OWNERSHIP**	Bureau of Land Management
ANIMALS	Deer, jackrabbits	**FEATURES**	Colorful rock formations, expansive views

To travel between Reno and Virginia City, pioneers and prospectors had to navigate Geiger Grade, which spans the steep eastern slopes of the Virginia Range. Today, winding Highway 341 allows cars to make this trek. In the nineteenth century, however, rough cut Toll Road was the only established passageway. The steep canyon alongside the road was a favorite hiding spot for bandits waiting to raid unsuspecting drivers of wagons hauling valuable ore mined from Virginia City. Retrace the steps of nineteenth-century fortune seekers by hiking Toll Road.

Out of the parking area on Toll Road, hike up the dirt road, which becomes increasingly rocky. The vegetation here consists of sagebrush mixed with juniper, piñon, and ponderosa pine trees. Tall grasses and even the occasional deciduous tree thrive in the canyon stream, which contains water until July most years. As you climb, enjoy the yellow, pink, and

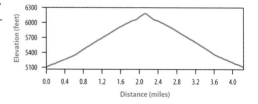

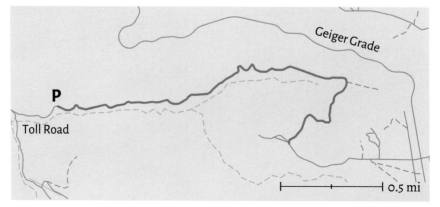

brick red cliffsides. Historical hydrothermal activity is responsible for altering the rocks to these exquisite colors; notice that the deepest reds occur down in the canyon, where hydrothermal activity continues today. Throughout the ascent, there are several short side roads that can take you into the canyon, a location that makes for a shady break spot.

After 1.6 miles of climbing, the road bends around the creek headwaters to the right. Excellent views of the Carson Range and Truckee Meadows open up. An additional 0.5 miles of hiking lead you to the first house in the Virginia Highlands. Turn around here, and enjoy the westward views during your descent. Because the top of this hike is also accessible by car, it is possible to use two cars to make this hike a very easy downhill trek.

From Reno. Take Highway 395/Interstate 580 south 10.0 miles to exit 25B for South Virginia Street. In 0.5 miles, continue onto South Virginia Street toward Virginia City. In another 0.5 miles, turn left onto Highway 341. In 0.7 miles, turn right on Toll Road. Continue for 2.9 miles. Although the pavement of Toll Road eventually ends, this dirt road is suitable for low-clearance two-wheel-drive vehicles. Park at 39.3709, -119.7003 in a large dirt turnout on the left side of the road near yellow rocks on the hillside. *20 mins.* If you wish to make this a one-way downhill hike with two vehicles, you can start the hike at the top of Geiger Grade. Drive the second vehicle past Toll Road, and continue on Highway 341 for 7.1 miles. Turn right on Cartwright Road, and in 0.7 miles park at 39.3683, -119.6789 on the dirt road. *15 additional minutes.*

Looking down the canyon

90 Mount Davidson and Mount Bullion

CLIMB TO THE TOP OF TWO PEAKS ABOVE VIRGINIA CITY, THE MOST FAMOUS MINING TOWN in the West. The completion of the steep ascents is rewarded with stunning panoramas and many calories burned.

At a Glance

DIFFICULTY	Hard	DISTANCE/TIME	7.5 miles/5 hours
ELEVATION GAIN	2,700 feet	TRAIL TYPE	Foot trail, dirt road
SOLITUDE	Light use	USERS	Hikers, OHVs
BEST SEASON	September–June	LAND OWNERSHIP	Bureau of Land Management
ANIMALS	Wild horses, jackrabbits	FEATURES	Expansive views

Hike among old silver mines on the steep and exposed eastern slopes of Virginia City. The faulted geology of the Virginia Range here gave rise to the veins of silver of the Comstock Lode, first discovered in 1859. The resulting mining boom was the largest in history and propelled Nevada into statehood. By the 1870s, Virginia City had 25,000 residents. Approximately 7 million tons of ore were processed in the Virginia City area during these years, which produced a quantity of gold and silver worth about $8 billion in today's dollars. The profits from this mining were largely controlled by West Coast investors, who used the money to transform San Francisco from a sleepy town in the 1850s to the largest city in the West with a population of more than 200,000 in the 1880s. By

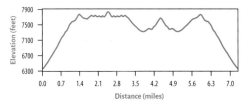

then, though, Virginia City's population began a steep decline because all of the profitable silver had been mined. Gold mining, however, continues to this day in the Virginia City area.

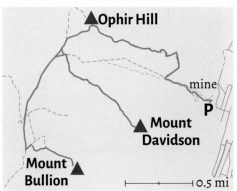

From the parking area, begin your hike by ascending a dirt road heading west. You will immediately see two old mines to your right, remnants of a bygone era. Never enter mine shafts! These structures can be unstable, and people have died after being trapped in collapsed shafts. Continue up the road, which takes you alongside Spanish Ravine.

In little more than 0.5 miles, you can continue on the steep road up the ravine

View of Carson Range from Mount Bullion

or turn right. The route to the right, although also steep, is more pleasant. This way eventually takes you to Ophir Hill, a point that is higher than Mount Bullion, your final destination. Unfortunately, the views from Ophir Hill are obscured by cell phone towers, one of the few features of the area anachronistic with respect to the 1860s.

Head past Ophir Hill, and in 0.2 miles make two lefts at two successive junctions to begin your southeast approach toward Mount Davidson. From the dirt road, a 0.1-mile foot trail will take you to the rocky top.

At 7,864 feet, Mount Davidson is the highest point in the Virginia Range and all of Storey County. Its exposed summit located at 39.3082, -119.6634 with a flagpole on top is visible throughout the hike and offers phenomenal views. On a clear day, you will be treated to excellent views of the Flowery Range and the Pine Nut Mountains to the south, Washoe Lake and the Carson Range to the west, the Pah Rah Range to the north, and much of central Nevada to the east.

After you have soaked in the panorama from the summit of Mount Davidson, retrace the 0.7 miles you just climbed along Mount Davidson's ridgeline. Turn left at the junction to begin your trip to Mount Bullion. Views of the Carson Range above you and Washoe Lake below you continue to amaze on this relatively flat section of the trail. This area is the only spot you may encounter OHVs because the Spanish Ravine and Ophir Hill section of this hike is too steep for most vehicular enthusiasts.

Continue down the road past turnoffs to Bullion Ravine. (A poorly marked trail down Bullion Ravine will lead you to the southern end of Virginia City.) After 0.7 miles, you will reach a saddle point, which is noteworthy in that it is

Virginia City at the base of Spanish Ravine

one of the few spots on this hike that is significantly forested and shaded. Amid the sagebrush, you will find an assortment of piñons, junipers, curleaf mountain mahoganies, and even a few ponderosa pines.

Climb about 300 feet over 0.4 miles on a dirt road heading to the east to reach the mounded top of Mount Bullion, located at 39.3044, -119.6722. Views on top of this peak are also outstanding.

Return to the shaded saddle, and climb back to Ophir Hill and around and down Spanish Ravine to the parking area.

From Reno. Take Highway 395/Interstate 580 south 10.0 miles to exit 25B for South Virginia Street. In 0.5 miles, continue onto South Virginia Street toward Virginia City. In another 0.5 miles, turn left onto Highway 341. Drive 13.5 miles on the curvy highway until you reach Virginia City. Turn right onto Taylor Street, which turns into Stewart Street. Continue climbing for a few hundred feet onto an unsigned road, and park on the dirt shoulder at 39.3106, -119.6532. The owners of the closest house have posted a sign asking hikers to park on the dirt shoulder instead of on the pavement of their road. *40 mins.*

Abandoned silver mine

91 Washoe Lake

THERE ARE SO MANY DIFFERENT THINGS TO ENJOY DURING THESE 2.5 MILES! APPRECIATE lakeside views, a spring-fed creek, wild horses, and snow-capped mountains on this easy stroll.

At a Glance

DIFFICULTY	Very easy	DISTANCE/TIME	2.5 miles/1.5 hours
ELEVATION GAIN	600 feet	TRAIL TYPE	Foot trail, dirt road
SOLITUDE	Medium use	USERS	Hikers
BEST SEASON	All	LAND OWNERSHIP	State Park, Bureau of Land Management
ANIMALS	Wild horses, water fowl, deer, rabbits	FEATURES	Lake, springs, caves, expansive views

Eleven streams from the Carson and Virginia Ranges flow to the bottom of Carson Valley to form Washoe Lake, a body of water that is approximately 6,000 acres. Washoe Lake is only 12 feet deep at its fullest, and in severe drought years, the lake can dry up completely by early fall. The lake provides excellent habitat for a number of bird species, including pelicans, herons, and a wide assortment of ducks. The notoriously strong winds in the Carson Valley, known as the Washoe Zephyr, frequently cause lake conditions to be choppy. Mark Twain once quipped that the "reason there are so many bald people [is] that the wind blows the hair off their heads while they are looking skyward after their hats."

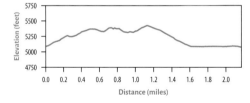

Enjoy this easy stroll alongside a spring-fed creek that flows into the lake. The creek supports luscious vegetation, and the upper stretches of the trail afford stupendous views of Washoe Lake and the surrounding mountains. From the parking area, head away from Washoe Lake to the east on the trail that passes along Deadman's Creek. Wildflowers here include wild roses, prickly poppies, desert peaches, giant blazing stars, and phlox. Willows and cottonwoods also line the creek bed. Other plants include sagebrush, rabbitbrush, bitterbrush, and stinging nettles. The hills surrounding

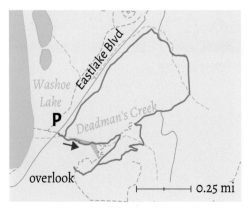

the creek are a favorite browsing spot for wild horses.

After you walk 0.3 miles along the creek, the trees end. Turn right on another dirt trail that crosses the creek, heads southwest, and climbs further. In another 0.3 miles and after a total of only 300 feet of climbing, you will reach a gazebo. Break here and savor the phenomenal views of the Carson Valley.

Retrace your steps, but only for 0.2 miles. At this point, turn right at a junction onto another dirt trail. In 0.1 additional miles, you will reach a cool, well-lit cave that provides you with shade and more excellent views should you stop here. Continue past the cave for 0.2 miles as the trail takes you down and up out of a dry ravine and to another junction. For a shorter hike, you can turn left here to return to your car for a total round-trip distance of 1.7 miles. Otherwise, turn right and reach a dirt road in 0.1 miles. Turn left onto the dirt road, and follow it to the edge of Eastlake Boulevard in 0.6 miles. Turn left to take a dirt trail that runs parallel to the road and takes you back to the parking area.

From Reno. Take Highway 395/Interstate 580 south toward Carson City. After 25.5 miles, take the exit for Eastlake Boulevard. In 3.0 miles, turn into a dirt parking area on the right side of the road at 39.2384, -119.7665. *30 mins.*

Wild horses near Deadman's Creek

Up to the gazebo

View from cave of Washoe Lake and the Carson Range

92 Mount Scott

SUMMIT MOUNT SCOTT FOR STUNNING VIEWS OF EAGLE AND WASHOE VALLEYS. THE DIRT road to the top is consistently gradual, giving you ample opportunities during your ascent to take in the views.

At a Glance

DIFFICULTY	Hard	DISTANCE/TIME	5.2 miles/3 hours
ELEVATION GAIN	1,000 feet	TRAIL TYPE	Dirt road
SOLITUDE	Medium use	USERS	Hikers, OHVs
BEST SEASON	September–June	LAND OWNERSHIP	Bureau of Land Management
ANIMALS	Wild horses, jackrabbits	FEATURES	Expansive views

Mount Scott is a prominent landmark to thousands of people in Reno and Carson City. This peak rises just east of Washoe Lake and helps separate the Washoe and Eagle Valleys. Despite its noticeable summit and impressive views, this mountain is less well known to hikers than those in the Sierra Nevadas.

Out of the parking area, begin your hike by walking on the dirt road to the right. This road takes you all the way to the summit, and aside from access roads that go to various cell phone towers at the top, there are no major junctions to pass through. Soon after you start the hike, the road will bend around some interesting rock formations on the hillside to the left. After the first bend, you will head north for the next 0.5 miles or so, and a large cinder rock pit actively mined for gravel is visible below you to the left. After another 1.2 miles, you cross through an unmarked point that is a four-way boundary between Washoe County, Storey County, Lyon County, and the municipality of Carson City.

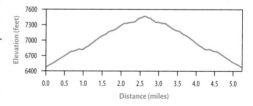

About 0.4 miles from the summit, you will see a few piñon trees at a relatively flat saddle. These trees offer the only shade on the hike. From here, climb to the Mount Scott summit, located at 39.2619, -119.7051, by meandering through the cell phone towers. To the west, enjoy excellent views of Washoe

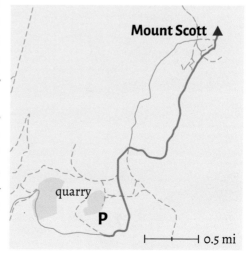

Lake below in front of the Carson Range. Mount Davidson (Hike 90) dominates views to the north. Views to the east extend for nearly 100 miles into central Nevada. Return the way you came.

Piñon pine with Washoe Lake and the Carson Range

From Reno. Take Highway 395/ Interstate 580 south toward Carson City. After 28.7 miles, get off at the College Parkway exit, and turn left at the off-ramp. After driving 0.4 miles on East College Parkway, turn left on Goni Road. Drive for 5.2 miles, and park off of Goni Road at 39.2362, -119.7246 near a junction between two dirt roads. The pavement on Goni Road will end, but the unpaved portion is suitable for low-clearance two-wheel-drive vehicles under dry conditions. *45 mins.*

View of Washoe Lake and the Carson Range from Mount Scott

93 Basalt Hill

HIKE PAST OLD MINES AND SUMMIT A PEAK IN NEVADA'S HISTORIC GOLD COUNTRY OUTSIDE of Virginia City.

At a Glance

DIFFICULTY	Hard	**DISTANCE/TIME**	5.0 miles/2.5 hours
ELEVATION GAIN	1,000 feet	**TRAIL TYPE**	Dirt road, off trail
SOLITUDE	Light use	**USERS**	Hikers, bikers, OHVs
BEST SEASON	All	**LAND OWNERSHIP**	Bureau of Land Management, open space
ANIMALS	Wild horses, jackrabbits	**FEATURES**	Expansive views, springs

Gold was first discovered in Nevada in 1849 by mountain man Abner Blackburn in Gold Creek. Take a short hike to the top of Basalt Hill to view this historic area.

Begin your hike by continuing up the dirt road past the water tower in the parking area. After 0.4 miles, the road begins to level out, and you will reach a junction. Either route is acceptable. The road to the right dips down into a canyon and will increase your elevation change, so the road to the left is shown on this map.

Basalt Hill, with its rounded dark top, is visible in front of you. Head up the road an additional 1.6 miles to reach the side of Basalt Hill and the top of the canyon. From here, turn right off the road and head cross-country up to the top in 0.5 miles. You will have to cross several large rock flows of basalt, but the sizes of these rocks are small enough to make your route bearable.

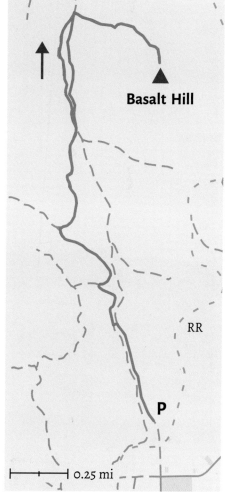

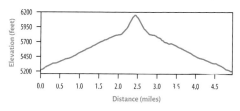

Basalt Hill

From the Basalt Hill summit located at 39.2569, -119.6710, enjoy views of the Pine Nut Mountains to the east and Mount Scott (Hike 92), which dominates views to the west. Mount Bullion (Hike 90) with its rounded rocky top is visible to the north.

Return the way you came. If desired, you can take the lower road through the canyon. On this route, you will pass a rather large spring that most times of the year waters a small pond that makes for an excellent watering hole for wild horses. The entrance to the Florida Shaft, a defunct gold mine, is visible on your right near this spring.

From Reno. Take Highway 395/Interstate 580 south toward Carson City. After 30.0 miles, merge onto Highway 50 heading east toward Dayton and Fallon. In 6.1 miles, turn left onto Highway 341. In 0.5 miles, turn left onto Industrial Parkway. Go 0.8 miles farther before turning left onto Cygnet Drive. In an additional 0.8 miles, you will reach the end of Cygnet Drive. Turn right onto a dirt road suitable for low-clearance two-wheel-drive vehicles, cross the railroad tracks, and park at the water tower at 39.2358, -119.6714. *45 mins.*

View of Mount Bullion and Davidson from the summit

Carson City and Beyond

The Wild Wild West

Carson City, which is only a 35-minute drive from downtown Reno, offers numerous hiking opportunities. Here, you can enjoy the scenic Carson River either from up high (Hike 100) or from along its banks (Hike 101). Just outside the city limits, marvel at a beautiful set of waterfalls with an easy hike to Kings Canyon Falls (Hike 99).

This chapter also covers desert landscapes east of the Virginia Range. Climb to the top of Rocky Peak (Hike 96) and Emma Peak (Hike 97) for adventurous and strenuous outings in the Flowery Range. At Patua Hot Springs (Hike 94), visit geothermal anomalies in the middle of stark desert lowlands. The hike at Grimes Point (Hike 95) will teach you that this desert landscape once was a fertile seaside environment, and the petroglyphs, pictographs, and caves lend a powerful lens into the prehistoric life of Native Americans. Lastly, the ruins at Fort Churchill (Hike 98) tell of the history of nineteenth-century Native Americans and European Americans in the desert.

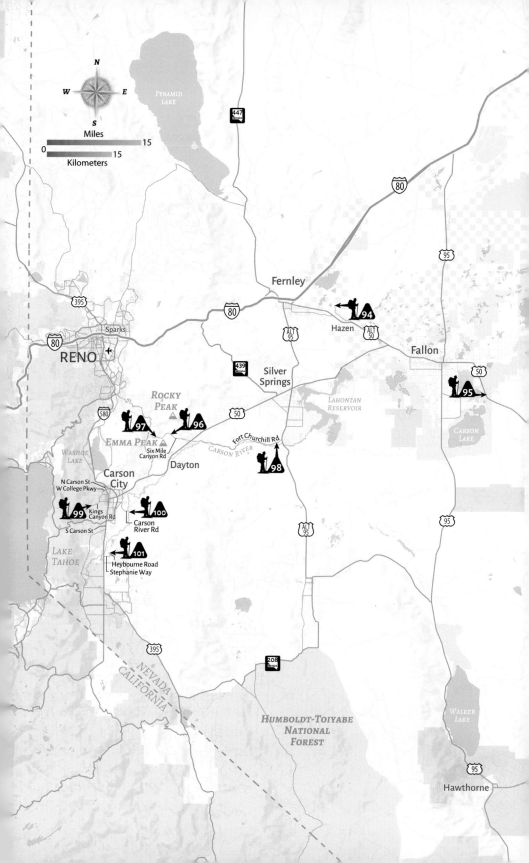

94 Patua Hot Springs

VISIT AN OASIS OF HOT SPRINGS IN THE MIDDLE OF AN ARID DESERT EAST OF RENO. THIS
flat hike in a remote portion of Nevada is suitable for recreationists of all abilities.

At a Glance

DIFFICULTY	Easy	DISTANCE/TIME	2.1 miles/1 hour
ELEVATION GAIN	100 feet	TRAIL TYPE	Dirt road, foot trail
SOLITUDE	Light use	USERS	Hikers, OHVs
BEST SEASON	September–June	LAND OWNERSHIP	Bureau of Land Management
ANIMALS	Jackrabbits	FEATURES	Hot springs

Of all the harsh landscapes faced by transcontinental pioneers lured by California's gold in the middle of the nineteenth century, the Forty Mile Desert east of Reno was the most feared. This barren stretch of hot desert had no drinkable water and no shade, so wagon trains crossed at night.

This hike to Patua Hot Springs lets you explore the rugged Forty Mile Desert and some of the region's interesting geothermal features. Because the elevation here is only 4,000 feet, making it among the lowest points in northern Nevada, the desert is particularly hot in the summer. As Earth's crust was stretched and thinned during the valley's formation, heat from underground could more easily reach the surface, thus resulting in the formation of the hot springs.

From the parking area, walk on the dirt spur road heading west. The vegetation, which is dominated by greasewood and shadscale, is different from the sagebrush that covers most of the lowlands of the Great Basin. These plants are adapted to

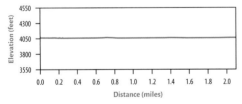

the hot, dry summers and the high salinity levels in the soil. Precipitation brings salts from the surrounding mountains, and the salt accumulates in this valley when the rain or snow evaporates. Look for a white crust of salt along the trail as you hike.

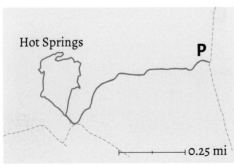

In 0.6 miles at the base of the hill, turn right at a junction. From here, you will see pockets of dense vegetation ahead to the north. These are willows and grasses that grow by the moisture of the springs. The first substantial hot springs are 0.3 miles to the north. Past these springs, head east for 0.3 miles to

see an even larger series of springs. The temperature of all of these springs is well above 100°F, too hot for bathing. We discourage bathing in any natural hot springs like these because, in addition to disrupting the habitat, you could pick up a rare but fatal brain-eating amoeba that can exist in warm waters.

Past the larger springs, complete your loop by walking another 0.3 miles to the south to return to the road and the first junction. From here, retrace your steps 0.6 miles to your car.

One of the hot springs

From Reno. Take I-80 east for 34.5 miles to exit 48 toward East Fernley. In 0.5 miles, merge onto Business I-80 west. In 0.7 miles, turn at the roundabout onto Alternative Highway 50 East/East Main Street. In 10.1 miles, turn left onto California Street. Cross the train tracks, and turn left at the first cross street, an unsigned dirt road. Drive on this dirt road, which is suitable for low-clearance two-wheel-drive vehicles, and park on the side of the road in 4.0 miles at 39.6008, -119.1004. There is room on the left side of the road to park, where a spur road meets the main dirt road. *55 mins.*

Shadscale vegetation

95 Grimes Point

ON THE SHORES OF ANCIENT LAKE LAHONTAN, EXPLORE ANCIENT PETROGLYPHS,
pictographs, and caves that contained Native American artifacts that are up to
10,000 years old.

At a Glance

DIFFICULTY	Easy	DISTANCE/TIME	4.4 miles/3 hours
ELEVATION GAIN	800 feet	TRAIL TYPE	Foot trail, dirt road
SOLITUDE	Medium use	USERS	Hikers
BEST SEASON	September–June	LAND OWNERSHIP	Bureau of Land Management
ANIMALS	Jackrabbits	FEATURES	Petroglyphs, pictographs, caves, interesting rock formations

There was an old western myth that deep in the Nevadan desert, an outlaw hid
his treasure in a cave. In the 1920s, four boys searching for this treasure in the
hills near Grimes Point discovered something more valuable: a cave filled with
prehistoric artifacts, some nearly 10,000 years old. Today, you can visit Hidden
Cave through public tours organized by the Bureau of Land Management twice a
month. Even if you cannot visit Hidden Cave during these scheduled tours, there
are petroglyphs, pictographs, and several smaller caves that make for an exciting
hiking adventure at Grimes Point.

Follow the signs for the **Petroglyph Trail** from the parking area. This trail
winds through boulders of basalt, which contain dozens of rock carvings display-
ing a mixture of abstract, animalistic, and anthropomorphic designs. In addition

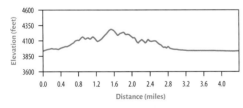

to the petroglyphs, the boulders contain
hundreds of cupules, small round pits
dug into the rock by prehistoric peoples.

In 0.3 miles, a junction heads back
down to the parking area. Instead of
returning to the parking area, turn left at
this junction to continue exploring the
hills past the petroglyphs on the **Overlook Trail**. In 0.5 miles, the trail reaches
a saddle between two hills. Turn left at
this junction to reach Grimes Point in
0.2 miles, the top of the first hill. From
the benches on top of Grimes Point, you
can take in excellent views of Lahontan
Valley, including the waters of Stillwater

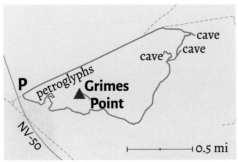

National Wildlife Refuge to the north and Carson Lake to the south. These waters are remnants of ancient Lake Lahontan, which 10,000 years ago completely submerged all of the land surrounding this hill.

From the Grimes Point overlook, walk 0.2 miles back down to the junction between the two hills. From here, hike straight through the junction and up to the second, taller hill, which is 0.3 miles away. Past the high point, continue on the ridgeline heading north for another 0.7 miles to enter the caves area.

Take a left at the faint junction and head left to the caves on the cliff 0.1 miles away. The beige bulbous rock formations on the cliff faces are evidence of deposition from the ancient sea. After you have enjoyed these strange formations, retrace your steps 0.1 miles to the junction, and walk straight through it to head east. The locked entrance to Hidden Cave is 0.1 miles away. Contact the Bureau of Land Management for touring information of Hidden Cave.

Lower past Hidden Cave, continue hiking for 0.2 miles on a spur trail that wraps around the hillside. There are several smaller caves along this hillside, but the most impressive one is a signed cave that contains ancient pictographs. While petroglyphs are rock carvings, pictographs are rock paintings. Pictographs are

Many panels of ancient petroglyphs are visible from the trail.

the rarer of the two because they are easily disturbed by weatherization. They typically are only found preserved in a dry desert cave like this one. Please be respectful and take only pictures.

Turn around at the pictographs, and hike 0.3 miles to the caves area trailhead. From here, turn left, and walk 1.3 miles on the dirt road back to the main trailhead to your car.

From Reno. Take I-80 east for 34.5 miles, and take exit 48 toward East Fernley. In 0.5 miles, merge onto Business I-80 west. In 0.7 miles, turn at the roundabout onto Alternative Highway 50 East/East Main Street. In 16.9 miles, continue onto Highway 50 East. In 19.5 miles, turn left into the parking area labeled "Grimes Point" at 39.4014, -118.6473. *1 hour, 20 mins.*

This dry landscape was the site of an enormous ancient lake.

Sheer rock formations carved by the ancient sea

Ancient pictographs are in this cave

96 Rocky Peak

SCRAMBLE TO THE CRAGGED TOPS OF ROCKY PEAK VIA THIS STRENUOUS ASCENT IN THE
little-explored Flowery Range. Those who successfully make it to the summit will
be treated to an incredible panorama.

At a Glance

DIFFICULTY	Epic	**DISTANCE/TIME**	7.6 miles/6 hours
ELEVATION GAIN	2,400 feet	**TRAIL TYPE**	Dirt road, off trail
SOLITUDE	Light use	**USERS**	Hikers, OHVs
BEST SEASON	March–June, September–November	**LAND OWNERSHIP**	Bureau of Land Management
ANIMALS	Wild horses	**FEATURES**	Expansive views, wildflowers

The climb to Rocky Peak is the preeminent hiking experience in the Flowery
Range. The views are breathtaking in all directions, and the peak caps off with

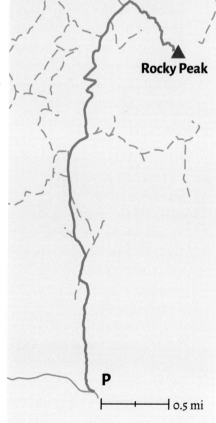

an entertaining, but easy, rock scramble. The
Flowery Range, named for its magnificent
springtime wildflowers, is a 15-mile spur of
the Virginia Range that separates Virginia
City from Dayton Valley. The best time to
hike Rocky Peak is in the spring or fall. Day-
time temperatures in the summer are too hot,
and snow in the winter can make navigating
around the large boulders near the summit
perilous.

Directly ahead of the parking area, you
will see a sign marking private property in
a small wash. This sign refers to property
owned by a homeowner whose house, which
is out of view from this point, lies on the
hillside to the right of the wash. Instead of
going immediately through the wash and
crossing the sign, head into the brush to the

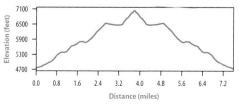

Glorious views of snow and desert from the rocky pinnacle that is the summit

left of the wash that runs alongside Six Mile Canyon Road. Within 200 feet, you will reach another dirt road with no signs posted. Begin hiking on this dirt road, which takes you back to the same wash, but farther upstream away from private property. Alternatively, high-clearance vehicles can park directly on this dirt road, which also begins at Six Mile Canyon Road.

Regardless, within 0.1 miles, power lines will soon accompany you on this dirt road as you hike north up the canyon. For the next 1.6 miles, walk on this dirt road with the large power lines not straying too far away from you at any point. You will climb about 1,200 feet during this trek and eventually reach a prominent junction at the first substantial plateau of the hike.

While the power lines continue straight up the steep hillside to the next ridge, take the dirt road to the right to climb the switchbacks of the road up farther. This climb will take you up an additional 800 feet over the next 1.1 miles.

At the end of this climb, you will reach a second, much larger plateau, which lies at the base of Rocky Peak. Continue hiking along the dirt road on this plateau for about 0.2 miles. At some point, you will have to leave this road and begin trekking off trail to the right, heading east through an open, but increasingly rocky landscape.

After you head off trail, you are approximately 0.8 miles away from Rocky Peak following most routes. The exact approach is unimportant, but avoid the southern face of Rocky Peak, which is dangerously steep. The high point is obvious but hidden from the second plateau. You will have to hike around several large and beautiful rock outcroppings before reaching a third, smaller open plateau that is right before the final summit block. The summit itself is adorned by an impressive rock outcropping with huge boulders. Many routes are difficult, but there is a route on the back east side that only requires light scrambling.

Views from the top are simply phenomenal. Marvel at Long Valley below you, a huge desert plateau that forms a largely uninhabited and rarely visited portion of the Virginia City Highlands. Mount Davidson (Hike 90) and Virginia City, all of the peaks on the east side of Lake Tahoe, the Dayton Valley, the Pine Nut Mountains, Lahontan Reservoir, the Virginia Range, and much more surround you in a beautiful 360° panorama. Return the way you came, enjoying exquisite views of the Dayton Valley on most of your way down.

From Reno. Take Highway 395/Interstate 580 south 10.0 miles to exit 25B for South Virginia Street. In 0.5 miles, continue onto South Virginia Street toward Virginia City. In another 0.5 miles, turn left onto Highway 341. Drive 13.7 miles on the curvy highway until you reach Virginia City. Turn left onto Six Mile Canyon Road (State Route 79). In 4.4 miles, park in a dirt shoulder on the left side of the road located at 39.3150, -119.5809. Along Six Mile Canyon Road, numerous parcels of private property are marked with "No Trespassing" signs, marking off both homes and mining claims. To avoid crossing these signs, make sure to park at the correct GPS coordinates. High-clearance vehicles should park 0.1 miles earlier on the road at 39.3156, -119.5833 (see hiking description). *50 mins.*

Wild horses frequent the first plateau of this hike.

97 Emma Peak

THE ASCENT TO THE TOP OF RUGGED EMMA PEAK IS CERTAINLY ADVENTUROUS. ON YOUR way, hike through a colorful canyon and remote forests of piñon and juniper trees.

At a Glance

DIFFICULTY	Hard	**DISTANCE/TIME**	4.0 miles/3 hours
ELEVATION GAIN	1,300 feet	**TRAIL TYPE**	Dirt road, off trail
SOLITUDE	Light use	**USERS**	Hikers, OHVs
BEST SEASON	March–June, September–November	**LAND OWNERSHIP**	Bureau of Land Management
ANIMALS	Wild horses	**FEATURES**	Expansive views

It is hard to avoid daydreaming on this hike to Emma Peak that every step represents a new opportunity to uncover a hidden treasure of gold and silver left by a nineteenth-century bandit. The scenery on this hike is also equally exciting.

From the parking area, hike around the gate, which blocks off a wide dirt road. In 0.3 miles, this road begins to bend sharply to the right, which is the start of a complete U-turn. Instead of following the U-turn, once the road bends right, head left and down off trail to reach another dirt road about 100 feet away from the road you are on.

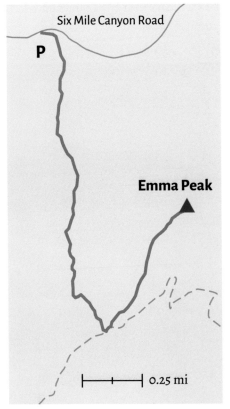

Continue heading south on this new dirt road, which meanders in and out of a colorful creek bed that is usually dry. Whether you follow the road or stay in the creek bed is not important, but do not follow any roads that go upslope. Instead stay in the creek bed for about 0.8 miles.

Although Emma Peak entices you by rising directly above you to the left during this trek, any shorter approach is far too steep and significantly more difficult. After you

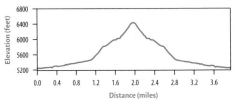

have gone about 0.8 miles, turn left and head up the open slopes. Your creek bed path will be blocked by a few large piñon trees and heavy brush, indicating that you should go upslope.

Your next target is the saddle between Emma Peak and Mount Grosh. The trail at this point roughly hugs a contour line as you bend back toward Emma Peak. Ignore the few very faint mining trails on this slope that do not lead anywhere in particular. There is a jeep road and an old flag on the top of the ridge. However, this area is the highest point that the jeep road reaches, so you will need to proceed northerly up the ridge off the jeep road.

After a bit of hiking along this ridge, Emma Peak becomes clearly visible in front of and above you. Although it is only about 0.6 miles of an off-trail trek to

Cottonwoods and piñons in front of Sugarloaf Butte

the top, careful route finding is required. Both the eastern and western slopes are very steep in spots, and you must either traverse over or around several sheer rock outcroppings. Hiking poles are strongly recommended.

Despite this rugged terrain, the actual peak is fairly flat and makes for an excellent breaking point that is shaded by a grove of juniper trees. Views between the trees are outstanding in all directions. The quaintness of Virginia City and its backdrop of Mount Davidson and Mount Bullion (Hike 90) are visible below you to the west. The rugged terrain of the Flowery Range, including the steep volcanic plug of Sugarloaf Peak, is striking to the north. Toward the east, marvel at the Carson River flowing through the town of Dayton, and enjoy views of Lahontan Reservoir in the distance. Descend carefully the way you came.

From Reno. Take Highway 395/Interstate 580 south 10.0 miles to exit 25B for South Virginia Street. In 0.5 miles, continue onto South Virginia Street toward Virginia City. In another 0.5 miles, turn left onto Highway 341. Drive 13.7 miles on the curvy highway until you reach Virginia City. Turn left onto Six Mile Canyon Road (State Route 79). In 2.1 miles, park in a dirt shoulder on the right side of the road located at 39.3062, -119.6147 in front of a gate. *50 mins.*

At the flag, you are well on your way to the top of Emma Peak.

98 Fort Churchill

EXPLORE THE RUINS OF A NINETEENTH-CENTURY DESERT FORT ON THE BANKS OF THE
Carson River. With history and riverside scenery, this easy hike has plenty to offer.

At a Glance

DIFFICULTY	Very Easy	DISTANCE/TIME	2.0 miles/1 hour
ELEVATION GAIN	100 feet	TRAIL TYPE	Dirt road, off trail
SOLITUDE	Medium use	USERS	Hikers
BEST SEASON	All	LAND OWNERSHIP	State Park
ANIMALS	Deer	FEATURES	Ruins, river

Fort Churchill was built in the 1860s to protect the Pony Express from Paiute
raids and soon became an important supply station for Union soldiers during the
Civil War. The site consisted of scores
of adobe buildings, the remnants of
which are protected in Fort Churchill
State Park.

From the parking area, follow the
foot trail that leads to the fort ruins. The
fort ruins occupy a large rectangle. Hike
either of the two "L"s of the rectangle
to reach the southwest corner of the
rectangle in 0.3 miles. At this corner,
leave the ruins, and hike south on a foot
trail for 0.4 miles until you reach the
Carson River.

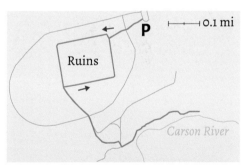

The Carson River at Fort Churchill in the fall

The flow of the Carson River varies substantially with the seasons, but the shade of the aspen and willow trees along its banks is always welcome. A foot trail that becomes increasingly less defined allows you to explore the Carson River for at least the next 0.5 miles. After you are finished enjoying the river, return to the ruins, and hike the remaining "L" of the rectangle before returning to your car.

From Reno. Take I-80 east for 18.8 miles, and take the USA Parkway exit (Highway 439). In 19.0 miles, turn right at the roundabout onto Highway 50 West. In 0.9 miles, turn left onto Ramsey Weeks Cutoff. In 3.4 miles, turn right onto Alternative Highway 95 South. In 4.2 miles, turn right onto Fort Churchill Road to enter Fort Churchill State Park. In 0.8 miles, turn left, and park in the state park's main parking area by the visitors center located at 39.2945, -119.2678. *55 mins.*

Adobe ruins at Fort Churchill

99 Kings Canyon Falls

EMBARK ON AN EASY STROLL TO THE SCENIC LOWER KINGS CANYON WATERFALLS OUTSIDE of Carson City. If desired, hike farther up the canyon to the more remote upper waterfalls.

At a Glance

DIFFICULTY	Very Easy or Easy	DISTANCE/TIME	0.6 miles/0.5 hours or 3.6 miles/2 hours
ELEVATION GAIN	200 feet or 1,700 feet	TRAIL TYPE	Foot trail, dirt road
SOLITUDE	Heavy use	USERS	Hikers
BEST SEASON	January–September	LAND OWNERSHIP	National Forest
ANIMALS	Deer	FEATURES	Waterfalls

Numerous fault lines have carved steep canyons on the east side of the Carson Range next to Eagle Valley. In Kings Canyon, two sets of scenic waterfalls less than a mile apart make for a quick and beautiful hiking experience just outside of Carson City.

From the parking area, follow the dirt trail to the right that heads up the hillside. The route switchbacks up through open sagebrush and bitterbrush vegetation over 0.2 miles. The last 0.1 miles of the trail is cut through the steep rock of the canyon, but the path itself is gradual to the base of the waterfalls. Enjoy the refreshing 25-foot waterfalls that cascade down open rocky terrain. The flow of the waterfalls varies considerably throughout the year and will be the greatest in early spring; in dry years, it will be little more than a trickle in the fall. There is no official trail beyond this point.

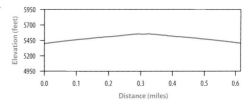

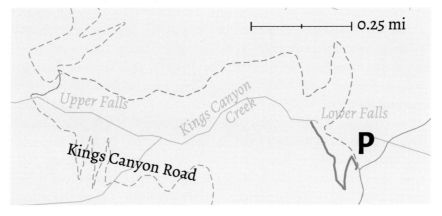

The trail to the lower falls

Return to the parking area the way you came.

If desired, you may also explore the upper waterfalls. While not quite as tall, what the upper waterfalls lack in height they make up for with their lovely forested setting. To reach the upper falls, you must hike the 0.3 miles back to the parking area. From the parking area, take the dirt road to the right that is lower than the trail on which you just hiked. This road soon crosses over Kings Creek and climbs 1,000 feet over 1.5 miles before you reach the upper falls nestled in a Jeffrey pine forest. A sturdy bridge takes you over the waterfalls. Continuing another several hundred feet will allow you to see their base clearly. Return the way you came, and enjoy wonderful views of Eagle Valley during your descent.

Waterfalls most commonly form at the interface between two types of rocks, and usually a softer rock that is more easily eroded lies at their bases. Every rock is classified as igneous, sedimentary, or metamorphic. Igneous rocks originate from magma, and sedimentary rocks are aggregates of sand. Metamorphic rocks are igneous or sedimentary rocks that are physically and chemically altered by heat and pressure. Fault activity in Kings Canyon has caused both the igneous granite of the Carson Range and the sedimentary rocks of Eagle Valley to become metamorphosed. While the lower Kings Canyon waterfalls flow from metasedimentary rocks to sedimentary rocks, the upper waterfalls farther west cascade from metaigneous rock to metasedimentary rock. From west to east, Kings Creek's course goes through the granite of the Carson Range, metamorphosed granite, metasedimentary rocks, and finally sedimentary rocks of Eagle Valley, with waterfalls forming at the rock interfaces. In this way, the beautiful modern-day landscape directly reflects ancient geological processes.

From Reno. Take Highway 395/Interstate 580 south for 26.9 miles to the US Business 395/N. Carson Street exit in Carson City. In 1.4 miles, turn right on West College Parkway. After 0.7 miles, turn left on Foothill Road/North Ormsby Boulevard. Turn right in 0.5 miles to stay on North Ormsby Boulevard. In 0.1 miles, turn right onto West Winnie Lane. After 0.7 miles, turn right on Ash Canyon Road. In 0.3 miles, turn left on Longview Way. In 0.8 miles, turn right on Kings Canyon Road. Continue on Kings Canyon Road in 1.1 miles by staying to the left. The paved road ends in a dirt parking lot located at 39.1534, -119.8157. *40 mins.*

Enjoying the lower falls

100 Prison Hill

ENJOY AN EASY STROLL ALONG THE CARSON RIVER BEFORE CLIMBING TO THE TOP OF A nearby desert peak to gain stunning views of the Carson Valley and surrounding mountains.

At a Glance

DIFFICULTY	Hard	DISTANCE/TIME	5.8 miles/4 hours
ELEVATION GAIN	1,200 feet	TRAIL TYPE	Foot trail, dirt road
SOLITUDE	Medium use	USERS	Hikers, OHVs
BEST SEASON	All	LAND OWNERSHIP	Bureau of Land Management
ANIMALS	Deer, coyotes, jackrabbits	FEATURES	River, expansive views

Originating in the Sierra Nevadas south of Lake Tahoe, the Carson River is a major waterway in western Nevada. Enjoy the riparian environment alongside the Carson River, and then climb to the top of nearby Prison Hill for outstanding views of Carson City and the surrounding mountains and valleys.

From the parking area, take the **River Trail**, which heads south along the Carson River. The river banks are home to several large Fremont cottonwood trees, favorite nesting sites for owls and other birds. In 0.7 miles, continue heading south on the **Mexican Ditch Trail.** This trail runs parallel to an irrigation canal before terminating at the Mexican Dam in 1.1 miles. Look for bald eagles, osprey, and other raptors hunting along the river.

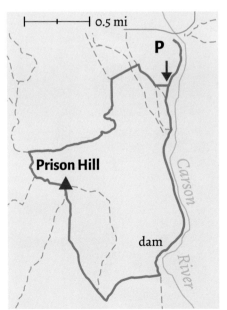

Cross over Mexican Dam, and in 0.2 miles, turn right at a junction to take a dirt road into the hills. According to signage at the parking area, you are now on the **Escape from Prison Hill Route,** although at this point this junction is unsigned. Stay on this road to climb 1,200 feet to the top of Prison Hill in 1.4 miles. Views of the Carson Range to the west, Mount Scott (Hike 92) to the north, and the Pine Nut Mountains to the south and east are phenomenal.

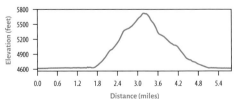

From the summit, take the jeep road heading west for 0.3 miles. At the junction, turn right to descend steeply into a canyon in 0.2 miles. Once in the canyon, you will arrive at an additional unsigned canyon. Turn right here, which puts you on the **Dead Truck Canyon Trail**. About halfway down the colorful canyon, you will pass an old, half-buried truck from which the trail gets its name.

In 0.9 miles, the trail exits the canyon, and several dirt roads crisscross a field of tall sagebrush. Find your way back to the River Trail by heading northeast on one of the roads over the next 0.8 miles. Once back on the River Trail, it is about 0.4 miles to the trailhead.

From Reno. Take Highway 395/ Interstate 580 south for 31.0 miles to the Fairway Drive exit. At the off-ramp, turn left onto Fairway Drive. In 1.5 miles, turn right onto East 5th Street. In 0.2 miles, turn right onto Carson River Road. In 2.0 miles, turn right into the well-marked parking area located at 39.1420, -119.7062. *45 mins.*

Sagebrush vegetation and the Carson Range in the background

Rocky outcroppings are scattered along the backside of Prison Hill.

101 Bently Heritage Trail

HIKE THROUGH A WORKING CATTLE RANCH THAT BORDERS THE SCENIC CARSON RIVER. With its sandy beaches and birding opportunities, this flat hike is excellent for children and adults.

At a Glance

DIFFICULTY	Easy	DISTANCE/TIME	4.8 miles/2.5 hours
ELEVATION GAIN	100 feet	TRAIL TYPE	Foot trail
SOLITUDE	Medium use	USERS	Hikers
BEST SEASON	All	LAND OWNERSHIP	Nature Conservancy, private land
ANIMALS	Deer, coyotes, jackrabbits	FEATURES	Expansive views, river

Perhaps the best part of hiking in Nevada is that 80 percent of its lands are publically owned, resulting in limitless recreation opportunities. The Bently Heritage Trail, however, is unique because it rests entirely on private land. The trail goes through a working cattle ranch alongside a beautiful stretch of the Carson River and was made possible by an agreement between the land owners, the Nature Conservancy, and local government agencies.

From the parking area, Genoa Peak and several other mountains of the Carson Range form a dramatic backdrop to the ranch's sagebrush vegetation. Hike 0.5 miles on the main trail until you reach a junction. The trail consists of three linked loops, but it is worthwhile to complete the largest outer loop on the perimeter of the trail system.

At the trail junction, turn left to hike

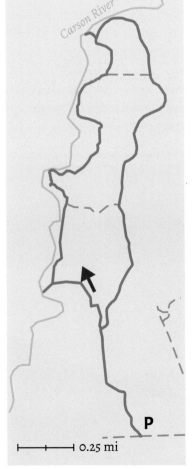

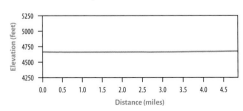

toward the Carson River. In 0.4 miles, turn left at another junction to head down to a sandy beach on the banks of the Carson River via a short spur trail. The trail loop contains several similar spur trails that lead to other views of the river that are worth exploring.

Back on the main trail, it is 1.6 miles to the northernmost point of the loop. Go straight through any trail junctions to stay on the largest outermost loop. Most of the junctions are well signed. The loop then bends back south through tall sagebrush along the eastern edge of the ranch and returns to the first junction in an additional 1.6 miles. From this junction, retrace your steps for 0.5 miles to return to the trailhead.

From Reno. Take Highway 395/Interstate 580 south for 34.4 miles. At this point, the interstate ends. Continue on Highway 395 (Carson Street) by turning left. Drive an additional 5.5 miles before turning left onto Stephanie Way. In 1.0 miles, turn left onto Heybourne Road. In 0.5 miles, turn left, following the signs for the Bently Heritage Trailhead, and park at the end of the road at 39.0486, -119.7656. *50 mins.*

The Carson River with the Carson Range in the background

This flat trail has constant excellent
views of the Carson Range

Acknowledgments

WE ARE GRATEFUL FOR MANY PEOPLE WHO HAVE INSPIRED AND HELPED US IN THE WRITING of this book.

Our parents:
Scott Miller, who believed his daughter was equally capable of adventure and acquiring wisdom as her brothers. Thank you for taking us outdoors and always wanting to learn. Your two rules sing in my ears like a guitar playing in an open field—nobody gets hurt, and everybody has fun. Anna Miller, who is my greatest role model. Your gifts and love have enabled our thriving.

Jeff Barile, who taught me to always value conservation and public lands. Maureen Barile, who taught me to how to write, to plan well, and to always stay safe. I am so grateful to have unconditionally supportive and loving parents.

Everybody who worked on this book:
Mark Sedenquist from Imbrifex Books, who gave us the opportunity and guidance in making this book a reality.
Vicki Adang, who edited our descriptions with care and consistency.
Sue Campbell, who designed the beautiful layout and style of the book.
Chris Erichsen, who put together the overview maps for the hikes.
Sarah Grant, who took lovely photographs of us.

Our children:
Juniper and Sage. With you on our shoulders and hiking poles in our hands, our hearts grow stronger and deeper in love with you and the world.

APPENDIX A: CHOOSE YOUR PERFECT HIKE

HERE ARE FIVE HIKES IN SEVERAL DIFFERENT CATEGORIES TO HELP YOU CHOOSE YOUR PERFECT hike. This list is to get you started and by no means is all inclusive.

Good for Children and Adults with Limited Mobility
27 Swan Lake
34 Sugarloaf
67 Stateline Point
80 Tahoe Meadows
99 Kings Canyon Falls

Teen Favorites
57 Summit Lake
63 Five Lakes
79 Incline Peak
86 Hidden Valley Canyon
97 Emma Peak

Waterfalls
5 Badenough Waterfalls
47 Hunter Creek Falls
53 Webber Falls
75 Mount Rose
99 Kings Canyon Falls

Lake Tahoe
65 Kings Beach Tahoe Rim Trail
67 Stateline Point
68 Sand Harbor
69 Chimney Beach
76 Mount Houghton and Relay Peak

Pyramid Lake
20 Dogskin Mountain
29 Pyramid Lake
30 Tule Peak
31 Incandescent Rocks
33 Virginia Peak

Wildflowers
43 Dog Valley

52 Webber Lake
55 Sagehen Creek
56 Castle Peak
80 Tahoe Meadows

Interesting Geology
13 Red Rock Cliffs
21 Moon Rocks
31 Incandescent Rocks
89 Geiger Grade
95 Grimes Point

Rock-Scrambling Opportunities
13 Red Rock Cliffs
16 Little Petersen
21 Moon Rocks
68 Sand Harbor
86 Hidden Valley Canyon

Spring
17 Goldstone Loop
41 Keystone Canyon
49 Huffaker Hills
74 Brown's Creek
96 Rocky Peak

Summer
3 Lakes Basin
54 Mount Lola
73 Church's Pond
78 Tamarack Peak
82 Ophir Creek

Fall Foliage
6 Babbitt Fire Tower
40 Peavine Peak
70 Marlette Lake
71 Upper Thomas Creek

APPENDIX B: HIKES ORDERED BY ELEVATION GAIN

30 Tule Peak- 4,000 feet

15 Petersen Springs- 2,900 feet

33 Virginia Peak- 2,900 feet

40 Peavine Peak- 2,900 feet

20 Dogskin Mountain- 2,700 feet

90 Mount Davidson and Mount Bullion- 2,700 feet

44 West Peavine- 2,600 feet

54 Mount Lola- 2,600 feet

88 Louse Benchmark- 2,600 feet

2 Adams Peak- 2,500 feet

10 Verdi Fire Tower- 2,500 feet

96 Rocky Peak- 2,400 feet

23 Freds Mountain- 2,200 feet

36 Spanish Springs Peak- 2,200 feet

75 Mount Rose- 2,200 feet

76 Mount Houghton and Relay Peak- 2,200 feet

73 Church's Pond- 2,100 feet

18 Cold Springs- 2,000 feet

56 Castle Peak- 2,000 feet

4 Beckwourth Pass Loop- 1,900 feet

83 Genoa Loop- 1,900 feet

6 Babbitt Fire Tower- 1,800 feet

11 Boca Ridge- 1,800 feet

25 Hungry Ridge Loop- 1,800 feet

7 Sardine Peak- 1,700 feet

71 Upper Thomas Creek- 1,700 feet

3 Lakes Basin- 1,600 feet

51 Sierra Buttes- 1,600 feet

85 Hidden Valley Peak- 1,600 feet

47 Hunter Creek Falls- 1,500 feet

60 Mount Judah and Donner Peak- 1,500 feet

66 Kings Beach Tahoe Rim Trail- 1,400 feet

70 Marlette Lake- 1,400 feet

78 Tamarack Peak- 1,400 feet

28 Spanish Benchmark- 1,300 feet

31 Incandescent Rocks- 1,300 feet

37 Olinghouse- 1,300 feet

38 Airway Loop- 1,300 feet

63 Five Lakes- 1,300 feet

97 Emma Peak- 1,300 feet

8 Stampede Overlook- 1,200 feet

24 Hungry Valley- 1,200 feet

59 Boca Hill- 1,200 feet

79 Incline Peak- 1,200 feet

100 Prison Hill- 1,200 feet

72 Thomas and Whites Creek Loop- 1,100 feet

82 Ophir Creek- 1,100 feet

89 Geiger Grade- 1,100 feet

26 Granite Hills- 1,000 feet

74 Brown's Creek- 1,000 feet

92 Mount Scott- 1,000 feet

93 Basalt Hill- 1,000 feet

22 Warm Springs Mountain- 900 feet

67 Stateline Point- 900 feet

68 Sand Harbor- 900 feet

84 Chalk Bluff- 900 feet

13 Red Rock Cliffs- 800 feet

34 Sugarloaf- 800 feet

50 Steamboat Hills- 800 feet

57 Summit Lake- 800 feet

87 Lagomarsino Petroglyphs- 800 feet

95 Grimes Point- 800 feet

17 Goldstone Loop- 700 feet

32 Seagull Point- 700 feet

41 Keystone Canyon- 700 feet

14 Sand Hills- 600 feet

16 Little Petersen- 600 feet

42 Evans Canyon- 600 feet

62 Martis Creek Lake and Lake Ella- 600 feet

69 Chimney Beach- 600 feet

91 Washoe Lake- 600 feet

5 Badenough Waterfalls- 500 feet

46 Steamboat Ditch- 500 feet

86 Hidden Valley Canyon- 500 feet

12 Truckee River Canyon- 400 feet

35 Griffith Canyon Petroglyphs- 400 feet

39 Sun Valley Park- 400 feet

48 Rattlesnake- 400 feet

58 Alder Creek- 400 feet

19 Silver Knolls- 300 feet

49 Huffaker Hills- 300 feet

52 Webber Lake- 300 feet

53 Webber Falls- 300 feet

55 Sagehen Creek- 300 feet

61 Coldstream Canyon- 300 feet

64 Martis Peak- 300 feet

66 Incline Flume Trail- 300 feet

77 Tamarack Lake- 300 feet

80 Tahoe Meadows- 300 feet

81 Chickadee Ridge- 300 feet

9 Little Truckee River- 200 feet

21 Moon Rocks- 200 feet

43 Dog Valley- 200 feet

99 Kings Canyon Falls- 200 feet

1 Frenchman Lake- 100 feet

27 Swan Lake- 100 feet

29 Pyramid Lake- 100 feet

45 Oxbow Park- 100 feet

94 Patua Hot Springs- 100 feet

98 Fort Churchill- 100 feet

101 Bently Heritage Trail- 100 feet

APPENDIX C:
HIKES ORDERED BY ROUND-TRIP MILEAGE

33 Virginia Peak- 12.0 miles

10 Verdi Fire Tower- 11.3 miles

76 Mount Houghton and Relay Peak- 11.3 miles

88 Louse Benchmark- 10.7 miles

70 Marlette Lake- 10.6 miles

54 Mount Lola- 10.4 miles

75 Mount Rose- 10.4 miles

87 Lagomarsino Petroglyphs- 10.2 miles

30 Tule Peak- 10.0 miles

40 Peavine Peak- 9.5 miles

65 Kings Beach Tahoe Rim Trail- 9.1 miles

11 Boca Ridge- 9.0 miles

6 Babbitt Fire Tower- 8.7 miles

20 Dogskin Mountain- 8.7 miles

7 Sardine Peak- 8.5 miles

83 Genoa Loop- 8.3 miles

36 Spanish Springs Peak- 8.2 miles

3 Lakes Basin- 7.9 miles

24 Hungry Valley- 7.7 miles

96 Rocky Peak- 7.6 miles

2 Adams Peak- 7.5 miles

90 Mount Davidson and Mount Bullion- 7.5 miles

71 Upper Thomas Creek- 7.4 miles

25 Hungry Ridge Loop- 7.2 miles

18 Cold Springs- 7.0 miles

23 Freds Mountain- 6.9 miles

14 Sand Hills- 6.8 miles

15 Petersen Springs- 6.8 miles

73 Church's Pond- 6.5 miles

57 Summit Lake- 6.3 miles

59 Boca Hill- 6.3 miles

44 West Peavine- 6.2 miles

52 Webber Lake- 6.2 miles

62 Martis Creek Lake and Lake Ella- 6.2 miles

72 Thomas and Whites Creek Loop- 6.2 miles

37 Olinghouse- 6.1 miles

68 Sand Harbor- 6.1 miles

47 Hunter Creek Falls- 6.0 miles

100 Prison Hill- 5.8 miles

56 Castle Peak- 5.7 miles

60 Mount Judah and Donner Peak- 5.5 miles

34 Sugarloaf- 5.3 miles

84 Chalk Bluff- 5.3 miles

92 Mount Scott- 5.2 miles

31 Incandescent Rocks- 5.1 miles

66 Incline Flume Trail- 5.1 miles

38 Airway Loop- 5.0 miles

55 Sagehen Creek- 5.0 miles

93 Basalt Hill- 5.0 miles

58 Alder Creek- 4.9 miles

63 Five Lakes- 4.9 miles

101 Bently Heritage Trail- 4.8 miles

12 Truckee River Canyon- 4.7 miles

22 Warm Springs Mountain- 4.7 miles

51 Sierra Buttes- 4.7 miles

85 Hidden Valley Peak- 4.6 miles

4 Beckwourth Pass Loop- 4.4 miles

41 Keystone Canyon- 4.4 miles

95 Grimes Point- 4.4 miles

74 Brown's Creek- 4.3 miles

89 Geiger Grade- 4.2 miles

82 Ophir Creek- 4.1 miles

97 Emma Peak- 4.0 miles

79 Incline Peak- 3.9 miles

78 Tamarack Peak- 3.8 miles

26 Granite Hills- 3.7 miles

81 Chickadee Ridge- 3.7 miles

42 Evans Canyon- 3.6 miles

77 Tamarack Lake- 3.6 miles

50 Steamboat Hills- 3.4 miles

46 Steamboat Ditch- 3.3 miles

61 Coldstream Canyon- 3.3 miles

5 Badenough Waterfalls- 3.2 miles

17 Goldstone Loop- 3.2 miles

28 Spanish Benchmark- 3.1 miles

67 Stateline Point- 2.9 miles

8 Stampede Overlook- 2.7 miles

80 Tahoe Meadows- 2.5 miles

91 Washoe Lake- 2.5 miles

9 Little Truckee River- 2.1 miles

16 Little Petersen- 2.1 miles

29 Pyramid Lake- 2.1 miles

32 Seagull Point- 2.1 miles

94 Patua Hot Springs- 2.1 miles

19 Silver Knolls- 2.0 miles

27 Swan Lake- 2.0 miles

35 Griffith Canyon Petroglyphs- 2.0 miles

98 Fort Churchill- 2.0 miles

69 Chimney Beach- 1.9 miles

49 Huffaker Hills- 1.8 miles

1 Frenchman Lake- 1.6 miles

48 Rattlesnake- 1.6 miles

13 Red Rock Cliffs- 1.5 miles

39 Sun Valley Park- 1.4 miles

43 Dog Valley- 1.4 miles

86 Hidden Valley Canyon- 1.2 miles

64 Martis Peak- 1.1 miles

45 Oxbow Park- 1.0 miles

21 Moon Rocks- 0.7 miles

99 Kings Canyon Falls- 0.6 miles

53 Webber Falls- 0.2 miles

APPENDIX D: HIKES ORDERED BY DIFFICULTY

FROM HIKING BOOKS TO PARK TRAIL MAPS, EVERY HIKING DESCRIPTION HAS ITS OWN CRITERIA used for gauging difficulty. These criteria are always subjective to varying extents and range widely depending on the author. Consider the following. Is a short, off-trail hike more difficult than a longer hike on a well-defined trail? Is a long, flat hike more strenuous than a short, steep climb?

In an effort to more objectively quantify difficulty, we calculated the number of calories a typical person will burn during each hike. Below is a list of the hikes in this book ranked in terms of decreasing number of calories burned with cutoffs delineating the epic, hard, easy, and very easy ratings. For adventures with two ratings and two versions of the hike, the calculation for the easier of the two options is shown.

The calculated number of calories burned is based on a 150-pound person carrying a 10-pound backpack traveling at 2 miles per hour. The calculations factor in the length of the hike, the elevation gain (steepness) of the trail, and the terrain factor of the walking surface. The terrain factor accounts for differences in the strenuousness of walking on, for example, a paved road versus a sandy trail versus a brushy trail. These calorie calculations were based on models developed by the U.S. Army that can be found in Richmond and coauthors' 2015 publication entitled "Terrain Factors for Predicting Walking and Load Carriage Energy Costs Review and Refinement" in the *Journal of Sport and Human Performance*. Our calculations assume dry, snowless terrain. Perceived difficulty can be much higher under muddy or snowy conditions.

Epic
- **30** Tule Peak- 4,350 calories
- **15** Petersen Springs- 3,670 calories
- **2** Adams Peak- 2,240 calories
- **44** West Peavine- 2,150 calories
- **33** Virginia Peak- 1,880 calories
- **20** Dogskin Mountain- 1,870 calories
- **96** Rocky Peak- 1,840 calories
- **54** Mount Lola- 1,720 calories
- **10** Verdi Fire Tower- 1,650 calories
- **88** Louse Benchmark- 1,650 calories
- **75** Mount Rose- 1,560 calories
- **87** Lagomarsino Petroglyphs- 1,560 calories
- **36** Spanish Springs Peak- 1,530 calories
- **40** Peavine Peak- 1,520 calories
- **76** Mount Houghton and Relay Peak- 1,410 calories

Hard
- **11** Boca Ridge- 1,380 calories
- **37** Olinghouse- 1,380 calories
- **23** Freds Mountain- 1,370 calories
- **4** Beckwourth Pass Loop- 1,360 calories
- **90** Mount Davidson and Mount Bullion- 1,360 calories
- **70** Marlette Lake- 1,320 calories
- **56** Castle Peak- 1,300 calories
- **73** Church's Pond- 1,280 calories
- **97** Emma Peak- 1,280 calories
- **18** Cold Springs- 1,240 calories
- **6** Babbitt Fire Tower- 1,230 calories

7 Sardine Peak- 1,180 calories

65 Kings Beach Tahoe Rim Trail- 1,180 calories

78 Tamarack Peak- 1,140 calories

71 Upper Thomas Creek- 1,100 calories

85 Hidden Valley Peak- 1,100 calories

83 Genoa Loop- 1,090 calories

3 Lakes Basin- 1,070 calories

51 Sierra Buttes- 1,050 calories

25 Hungry Ridge Loop- 1,040 calories

8 Stampede Overlook- 970 calories

84 Chalk Bluff- 940 calories

24 Hungry Valley- 890 calories

86 Hidden Valley Canyon- 850 calories

59 Boca Hill- 840 calories

28 Spanish Benchmark- 810 calories

47 Hunter Creek Falls- 810 calories

79 Incline Peak- 800 calories

100 Prison Hill- 800 calories

60 Mount Judah and Donner Peak- 790 calories

31 Incandescent Rocks- 770 calories

38 Airway Loop- 760 calories

13 Red Rock Cliffs- 740 calories

32 Seagull Point- 740 calories

72 Thomas and Whites Creek Loop- 740 calories

82 Ophir Creek- 720 calories

92 Mount Scott- 720 calories

93 Basalt Hill- 710 calories

Easy

14 Sand Hills- 700 calories

57 Summit Lake- 700 calories

63 Five Lakes- 700 calories

89 Geiger Grade- 670 calories

34 Sugarloaf- 660 calories

62 Martis Creek Lake and Lake Ella- 660 calories

22 Warm Springs Mountain- 650 calories

26 Granite Hills- 630 calories

65 Incline Flume Trail- 630 calories

68 Sand Harbor- 630 calories

52 Webber Lake- 620 calories

74 Brown's Creek- 580 calories

50 Steamboat Hills- 570 calories

55 Sagehen Creek- 570 calories

95 Grimes Point- 550 calories

35 Griffith Canyon Petroglyphs- 540 calories

58 Alder Creek- 540 calories

41 Keystone Canyon- 530 calories

16 Little Petersen- 510 calories

12 Truckee River Canyon- 500 calories

17 Goldstone Loop- 480 calories

101 Bently Heritage Trail- 470 calories

67 Stateline Point- 450 calories

94 Patua Hot Springs- 450 calories

42 Evans Canyon- 440 calories

77 Tamarack Lake- 430 calories

5 Badenough Waterfalls- 410 calories

9 Little Truckee River- 410 calories

46 Steamboat Ditch- 410 calories

81 Chickadee Ridge- 400 calories

Very Easy

61 Coldstream Canyon- 360 calories

29 Pyramid Lake- 340 calories

91 Washoe Lake- 310 calories

69 Chimney Beach- 300 calories

48 Rattlesnake- 280 calories

80 Tahoe Meadows- 260 calories

49 Huffaker Hills- 240 calories

43 Dog Valley- 230 calories

19 Silver Knolls- 220 calories

27 Swan Lake- 200 calories

39 Sun Valley Park- 200 calories

98 Fort Churchill- 200 calories

1 Frenchman Lake- 180 calories

21 Moon Rocks- 180 calories

64 Martis Peak- 150 calories

45 Oxbow Park- 100 calories

99 Kings Canyon Falls- 100 calories

53 Webber Falls- 50 calories

Index